The Power of People Skills

A Manager's Guide to Assessing and Developing Your Organization's Greatest Resource

DOUGLAS STEWART

A Wiley Press Book JOHN WILEY & SONS, INC.
New York • Chichester • Brisbane • Toronto • Singapore

Publisher: Stephen Kippur
Editor: Elizabeth G. Perry
Managing Editor: Katherine Schowalter
Production Services: G&H/SOHO, Ltd.
Illustrations by Mina Yamashita

Library of Congress Cataloging-in-Publication Data

Stewart, J. Douglas (John Douglas), 1931-
The power of people skills.

"A Wiley Press book."
1. Personnel management. 2. Interpersonal communication. I. Title.
HF5549.S854 1986 658.3 85-31529
ISBN 0-471-01187-8

Printed in the United States of America

89 90 10 9 8 7 6 5 4 3

This book is dedicated to my parents, Elmer and Evelyn Stewart, who have lovingly given me a lifetime course in managerial people skills.

Acknowledgments

Writing a book is like moving a piano—you have to be either exceptionally strong or very foolish to attempt it alone. This book could not have been moved from concept to reality without the help of many generous managers and friends, all of whom contributed significantly to its development.

Primary among them has been Marilyn Worthington, my partner and toughest critic. She has had an active role in formulating and clarifying ideas and concepts, and her sharp editorial pencil was often the only thing between the book you hold and something closer to *War and Peace.* Her insistence on a balanced life-style has narrowly kept me from flunking my own workaholic assessment.

Don Strel, Steve Buchholz, and Sheila Sullivan contributed valuable suggestions from their managerial vantage points. Tom Kubistant, Harry Woodward, David Shapiro, Brenda Warner, Tavo Holloway, Jim L'Allier, Evelyn Stewart, Holly Field, Bob Bly, and Richard Bradford helped with useful ideas and editorial feedback.

My thanks to business editor Bob Storey, who edits my weekly column in *The New Mexican,* where many of these ideas originally appeared. Thanks also to Anne Hillerman, friend and editorial editor, for her valuable input into the manuscript process.

Special thanks to Betsy Perry, my Wiley editor and consultant, who successfully bridged the considerable distance between The Big Apple and The City Different, graciously fielding many anxious-author phone calls in the process. Katherine Schowalter's professional care and skills transformed the manuscript into a book. All authors should have such a supportive editorial team.

Mina Yamashita, who produces delightful drawings under even the tightest of deadlines, deserves special credit. I'm also grateful to my aunt, Mary Mooney, for her marketing advice from St. Petersburg, Florida, that if this book doesn't contain shooting or sex, it probably won't sell.

Finally, my appreciation goes to all of *The New Mexican* business page readers who have shared their Saturday mornings with me. Their response to my column has been gratifying and encouraging. May they, and you, enjoy this book as much as I have enjoyed writing it.

Preface

It doesn't matter where you are, if it doesn't matter where you're going.
—Ridin' the Rails, *1928*

This book is about people skills, the timeless skills that improve interpersonal communications and help managers and employees work together more productively. People skills have become the basic tools with which the contemporary manager carries out his or her organizational responsibilities. While computerized robots are learning to make products, managers are learning to develop employees' potential.

Since I think that it does matter to most managers where they're going, this book is also about feedback, the information from "out there" that lets us know where we are and how we're doing. In the complex world of modern organizations, that is not always easy to discover.

To help you solve that problem, this book includes a number of practical assessments, checklists, and worksheets designed to give you the feedback necessary to strengthen your people skills. It also contains a glossary of terms to make using the material simpler and more understandable.

The book has a nonlinear, "random access" structure, allowing you to start and finish anywhere you choose. Begin with topics of special interest or concern, and you'll find internal references that suggest where in the book to go next for additional information.

The book is also designed to function as a resource for consultants, teachers, trainers, and other human resource developers. The assessments and the modular structure make a logical bridge into training sessions or classes on each subject. A Leader's Guide is available to assist you with that process.

Above all, this book is designed to be useful. Mark in it, make notes, doodle, do calculations—use it as a tool to reinforce your people skills. In short, *use it up!*

The book is easily replaced. Good employees are not.

Douglas Stewart
Santa Fe, New Mexico

Contents

Contents

Introduction

While shopping recently in a local supermarket, I overheard a fragment of anonymous conversation from the next aisle, behind the canned goods. "Down at work . . ." a woman's loud, clear voice began to an invisible listener. The intensity in her voice told me, even across the canned peas, that "down at work" was a very important place to her, a place where significant things happened.

"Down at work . . ." is the place where most of us spend the majority of our waking adult lives, the place where victories are won, defeats shared, and our adult personalities shaped and honed. "Down at work . . ." is our home away from home, the culture in which workers' talents and skills are melded through personal interactions to create the world's goods and services. For the wage-earner, there is no more important place.

This book is written with the explicit purpose of helping managers create a work culture that is as positive and rewarding a place as possible. It is based on the premise that people are an organization's greatest resource, and that a manager's people skills are the most significant factor in shepherding and nurturing that resource.

Earlier in this century, things were different. In an era dominated by agriculture and small shops, the majority of workers were self-employed. The worker had control over the workplace. Now only a small fraction of the work force is self-employed, and control of the work culture has passed to supervisors and managers. No matter at what level of the organization he or she functions, almost every wage-earner has a manager-employee relationship with someone.

In that simpler era, most wage-earners had several important resources for personal and emotional support, from birth to death: family, friends, church, school, and work. The pallbearers at the funeral of my grandfather, a self-employed carpenter in rural Ohio, were the same schoolboy teammates, teenage rivals, fellow church ushers, and loyal business customers who had shared his days across a lifetime.

Today, in an era when statistics indicate that we are changing addresses, spouses, houses, diets, cars, colas, and jobs at a frantic pace, that quality of birth-to-death support is seldom available. In our mobile population, school, church, and family are no longer the pillars to which one can anchor a lifetime. While our class reunions have become conventions of virtual strangers, "down at work" has become the center that fulfills many more personal needs than just earning a regular paycheck, as important as that may be.

I was embarrassingly far along toward middle age before I discovered that there are actually *three* ways to make money or get ideas carried out: work for yourself, work for other people, or have other people work for you. I also discovered that, almost without exception, having other people work for you—managing—is by far the most profitable.

As obvious as that fact appears now, I was at first stunned by the realization, and then upset. Why, in more years of education than I admit in public, hadn't any teacher told me that? Why hadn't at least one of my alumni-soliciting institutions prepared me for the simple fact that no matter what technical and professional skills they taught me, it was going to be managerial people skills that would help get me wherever it was I wanted to go?

I don't think that I'm alone. Working with client organizations of all sizes has shown me that most managers acquire a technical or professional education that is very light on people skills, if those skills are included at all. Most of us started out as doers, then awoke one morning to discover that we were managers. People—not things, systems, gadgets, numbers, strategies, formulas, equipment, tools, airline schedules, or stock quotes—were now our major responsibility.

It's hard for a doer to become a manager—hard to delegate to others the things one does best, hard to give up the sense of satisfaction that comes with accomplishing the familiar, only to step into the unknown waters of managing people. It feels infinitely more secure to keep answering technical questions than it does to take on the interpersonal questions that have puzzled men and women since staff meetings were held in caves.

And yet it must be done—an organization's human resources must be managed. And not by a single department with that name on the door, but by each manager in the organization. We are moving into an era of knowledge and service industries, where the human brain and spirit is the treasured resource that will make the bottom-line survival difference for all organizations. In such an era, each manager's people skills "down at work" become absolutely crucial.

This book is written to help the contemporary manager develop and strengthen those people skills. It is a result of my own research, the research of others, and contemporary management literature. My primary source, however, is nearly forty years' experience as consultant, teacher, designer, friend, psychologist—experience of managing, and of being managed. Frankly, it is the latter "down at work" experiences that I remember most vividly.

"Down at work . . ." Where the people are.

Using the Assessments

The assessments in this book are designed to provide the maximum amount of information for you, the manager, with a minimum amount of effort. By purchasing the book you've also purchased the right to use the "Employees" version of the assessments within your own organization. Use them as often as you like, for the more feedback you get from your employees, the more quickly you can improve your people skills.

These assessments are not designed or intended to be used for evaluation or qualifying. There is no scoring; that is, you can't flunk listening. The assessments are designed only to give you specific feedback, both from yourself and from your employees, in an organized and systematic way.

Given these limitations, use the assessments for analyzing your people skills, as a basis for personal or staff discussions, as economical training components, or as indicators of a need for change, additional skill-building, or a shift of managerial emphasis.

Just using a managerial performance assessment with your employees sends the message that you are as interested in improving your own performance as you are in helping them improve theirs. It also shows them that you are willing to put yourself on the line to do it. This is a very powerful example to provide for employees. It also makes it much easier for your employees to receive performance feedback from you, for it's now a two-way street.

Reading the Results

Most of the assessments in the book give you two dimensions of information. That is, from the assessment results you will know not only how you and your employees perceive a given skill level, but also how important that skill is thought to be within a particular job setting.

This two-dimensional feature of the assessments is the main reason there is no scoring. Comparing scores on any given skill level, for example, makes no sense without looking at it in the context of how important that skill is to high performance in a given situation or job. "Low listening skills" are of little importance to hockey star Wayne Gretzky skating down the ice with the puck, just as "low leg strength" would be of little importance to a manager faced with an employee's performance problem.

By looking at both a skill's level and its importance, the assessments allow you to keep the skill ratings in perspective. This gives you the choice of whether or not something needs to be done about it, based on your own interpretation of the information relevant to your situation.

The primary things to look for in your assessment information are gaps. Watch for differences on both your own and the employees' assessments between what is important or wanted and the current skill level. Watch also for gaps between how you perceive your skill level and the perceptions of your employees. Gaps here may indicate either that you are not coming across the way you think you are—not unusual for most of us—or that your perceptions of how you come across are not based on realistic or reliable information.

Figure 1 is an example of a completed assessment, the "Manager" version of the Listening Skills Assessment. Note that the average employee scores for each question have been put in place, under the appropriate symbols for square and circle, along with the manager's self-assessment. This provides an easy and quick comparison between the results of the "Manager" and the "Employee" assessments.

Gaps that may require immediate attention occur in questions 3, 5, and 7, where the manager's circle is two or more numbers to the *right* of the square. This indicates an important difference between what listening skill levels the manager thinks are important and his or her current skill level.

Other significant gaps are shown by questions 2 and 6, where there is a marked difference between the employees' averaged scores and the manager's skill level self-assessment. It is apparent that the manager does not come across to employees in the same way as his or her self-perception.

Another important gap appears in question 4, where employees think that "giving full attention to the speaker" is much more important than the manager does.

In cases where there are significant gaps (two or more numbers) between the perceptions of manager and employees, it is up to the manager to discuss those differences with employees if noticeable improvement is going to occur.

The assessment itself will not improve your people skills. But the resulting sharpened self-awareness of how you come across to other people, and your discussions with them, can lead to the positive development of your people and your people skills.

The problem with using any kind of feedback is that you may not always like what you discover, but this shouldn't keep you from using it. Closing your eyes is one way to avoid seeing an ugly landscape, but you'll also miss a lot of sunsets and rose gardens.

If you discover something disconcerting from using the assessments, try to avoid the temptation to dismiss the information as "inaccurate" or to discredit the assessments themselves. Give the information careful thought—check it out in other ways. Far better that you discover a people skills problem with your own assessment than to get the news from unexpected sources.

The assessments are snapshots of skill level perceptions at a given time. They are not carved in stone, any more than are the situations or behavior they tell you about. All of the assessed areas can be changed, if you feel that

Date 12/2 **MANAGER**

∇ Listening Skills Assessment

Directions: Place a <u>square</u> around a number to indicate how <u>important</u> you think that skill is for good listening.
Place a <u>circle</u> around a number to indicate your estimation of your present <u>skill level</u> in listening to your employees.

Suggestion: Have your employees fill out the "Employee" version. Place their averaged scores in the appropriate places and compare their perceptions with yours.

Scale: **High/Excellent - 5 4 3 2 1 - Low/Poor**

Skills		**Employees** □	○
1. Regarding what the speaker says as important--at least to the speaker.	5 [(4)] 3 2 1	4.2	3.7
2. Listening without interrupting.	[5] (4) 3 2 1	4.8	2.6
3. Not rushing the speaker.	5 [4] 3 2 (1)	3.6	1.4
4. Giving full attention to the speaker.	5 4 (3) [2] 1	4.6	1.6
5. Not responding judgmentally.	[5] 4 3 (2) 1	4.4	1.6
6. Adjusting to the speaker's pace.	5 [(4)] 3 2 1	3.4	2.1
7. Listening objectively.	[5] 4 3 (2) 1	4.7	2.2
8. Responding both to what is said and to what is left unsaid.	5 4 [(3)] 2 1	3.6	2.9
9. Checking to be sure that he or she heard correctly.	5 [4] (3) 2 1	41	2.8
10. Maintaining confidentiality.	[(5)] 4 3 2 1	4.9	4.2

Overall rating of the quality of your listening skills:

<u>Very high</u> - 10 9 (8) 7 6 5 4 3 2 1 - <u>Very low</u> (circle one)

Your employees' averaged rating: 7.2

Note: Circled items in the 1-2 area may require immediate attention to improve your listening skills. Also, give close attention to items in which the circle is two or more numbers to the <u>right</u> of the square, as this indicates a gap between <u>importance</u> and <u>skill level</u>.

Figure 1. *An example of a completed assessment*

change is needed. That is, after all, what people skills are about—"growing people." And growth requires change, difficult as that sometimes may be.

Finally, because the assessments are snapshots, using them several times will give you a more accurate picture of your change and development. They take only a few minutes, and the additional feedback will help you chart an even more accurate course toward greater power with people skills.

∇ 1. Why Is It So Lonely at the Top?

Even successful managers often confide that "it gets lonely at the top." Why is it that the more successful managers become, the more isolated they may be in their own organizations? "That's the price of success," managers say, as though being lonely at the top is an accepted fact of business life. Is corporate loneliness a necessary price to pay for rising to the top?

Unfortunately, if the manager's situation is left to run its typical course, isolation at the top of the managerial pyramid can be the result. As a manager acquires more power and authority, some employees try to get closer; i.e., power by proximity. Others start to give the manager a wider berth; "power nearby makes me nervous."

Whatever the reason, the result is the same; managers may not know what is really going on in their own companies. I've talked with managers who felt they had a better idea of what was going on with their competition than they did with their own people. And they weren't sure what they could do about it.

One major answer to this isolation dilemma is *better feedback*. For example, even if your life depends on it, you can't run if your foot is asleep; there's no feedback from the foot to your brain and back through your nervous system to your muscles. It is equally difficult to manage any aspect of an organization without adequate information concerning how your employees feel about their job situations, your managerial performance, and the other necessary information that gives you the pulse of your work unit or organization.

Getting Feedback

There are a number of ways, of course, that you can get feedback from your employees:

- The **suggestion box** has been a standby for years. It can be convenient, anonymous when necessary, and it is a familiar system. It does require that feedback be coherently written—not everyone's forte—and it doesn't provide the opportunity to clarify the communication if the feedback is given anonymously. It quickly loses its effectiveness without some sort of managerial response to submitted suggestions.

- The **open door policy** method of allowing employees to have easy access to managers during scheduled hours can be helpful in supplying feedback, providing that the number of people who report to you is not too large, and the manager leaves enough room in the schedule that employees really do have free access to the manager. After the first few employees are turned back from the manager's "open door" because "she's too busy," the system—and often the manager—loses credibility. A few months later, if you ask the manager about open door policy feedback, the likely response will be, "Well, I tried it once and it didn't work."

  To make it work best, announce and discuss the open door system with employees face-to-face, and clearly post *and adhere to* schedules when the manager's door is open. A manager trying an open door policy for the first time can assume that employees will test his or her sincerity—the door had better be open when scheduled.

This method is especially useful when a manager high in an organization wants to ensure direct access from employees several levels down in the organization.

- ∇ The **walk-around management** system mentioned in Peters and Waterman's *In Search of Excellence* is also an effective way for managers to stay in closer touch with their employees. It provides upper-level management an opportunity to get feedback from employees at all levels, as well as share the organization's mission on an ongoing basis. Employee morale is reinforced if managers can give employees they meet positive feedback on specific instances of high performance.

  The major drawback, until it is widely accepted in organizational systems, is that the walk-around manager appears not to have anything else to do. However, it is probably one of the best systems in use for helping a manager take the pulse of the organization. Managers trying it for the first time report being amazed at how much information employees share when the manager is at *their* work station, rather than closed off in the manager's office.

- ∇ **Problem-solving groups**—"rap sessions," quality circles, focus groups, and other employee problem-solving groups—can also give managers valuable feedback on everything from production economies to managerial performance. Most groups meet and take time, on a regular basis, but even one good cost-saving or money-producing idea from such a group can more than pay for the time involved.

- ∇ **Reports** have been a method for providing information to the person in charge ever since we were in grade school. Unfortunately, with some managers, it is also the *only* method by which they get feedback. Although reports are one of the best ways to organize information, they can be time-consuming to prepare, cold and overly factual, and a burden to read once they reach their destination. If you're in a superior position, there is also the problem that people tend to tell you what they think you want to hear.

  Because reports are time-consuming to read and digest, the preparer always suspects that the recipient doesn't look at them. This can leave the employee feeling that the reporting process is an exercise in time-wasting futility. To help any reporting system function as it was intended, the manager needs to be sure that at least these three things occur:

  1. The reporting system should be as simple and efficient as possible. If it is perceived by employees as an interruption and a competitor for other work responsibilities, it is much less likely to be carried out as planned. The employees' frustration is much the same as would occur if you asked them to do two things at once.
  2. The employees must understand the need for the particular report. There is nothing more annoying than to have to do things that you feel are nonessential when you have essential things to do. "Don't ask questions,

just bring it to me on time!"—or the endless variations on the same theme—is not a managerial approach that reinforces an effective report-writing system.

3. Reports, once written, need to be acknowledged. Reports that just disappear into the void, a bureaucratic time-warp of unknown dimensions, only reinforce the employees' suspicion that the reporting system was invented by people who either wanted to punish employees or wanted numbers to crunch so that they could look busy and keep their jobs. Unfortunately, there is often just enough truth in those suspicions to keep them alive.

An additional drawback to reports is that they often end up containing only factual information, leaving out the personal dimension, which is of prime importance to the effective manager of people. If employees have been burned once by a breach of confidentiality, they may fear putting sensitive personal information or opinions into writing.

∇ **Informants**—the employees who have a direct pipeline to the manager and report all they see and hear—have been a source of feedback to those in power ever since "organization" meant two of our ancestral families sharing a cave. Although a tempting source of information for a manager, it is one of the least desirable ways for a manager to get feedback about what is going on in the organization, for these reasons:

- It turns employee against employee and encourages feelings of distrust within the work unit. Managers who must resort to such covert methods of obtaining feedback may already have a trust problem with their employees.
- Employees spot an informant much quicker than either manager or informant suspects. After that, employees may use the informant for their own purposes, sending messages to the manager that they don't feel comfortable sending any other way. What is worse, some employees are overcome by the temptation to send the manager false information via the informant, just for spite. The manager is then left with the almost impossible task of attempting to sort out the valid and the invalid information delivered by the informant, without being able to check back to the source.

  Given that kind of information, it is easy for the manager to end up fighting the wrong battle with the wrong weapons.

∇ **Questionnaires and surveys** can give useful information on managerial performance, employee attitudes and values, and reactions to managerial decisions. When well-designed, they can be quick and easy to use, anonymous when that is important, simple to analyze statistically, and able to provide feedback from large numbers of employees when necessary.

Feedback Hurdles

No matter how much a manager may want employee feedback, there are a number of hurdles that the manager must clear before it can happen:

- **The manager's own resistance to asking for feedback.** It is unlikely that employees will volunteer significant feedback on a manager's performance if there are no managerial signals that it is desired. That's only human nature. Employees see no point in sticking their necks out unnecessarily.

  Avoiding employee feedback is like running track without keeping any times. It's up to the manager to give employees the signal to "Start the timing clock—I want to know how I'm doing."

- **Employees' past experience.** Your employees' willingness to give you feedback will depend to a great extent on how they were treated in the past when they offered feedback to their managers. If feedback was met with criticism, ridicule, silence, anger, or other defensive behavior, then it may take you a while to build up their trust level.

- **Risk involved.** The freedom with which employees feed useful information back to a manager is often in direct proportion to how much risk the employees perceive is involved. Managers must come to grips with the fact that if they have the power to hire and fire, some employees, if not most, will be unable or unwilling to tell a manager what's really on their mind.

  Although not all managers may have the versatile interpersonal skills necessary to clear this hurdle completely, it can be minimized by using a method of gathering feedback information that is appropriate either to the sensitivity of the information you want, or to the people involved.

  For example, if you want employee feedback on your interpersonal skills, a rather sensitive area, you are probably better off using an anonymous method of acquiring the information. Information on employees' thoughts about the pros and cons of a new insurance package can probably be gathered with reasonable accuracy in a staff meeting. It is the sensitivity of the feedback area—how close it hits to home—that helps determine the feedback system to use.

  A second aspect of risk is the personalities of the employees involved. Some employees are able and willing (sometimes *overly* willing!) to give you feedback face-to-face. Others would rather do it less directly, while there are a few who, if they had their druthers, would much prefer to leave you a note in a hollow tree. It is up to the manager to be sensitive enough to employee differences to know which feedback system to use with which employees.

- **Manager-as-Parent.** Employees who need a lot of support and direction from their manager are often reluctant to give any negative feedback. It is just too unsettling for them to think that the person to whom they are responsible might be wrong.

This kind of employee thinking is very flattering for the manager, but it also provides distorted feedback information. As an answer, "Yessir, boss, sir" may give a manager great feelings of power and authority. It should also give the manager a distinct warning signal that he or she at that moment has no idea at all what the employee is thinking or feeling.

Other employees who have always rebelled against authority may see the manager as parent or authority figure, and distort the feedback accordingly.

∇ **"Us vs. Them."** In many organizations, an adversarial positioning exists between management and workers, between honchos and peons, between the brass and the grunts. This contending relationship can affect both the quantity and the quality of feedback available to managers from their employees. I have worked with organizations where the polarity was initially so bad that it was almost impossible for managers to get reliable feedback. For the managers, it was like trying to sail a ship in a dense fog; they knew they were moving, but they didn't know where.

In a polarized situation, the employee attitude regarding constructive feedback is often, "Why help *them*?" Here the manager needs to convince employees that the feedback on the manager's performance is for the mutual benefit of both employees and manager. It is also necessary for management to work on the other factors that have brought the employees' trust level this low. Failing in that, the situation is likely to continue.

A corollary to the "us vs. them" theme can occur any time there is an adversarial relationship between manager and employee, either individually or as a group. It is known simply as the "Let the S.O.B. fail!" syndrome. Employees reason that if inadequate or inaccurate feedback will hasten the demise of the offending manager, then so be it.

Obviously, the manager must clear up the adversarial relationship before the employee feedback channels will start delivering useful information. The major problem occurs when the manager is blissfully unaware that the syndrome is in operation.

∇ **Fear of reprisal.** Some managers have the unfortunate personality characteristic of taking any employee feedback that can be construed as negative as a personal attack. Many also have the equally unfortunate characteristic of believing that the best, or *only,* response to such a perceived attack is an even more vigorous counterattack. Once that occurs, unless the employee is blessed with more control than the manager, the battle is truly joined, and all hope of constructive feedback is lost in the gunsmoke.

This is not always an accident or personality quirk, for it is an excellent way for the uncertain manager to avoid getting feedback on behaviors or actions. When an employee realizes that giving the manager negative feedback means war, he or she quickly learns to avoid the field of combat. After all, the manager does control the ultimate weapon—the employee's job.

The manager who does *not* attack when employees' feedback is negative may be operating on the principle "Don't get angry—get even." Some managers have memories like elephants for employees they feel have crossed them, with tusks to match. For employees this can be more threatening than an open counterattack, for they never know when or how the "get even" manager will attempt to settle the score.

It doesn't take long for employees to learn the rules of this kind of feedback game, because the manager holds all the high cards—approval, pay scale, favored status, promotions, good assignments, overtime—the job itself. Employees aren't stupid. If the manager is reprisal-oriented, they quickly discover that the safest strategy for answering a request for feedback is, "Sure, boss, whatever you want to hear."

∇ **"Head of the Messenger."** For some managers, it isn't the employee giving them negative feedback that's the problem, it's the *news* that employee brings, for which the employee is made to suffer. I know of one bank president who went through five comptrollers before he found one who would give him the numbers he wanted to hear.

The managers who consistently transfer their negative response to a bad news message over to the messenger soon train their employees to avoid bringing "bad news to the palace of the king." The employees remember all too well what happened to the head of the last member of their work unit who foolishly carried such a message. Good news appears to be a whole lot safer.

As a manager, ask yourself:

- Which messages do I reward, and which do I punish?
- Do I clearly and consistently distinguish between the message and the messenger?

Examine your answers to those questions carefully, and you'll discover what kind of feedback messages you're training your employees to deliver.

Pros and Cons

Even if you think you have the potential for a good feedback system, you still need to decide if you really want feedback, especially on your performance as a manager. There are, after all, pros and cons—two sides to this feedback coin.

On one side, not receiving employee information on your performance can help maintain a comfortable status quo. There's no need for you to change if you aren't aware that any change is needed. No sense rocking the boat if you don't have to.

No employee feedback on your managerial performance also helps keep self-perceptions and illusions intact. Managers who think they are truly great people managers and respected by their employees—but who have never checked it out—may be operating under the same illusions as the emperor with his new clothes.

Some managers fear that even asking employees for feedback on their performance could imply that they might be wrong or weak in some areas, thus undermining themselves as "experts" or authority figures.

On the other side of the coin, if you can honestly solicit feedback from your employees about your managerial performance, and objectively hear it, you can establish a model of willingness and openness to discuss performance improvement with your employees, theirs as well as yours. This can serve to improve organizational performance all across the board.

Using Feedback

Once you've made a firm commitment to request employee feedback on your managerial performance, there are two basic ground rules you may want to remember:

1. The old saying, "Use it or lose it!" is especially true of employee feedback. Employees can't be expected to take the risk of giving you honest feedback if they aren't rewarded by having you make some response to it. This is true even if that response is limited to explaining in a nondefensive way why *no* action can be taken at this time.
2. If you ask for feedback on your managerial performance, your employees have every right to expect that you will at least make an effort to change areas that may need improvement. In short, *if you aren't willing to change, then don't ask for feedback.*

   Keep in mind, however, that if you as the manager aren't willing to change, you probably shouldn't expect your employees to change, either.

In Conclusion

Used judiciously and well, feedback can be a major factor in improving both your own and your employees' performance. If you haven't had the opportunity to get feedback on your managerial performance and would like to start out in a modest way, I suggest using the Managerial Support Assessment at the end of this chapter. It is easy to use, anonymous, and can give you useful information on how your employees perceive your support of their performance.

It gives you the chance to ask, as does New York's Mayor Ed Koch, "How am I doin'?"

∇ ***For additional information, see:***

Chapter 2. When Manager and Employees Communicate
Chapter 4. Feedback Is Free
Chapter 5. Growing the Corporate Culture

Date ______________

∇ Managerial Support Assessment

Directions: Place a square around a number to indicate how important you think that item is for adequate managerial support.
Place a circle around a number to indicate your estimation of your present performance level in providing support for your employees.

Suggestion: Have your employees fill out the "Employee" version. Place their averaged scores in the appropriate places and compare their perceptions with yours.

Scale: **5-Always 4-Usually 3-Occasionally 2-Seldom 1-Never**

Items		**Employees** ☐ O
1. I am available when my employees have a problem or need help.	5 4 3 2 1	___ ___
2. If employees make an honest mistake, rather than being critical, I help them learn from it.	5 4 3 2 1	___ ___
3. I am fair when dealing with my employees.	5 4 3 2 1	___ ___
4. I make quick decisions when an employee needs an answer in order to get a job done.	5 4 3 2 1	___ ___
5. If I reprimand an employee, it is just and called for.	5 4 3 2 1	___ ___
6. I help my employees set reasonable performance goals.	5 4 3 2 1	___ ___
7. I hold regularly scheduled performance reviews with my employees.	5 4 3 2 1	___ ___
8. My employees feel that I will back them up when necessary.	5 4 3 2 1	___ ___
9. I attempt to ensure that my employees are compensated as well as possible for their work.	5 4 3 2 1	___ ___
10. I have realistic expectations of my employees' performance.	5 4 3 2 1	___ ___
11. When I delegate a task, I provide the authority to carry it out along with the responsibility.	5 4 3 2 1	___ ___
12. If there is a problem with an employee's performance, I criticize only the problem behavior, not the employee as a person.	5 4 3 2 1	___ ___
13. I give my employees a balance of both positive and negative feedback on their performance.	5 4 3 2 1	___ ___

continued

Managerial Support, continued.

14. I check in with individual employees and/or work units, even when there is no specific problem. 5 4 3 2 1 ___ ___

15. I praise my employees appropriately for good work. 5 4 3 2 1 ___ ___

Overall rating of the quality of your managerial support skills:

Very high - 10 9 8 7 6 5 4 3 2 1 - Very low (circle one)

Your employees' averaged rating: ___________

Note: Circled items in the 1-2 area may require your immediate attention, as they can be indicators of low support skills. Also notice items in which the circle is two or more numbers to the right of the square, as this indicates a gap between importance and skill level.

Date _____________ EMPLOYEE

∇ Managerial Support Assessment

Directions: Place a <u>square</u> around a number to indicate how <u>important</u> you think that item is for adequate managerial support.
Place a <u>circle</u> around a number to indicate your estimation of your manager's present <u>performance level</u> in providing support for employees.

Scale: **5-Always 4-Usually 3-Occasionally 2-Seldom 1-Never**

Items

1. My manager is available when I have a problem or need help.	5 4 3 2 1
2. If I make an honest mistake, rather than being critical, my manager helps me learn from it.	5 4 3 2 1
3. My manager is fair when dealing with people.	5 4 3 2 1
4. My manager makes quick decisions when I need an answer to get a job done.	5 4 3 2 1
5. If I am reprimanded by my manager, it is just and called for.	5 4 3 2 1
6. My manager helps me set reasonable performance goals.	5 4 3 2 1
7. My manager holds regularly scheduled performance reviews.	5 4 3 2 1
8. I feel that my manager will back me up when necessary.	5 4 3 2 1
9. My manager attempts to ensure that employees are compensated as well as possible for their work.	5 4 3 2 1
10. My manager has realistic expectations of my performance.	5 4 3 2 1
11. When my manager delegates a task, the authority to carry it out is provided along with the responsibility.	5 4 3 2 1
12. If there is a problem with my performance, my manager criticizes only the problem behavior, not me as a person.	5 4 3 2 1
13. My manager gives me a balance of both positive and negative feedback on my performance.	5 4 3 2 1
14. My manager checks in with me and/or my work unit, even when there is no specific problem.	5 4 3 2 1
15. My manager praises me appropriately for good work.	5 4 3 2 1

Overall rating of the quality of your manager's support skills:

<u>Very high</u> - 10 9 8 7 6 5 4 3 2 1 - <u>Very low</u> (circle one)

∇ 2. When Manager and Employees Communicate

The key to success is not information. It's people.
—*Lee Iacocca, Chrysler Corporation*

Contrary to what most of us may think, communication is not a natural human function. Talking was possible only after the invention of language, and writing possible only after someone else designed a symbol system for the talking.

Talking made possible the organization of our ancient ancestors into families and communities, and writing made possible larger organizations like the Roman Empire. Electronic communication makes the contemporary business world possible. Given that breadth of communication history, why aren't we better at it?

The primary reason is that the successful use of communication, like other inventions, involves two inseparable elements: *motivation* and *skill*. No matter how good the orator, without motivation there is still no speech; no matter how strong the intent, if we don't know the language we are still strangers in a strange land.

In terms of manager-employee communication, let's look at both elements, motivation and skill, with an eye toward the improvement of each.

Motivation

As in other human activities, there are two sides to the communication coin: a push-pull. There are good reasons why managers and employees are motivated to communicate with one another, and often equally strong reasons why they are not. In order to eliminate as many barriers to quality manager-employee communication as possible, let's take a look at some of the motivational issues that can block good communication.

- **Privacy.** Some people choose to share their personal lives with only a few close friends. Generally, this isn't a problem in the workplace, except when problems in personal life spill over into the work environment and affect performance.

  If that appears to be the case, a go-slow approach to opening the communication channel will usually be more effective.

  Don't: "I'll bet you're having problems at home. Tell me about it—maybe I can help."

  Better: "Your performance doesn't seem to be up to your usual standards lately. Is there anything you can tell me that might help us get you back on track?"

- **Lack of information.** No problem here—as long as the work environment is open and supportive enough that anyone can say, "Frankly, I don't know" without fear of repercussions. When people feel they *must* give an answer, the communication channels are full of ambiguities, sandbagging, bluffing, and stonewalling.

  Don't: "Well, why *don't* you know? I thought you were supposed to be the expert around here."

  Better: "Thanks for being up-front about it. Find out and get back to me right away, will you?"

- **Maintaining ambiguity.** For a number of reasons, not everyone *wants* to be clear in all communications. If that occurs, it is more likely to be rectified by reinforcing clarity rather than punishing the ambiguity. That only lets the other person confirm that his or her ambiguity strategy is working.

  Don't: "Come on, will you just put it in plain English for me!"

  Better: "Let me tell you what I think you just said and see if you can help clarify it for me."

- **Withholding information/sabotage.** If you know or suspect that this is the case, generally the best strategy is to confront the person within a supportive context, to minimize defensiveness. If the other person becomes defensive, messages may continue, but problem-solving communication stops.

  Don't: "I think you're stonewalling me. Now just tell me what's *really* going on." (If you have enough authority or power, you may get the information—this time. By next time, the person is likely to have put larger or more clever stones in his or her wall.)

  Better: "I have a feeling that there's something else to it. I realize you probably have good reasons for that, which I'll be happy to discuss, but I do really need to know what's going on. Can you help me with the rest?"

  If people want to withhold communication badly enough, even in the face of physical torture, they will. Your only recourse is to create an emotional climate in which they feel comfortable communicating. If you come across as The Inquisition, you won't be able to trust whatever information you do get. People don't like to be intimidated. If they are not in a position to get angry, they will at least attempt to get even. Inaccurate or partial information is an effective way to do that.

∇ **Anger.** Since anger is a stress-producing emotion, angry people tend to react in one of the two ways typical of a stress response: fight or flight, attack or leave the scene.

If the response is fight, the communication channels are likely to be overloaded! The reaction can be either a personal attack on the person at the other end or a very autocratic, "Do as I say because I said so!" response. In either case, true communication stops until the channels are not so emotionally charged.

The best way to defuse fight-oriented individuals is to recognize their anger, hear them out, be sure that you are clear about the nature of the problem that upset them, and then suggest some possible solutions. Until their anger is defused, communication will be a one-way street, so deal with the anger first.

Don't: "If you'll just be quiet for a minute, I'll tell you how to take care of it!"

Better: "You really sound angry! Can you tell me more about it? . . . Let me see if I have this straight. You . . . I have a couple of ideas that might help—want to hear them?"

For the angry person in flight, the communication channels may be empty. As far as meaningful communication is concerned, they've gone elsewhere. To restore the link, you will need to develop a trusting and nonthreatening communication environment so that they are willing to resume contact.

Until you can build that trust level, you are likely to be avoided, stonewalled, or—even more difficult to handle—totally agreed with ("Right, boss, anything you say."). Until the negative flight emotions are resolved, positive communication motivators won't have a chance to operate.

Don't: "Look, I know you must be upset about this. So just speak up and tell me about it."

Better: "I can imagine in your situation I'd be pretty upset. Is there anything that you're thinking or feeling you can tell me about?"

∇ **Fear of retribution.** This communication lesson starts early and is with us for life. If we tell ourselves, "Keep your mouth shut," "Discretion is the better part of valor," or, "Bite your tongue," someone is not finding out what we're really thinking or feeling.

Why are we so reticent in some situations? Usually it's because at an early age we were chastised by those in authority—parents, teachers, and so forth—for "speaking out of turn." We soon learn there are times to have open communication, and times when it is much safer to shut down communication.

We may have been victim of a "head of the messenger" experience by someone who hadn't learned to distinguish message from messenger. We quickly learned, "If you can't tell me good news, be quiet." We may have shared with authority figures thoughts or feelings that were threatening or clashed with theirs, and the ax fell. That taught us, "If it isn't in line with the boss's thinking, hold your tongue."

In the Middle Ages, only the court jester's head was safe when there were disagreements with the king. Unfortunately, in some organizations today that still holds true.

This is a tough one for a manager to deal with if the fear runs deep and was acquired before the manager joined the organization. The best approach is to build a trust level that connotes safety, and then demonstrate sharing thoughts and feelings yourself. You can assume that employees who have a fear of retribution will test these waters very carefully. The first time they or any of their co-workers pay a price for saying what they think or feel, they'll pull back in their communication shell faster than a sea turtle in the middle of Interstate 75.

Don't: "If that's what you *really* think, you're wrong, dead wrong."
Better: "I can't agree with you on this one, but I appreciate your putting your opinion on the table."

∇ **Personal dislike.** Our natural tendency is to communicate with people we like and ignore the ones we don't. There may be no problem with that around the neighborhood, but it doesn't help solve problems in the organizational community. Chances are we probably won't like everyone we must work with.

The method that seems to work best for this communication problem is to make a deliberate shift in what we tell ourselves—a reflection of our beliefs and attitudes—about our communication with other people.

Don't: (to self) "I only communicate openly with people I like."
Better: (to self) "There is no necessary connection between liking someone and open communication. I sometimes will need to communicate with people whether I like them or not."

∇ **Self-consciousness/shyness.** In terms of communication, shyness may take dramatically different forms. People who are passively shy or self-conscious may appear to be quiet, aloof, standoffish, loners, or overly modest. They often will not speak out in large meetings, no matter how intense their feelings or how original their ideas, giving others the impression that they have nothing to say.

The aggressively shy, on the other hand, are apt to be loud and boisterous, talkative, the life of the party, and to dominate loosely structured meetings. Examine the content of their communications, however, and you'll find they've revealed nothing significant of themselves. Like the passively shy, they've figured out a way to keep people at a distance. They just operate on the other side of the same street.

With both types of shyness, a safety net of mutual trust needs to be established before the person will communicate in-depth thoughts and feelings. In both cases you're generally better off communicating on a one-to-one basis.

PASSIVELY SHY:

Don't: "Oh, come on, you're just being modest! Tell us what you really think about it."

Better: "You've had a lot of experience in that area. Can you share with us what you think about it?"

AGGRESSIVELY SHY:

Don't: "Quit acting the fool and give us your opinion on this thing."

Better: "We value your opinion on this thing, too. What do you think about it?"

∇ **Lack of skill.** What may appear to be low communication motivation is often caused by a lack of adequate communication *skills*. This is especially true of those with perfectionist tendencies, for what they can't do well, they'd rather not do at all.

The answer for anyone in this situation is training and experience, with the areas of weakness determining the nature of the training. It may require a little nudge from the manager for it to happen, but communication skills can definitely be improved.

Communication Modes and Media

A number of excellent reference books and training programs deal with the *hows* of verbal, nonverbal, and written communication skills, so we won't go into detail here. What often gets overlooked, however, is the *which.* Not the which of meeting or memo, but which mode to use with each individual with whom we wish to communicate.

Research indicates that we communicate in four basic modes: visual images, visual text, words, and kinesthetic (physical) actions. We take in information this way, process it internally, and use it in communicating that information to others.

If we were all equally proficient with all four modes, there would be no problem; we could put our messages to others in any mode we liked. Most of us, however, prefer only one or two modes as our mode of choice. Communication in that mode is more easily received and processed than in the others.

Observe your co-workers. One frequently says, "Can you get that to me in writing?" Another says, reaching for pencil and napkin, "Here, let me draw it for you." Another advises, "No, a letter's not necessary, just tell it to me over the phone." Still another says, "I'm beginning to get a real feeling for what you mean . . . I think I've got a handle on it."

Think of these four modes—visual, textual, verbal, and physical—as four different languages and your work unit as your own United Nations. Unless you're fluent in all four, there will be some people in your work unit with whom you won't communicate as easily as with others. In answer to the often-exasperated question, "Oh, come on, do I have to draw you a *picture*?" the answer may well be, "yes!"

Putting the Modes to Work

Obviously, most adults can communicate to some degree in all modes. This doesn't mean that we never send a visually oriented person a memo or ask him or her to write a report. As with languages, some have become proficient in several modes, although most of us still have one mother tongue that we prefer. Here are several ways you can put this information to use in your work unit:

For the visually oriented:

- Graphs and flowcharts.
- Symbols.
- Graphics (photographs and drawings).
- Color.

For the verbally oriented:

- Telephone.
- Tape recordings.
- "Walk and talk" meetings.

For the minimal reader on the go:

- Major points set off by bullets.
- Lists rather than prose.
- Short sentences.
- One-page messages, with space for return comments.
- Long topics broken up into smaller units.
- Inclusion of "Return by [date]."

Like a good TV commercial, and for the same reason, use as many different modes in the same communication as you can: sound, text, and images.

In Conclusion

Given the opportunity to speak in our strongest communication language, be it images, text, talk, or physical actions, most of us know *how* to communicate. The main communication issue then becomes the *why*—our intent. The manager who can help create a work environment where employees feel safe to truly express themselves will have leaped the biggest hurdle to meaningful manager-employee communication.

∇ ***For additional information, see:***

Chapter 3. If I'm Talking, Who's Listening?

Chapter 4. Feedback Is Free

Chapter 12. Meetings—Power or Punishment?

Chapter 17. Team-Building for All Seasons

Date________________

∇ Manager-Employee Communication Assessment

Suggestion: Have your employees fill out the "Employee" version. Place their averaged scores in the appropriate places and compare their perceptions with yours.

Scale: **5-Always 4-Usually 3-Occasionally 2-Seldom 1-Never** (circle one)

		Employees
1. Do you generally find talking to your employees an enjoyable experience?	5 4 3 2 1	___
2. Are you as willing to compliment your employees for their good work as you are to find fault with their mistakes?	5 4 3 2 1	___
3. Do you help your employees feel as though they are important people?	5 4 3 2 1	___
4. When you're working with your employees on a problem, are you able to ask questions that help them get to the heart of the matter?	5 4 3 2 1	___
5. Do you help your employees feel at ease when you're talking to them?	5 4 3 2 1	___
6. When your employees have something rather difficult to discuss, do you help make it easier for them to say what is on their mind?	5 4 3 2 1	___
7. When your employees talk with you, do they feel really understood?	5 4 3 2 1	___
8. Do you admit it to your employees when you are wrong?	5 4 3 2 1	___

Scale: **5-Never 4-Seldom 3-Occasionally 2-Usually 1-Always** (circle one)

9. Do you talk too long to hold your employees' attention?	5 4 3 2 1	___
10. When your employees talk to you, do they feel as though they are talking to a blank wall?	5 4 3 2 1	___
11. When you are talking with your employees, do you end up discussing only those things that are of interest to you?	5 4 3 2 1	___
12. When you give your employees instructions, do they find it difficult to understand what you want them to do?	5 4 3 2 1	___
13. When you are discussing something with your employees, do they feel as though they are being cross-examined?	5 4 3 2 1	___
14. Does talking with your employees cause them to feel stupid or diminished?	5 4 3 2 1	___
15. Do you seem to contradict your own previous instructions?	5 4 3 2 1	___

Overall rating of the quality of your manager-employee communications:

Very high - 10 9 8 7 6 5 4 3 2 1 - Very low (circle one)

Your employees' averaged rating: ____________

∇ Manager-Employee Communication Assessment

Scale: 5-Always 4-Usually 3-Occasionally 2-Seldom 1-Never (circle one)

1. Do you generally find talking to your manager an enjoyable experience? 5 4 3 2 1
2. Is your manager as willing to compliment you for your good work as to find fault with your mistakes? 5 4 3 2 1
3. Does your manager help you feel as though you are an important person? 5 4 3 2 1
4. When you're working with your manager on a problem, is your manager able to ask questions that help you get to the heart of the matter? 5 4 3 2 1
5. Does your manager help you feel at ease when you're talking to him or her? 5 4 3 2 1
6. When you have something rather difficult to discuss, does your manager help make it easier for you to say what is on your mind? 5 4 3 2 1
7. When you talk with your manager, do you feel really understood? 5 4 3 2 1
8. Does your manager admit it when she or he is wrong? 5 4 3 2 1

Scale: 5-Never 4-Seldom 3-Occasionally 2-Usually 1-Always

9. Does your manager talk too long to hold your attention? 5 4 3 2 1
10. When talking with your manager, do you feel as though you are talking to a blank wall? 5 4 3 2 1
11. When you talk with your manager, do you end up discussing only those things that are of interest to him or her? 5 4 3 2 1
12. When your manager gives you instructions, do you find it difficult to understand what you are supposed to do? 5 4 3 2 1
13. When you are discussing something with your manager, do you feel as though you are being cross-examined? 5 4 3 2 1
14. Does talking with your manager cause you to feel stupid or diminished? 5 4 3 2 1
15. Does your manager seem to contradict his or her own previous instructions? 5 4 3 2 1

Overall rating of the quality of your manager-employee communications:

Very high - 10 9 8 7 6 5 4 3 2 1 - Very low (circle one)

∇ 3. If I'm Talking, Who's Listening?

I know you believe you understand what you think I said, but I am not sure you realize that what you heard is not what I meant.

—*Anonymous*

Do you frequently find yourself in a verbal communication maze, either at home or on the job? Does it often seem as though you and your employees could use some brushing up on listening skills?

According to Madelyn Burley-Allen, author of *Listening: The Forgotten Skill*, a 1980 survey of Fortune 1000 company presidents indicated that the two most anxiety-producing work situations for top management were the failure of employees to accept and/or carry out responsibilities, and the failure of managers to receive critical information. Both of these problem areas imply inadequate listening skills.

To put the value of good listening skills in a bottom-line context, imagine that if each of the hundred million or more American workers made one small five-dollar mistake per year because of poor listening. The annual cost to American business would be half a *billion* dollars!

Is this estimate realistic? A study of one hundred business and industrial organizations revealed that listening seems to be less effective the farther down the organizational chart you go, from a high of 90 percent for members of the board of directors to an alarming low of 20 percent for employees listening to a supervisor. This indicates not only that there is room for improvement of managerial listening skills, but also that there is a high need for managers to train their employees in more effective listening.

Dr. Ralph Nichols, in his book *Are You Listening?*, summarizes several studies that indicate how much of our total interpersonal communication uses the four basic skills of reading, writing, speaking, and listening. Unfortunately for good interpersonal communication, the amount of formal training we receive in each skill is in inverse proportion to the amount we use the skill in actual practice.

Skill	Of Total Communications, % of Use in Practice	Formal Training in Skill
Writing	9%	8–12 years (or more)
Reading	16%	6–8 years (or more)
Speaking	35%	1–2 years (or more)
Listening	40%	0–1/2 year (or more)
	100%	

The Importance of Good Listening

Is good listening really that important? Besides, isn't it something that we all do naturally anyway? Yes, it is. And no, it isn't.

We tend to equate "listening" with "hearing," and that is simply not the case. Good listening implies:

- Heightened awareness of what you hear.
- Accurate reception of the information presented to you.
- Integration of the information in such a way that it is useful to you.

For example, if I *hear* a strange sound in my automobile engine but ignore it until the engine stops late on a Saturday night halfway between here and there, I certainly didn't *listen* to the engine in the same way that a trained mechanic would have: I didn't attach any *meaning* to the "ka-thunks."

Likewise, if my manager's secretary pointedly says, "I'm really not sure you want to ask about that raise this morning," but I charge into the manager's office anyway, I have no one to blame but myself if an upset manager turns me down cold. I *heard* the secretary's words, but I didn't *listen* for the meaning.

For a manager, good listening provides a number of positive results:

∇ **Prevents misinformation.** The number of costly mistakes that are the result of someone not listening to facts, figures, instructions, and situations is incalculable, probably far exceeding our half-billion-dollar estimate. For example, how much would your raise have been worth had you really *listened* to your manager's secretary and brought up the issue at a more opportune time?

∇ **Improves morale, rapport, and trust level.** Much of our self-concept is based on how others treat us, and listening is no exception. If you truly listen to employees' thoughts, feelings, and ideas, they will feel better about themselves, you, and the working relationship.

They are also more likely to give you productive ideas and suggestions, since it is human nature to volunteer information only if we feel it is really going to be listened to.

∇ **Enhances teamwork.** If people in any group—family, office, or factory—are taking the time and energy truly to listen to one another, then teamwork, cooperation, and group effectiveness improve immensely. No one likes to work with someone who doesn't listen to ideas, suggestions, or other points of view. Good communication is vital to good team performance, and listening is an important ingredient.

But if listening is such an essential part of good communication, why aren't managers and employees better at it? What gets in the way between hearing and listening?

Barriers to Good Listening

A number of factors can impede the listening process:

∇ **Habits.** You may have acquired poor listening habits from parents, friends, or family, or developed them on your own. Consciously or unconsciously, such habitual behaviors as interrupting, jumping to conclusions, distracting the speaker, or changing the subject tend to undermine your best listening intentions.

∇ **Filters.** Everything you hear is passed through what might be called your filter system: your beliefs, experiences, customs, expectations, assumptions, prejudices, and cultural background. If a speaker is saying something that is significantly different than your filter system, it can set up a conflict within you that seriously interferes with your ability to listen objectively.

∇ **Physical environment.** Annoying or distracting sounds, physical discomfort, visual distractions, fatigue, or lack of privacy can all interfere with effective listening.

- ∇ **Competitiveness.** If you have an excessive need to dominate the conversation, for whatever reason, you'll spend more time thinking about what *you* want to say, the impact it will have, and how you can get back into the conversation, than you will spend really listening to the speaker. Also, listening can be considered a passive act, felt by some as a discomforting loss of control.

- ∇ **Shyness.** If you are uncomfortable or self-conscious in social situations, you may be so concerned with what you are going to say next, or with what others are thinking of you, that you don't hear what they are saying to you.

- ∇ **Bad news.** If others are telling you something you don't want to know—bad news—you may subconsciously tune it out. Asked about it later, you may not remember hearing it.

- ∇ **Difference in rate.** The average rate of speech is 100 to 150 words per minute, while the average thinking rate—"talking to yourself"—is 250 to 500 words per minute. If you are distracted, or have "more important things on your mind," then you are likely to fill in this difference in speed with your own thoughts—and soon you're not listening to the other person at all.

Good listening isn't easy, especially when we consider that words alone are not even the most important part of the communication process. Here are the percentages that make up the average verbal exchange between two people who are "talking" and "listening" to one another:

Nonverbal (gestures, body motion, expressions, stance, etc.)	55%
Tonality (*how* we say the words)	38%
Words (*what* we say)	7%

Surprised? Most people are. But think of all the ways you can say the word "No," including the gestures and expressions, and the different messages a careful listener would get from each of them.

Good listening, then, is more often being aware of *how* something is said rather than *what* is said. In many cases, good listening is also realizing what has been left *unsaid* (a skill brought to a high art by teenagers for listening to parents: "But, Dad, you didn't say *not* to take your car out to the drag strip. Besides, look at the trophy . . .").

Active Listening

Most experts agree that there are three basic components to active listening, the sincere attempt to understand as much as possible of what is being communicated to you:

- **Selective listening** is sorting out from the information you are receiving only those things that are pertinent to what is being discussed. For example, if you're talking to Sandy about frequent lateness, you ignore the account of the family's weekend fishing trip or the kids' dance recital and focus on the problems with Sandy's car pool.

  Too often we think that being polite requires us to listen and respond to everything, whether it is pertinent to the discussion or not. Doing so encourages the speaker to take off on tangents.

- **Responsive listening** is letting the speaker know that you are paying attention and understanding what is being said. We do this verbally and nonverbally, using smiles, nods of the head, "hmm," "really," laughing, and other indicators that we are following and interested in what is being said. Appropriate questions to clarify meaning also let the speaker know we are listening.

- **Empathic listening** is letting the speaker know that we understand what is being said, usually by reflecting it back to the speaker and checking for accuracy.

  For example, "So from what you've told me, Sandy, I gather that one member of your car pool is consistently late, so that when he's driving, you're also late. Is that correct?" This gives the speaker a chance to clarify the information if it didn't come across to you in the way that the speaker intended.

  The use of empathic listening does not imply that you necessarily agree with the speaker, only that you understand what was said.

  Good empathic listening makes use of all three communications components: words, tonality, and nonverbal cues and messages. It also checks with the speaker if there is a mixed message, that is, if all three components of the communication process don't seem to be sending the same message.

  For example, "Sandy, you're telling me the car pool is the cause of your being late, but you look a little nervous. Are you sure that's the only reason?"

Improving Listening Skills

Following are a few suggestions to help improve your listening skills and those of your employees:

- **Talk less.** You can't listen if you are doing most of the talking.

- **Avoid hasty judgments.** Keep an open mind until all of the speaker's facts are in. A premature judgment tends to close your mind to further information and distort your listening.

∇ **Focus on what you can learn.** Even the most boring speaker usually has something useful for you in what he or she says—or doesn't say. As Harry Truman observed, "The only things worth learning are the things you learn after you know it all."

∇ **"Read" the nonverbals.** The speaker's hands, eyes, face, mouth, and body provide additional information about the meaning of the words. This focus on the visual as well as the verbal also helps you concentrate, while letting the speaker know you are listening. It also alerts you to mixed messages that may indicate a gap between what the speaker is saying and really thinking or feeling.

∇ **Make notes.** Most of us don't have a perfect memory, and when accurate recall of the information is important, write it down. This is also a good signal to the speaker that you are listening. Reading your notes back to the speaker is also an excellent way to check your listening accuracy. If you think taking notes will make the speaker uncomfortable, ask permission first.

∇ **Let the speaker finish** what he or she has to say. By interrupting, you imply that what you have to say is more important than what the speaker was saying, or that you've heard it before. This "Me first—you later" message does not make for healthy or trusting communications.

∇ **Ask questions** to clarify your understanding of what was said and to check out assumptions you may have made while the speaker was talking. As someone once said, "The only dumb question is the one you didn't ask."

In Conclusion

Quality listening isn't easy. It requires energy, concentration, and consistent feedback to the speaker. Unlike merely *hearing*, it also takes practice.

Is it worth it? Imagine the benefits to both your personal and job situations if everyone actually listened and accurately understood what was said. The rewards would be well worth the effort to actively listen.

∇ ***For additional information, see:***

Chapter 2. When Manager and Employees Communicate
Chapter 4. Feedback Is Free

∇ Listening Skills Assessment

Directions: Place a square around a number to indicate how important you think that skill is for good listening.
Place a circle around a number to indicate your estimation of your present skill level in listening to your employees.

Suggestion: Have your employees fill out the "Employee" version. Place their averaged scores in the appropriate places and compare their perceptions with yours.

Scale: **High/Excellent - 5 4 3 2 1 - Low/Poor**

Skills		**Employees** □	O
1. Regarding what the speaker says as important--at least to the speaker.	5 4 3 2 1	___	___
2. Listening without interrupting.	5 4 3 2 1	___	___
3. Not rushing the speaker.	5 4 3 2 1	___	___
4. Giving full attention to the speaker.	5 4 3 2 1	___	___
5. Not responding judgmentally.	5 4 3 2 1	___	___
6. Adjusting to the speaker's pace.	5 4 3 2 1	___	___
7. Listening objectively.	5 4 3 2 1	___	___
8. Responding both to what is said and to what is left unsaid.	5 4 3 2 1	___	___
9. Checking to be sure that he or she heard correctly.	5 4 3 2 1	___	___
10. Maintaining confidentiality.	5 4 3 2 1	___	___

Overall rating of the quality of your listening skills:

Very high - 10 9 8 7 6 5 4 3 2 1 - Very low (circle one)

Your employees' averaged rating: ___________

Note: Circled items in the 1-2 area may require immediate attention to improve your listening skills. Also, give close attention to items in which the circle is two or more numbers to the right of the square, as this indicates a gap between importance and skill level.

Date ______________ EMPLOYEE

∇ Listening Skills Assessment

Directions: Place a square around a number to indicate how important you think that skill is for good listening.
Place a circle around a number to indicate your estimation of your manager's present skill level in listening to employees.

Scale: **High/Excellent - 5 4 3 2 1 - Low/Poor**

Skills

1. Regarding what the speaker says as important--at least to the speaker.	5 4 3 2 1
2. Listening without interrupting.	5 4 3 2 1
3. Not rushing the speaker.	5 4 3 2 1
4. Giving full attention to the speaker.	5 4 3 2 1
5. Not responding judgmentally.	5 4 3 2 1
6. Adjusting to the speaker's pace.	5 4 3 2 1
7. Listening objectively.	5 4 3 2 1
8. Responding both to what is said and to what is left unsaid.	5 4 3 2 1
9. Checking to be sure he or she heard the speaker correctly.	5 4 3 2 1
10. Maintaining confidentiality.	5 4 3 2 1

Overall rating of the quality of your manager's listening skills:

Very high - 10 9 8 7 6 5 4 3 2 1 - Very low (circle one)

∇ 4. Feedback Is Free

Rebuke in private, praise in public.
—*William Lee Hanford,*
letter to his son, 1833

Giving employees constructive feedback is one of the most important functions a manager can perform. Unfortunately for employee morale, productivity, and high performance, it is also one of the most neglected.

Many management experts feel that, contrary to a claim we've heard since childhood by a well-known cereal manufacturer, feedback is "the breakfast of champions." It is virtually impossible to know whether job performance is meeting necessary requirements—let alone improve that performance—unless there is adequate and accurate feedback.

Growing up near Michigan's Lake St. Clair, I thought I was a pretty good sailor—until my first collegiate race, when an opponent in an identical boat passed me to windward like I'd forgotten to raise the anchor. *That* was feedback! Not very pleasant for a hotshot college freshman, but at least it left no doubts as to the performance criteria I was going to have to meet to be a competitive collegiate sailor.

Not all managers are comfortable with feedback, no matter on which end of the process they find themselves. Some can handle receiving it, but would rather not give it to their employees. Others are just the opposite, giving it generously but becoming defensive if it comes back the other way. Some would rather just avoid the whole thing, like some dangerous weapon.

There are managers who are sufficiently concerned about receiving possibly negative feedback that they don't undertake projects that they are otherwise perfectly competent to handle.

The impression that employees get from such managers is that feedback, especially positive feedback, must be a very rare commodity. If that's so, employees reason, positive feedback will be doled out by managers only on certain special occasions, such as the thirtieth of February.

Reasons for Not Giving Feedback

Why do some managers apparently think that feedback can't be freely dispensed? The reasons vary from manager to manager, and not all are equally clear, even to the managers involved. Here are several that have been collected from managers all across the country:

- "I don't have time."
- "They already know how well they're doing."
- "If anything goes wrong, I'll tell them."
- "They're professionals—they shouldn't need to be told."
- "I don't want to interrupt their work."
- "If I told them they were doing a good job, they'd want more money."
- "The only feedback anyone ever gave *me* on the way up was a kick in the backside if I screwed up."
- "I told him how he was doing three years ago, and nothing has changed since."
- "A manager should maintain a certain professional distance from employees."
- "If I told them how they were doing now, I wouldn't have anything to talk about in this year's performance review."
- "I'm keeping them from getting swollen egos."

Unfortunately, employees do not work in a vacuum. In the absence of feedback from their managers, employees will make up their own. And it often isn't accurate. Incompetent employees may think they're doing a great job if the manager never says anything. Even more common are capable employees who have a negative impression of their performance because their manager has not given them positive feedback.

Improving Feedback Skills

If you would like to improve your employee feedback skills, there are several things you can do:

∇ Give feedback **directly.** There's a basic law of communication—both interpersonal and electronic—that states that the more relay stations a message goes through, the more likely it is to be distorted. In many situations, therefore, second- or third-hand feedback can be worse than none at all. The sender doesn't know if it was delivered accurately. The receiver, realizing it is probably distorted, either regards it suspiciously or doesn't bother to act on it at all. The employee also wonders why the manager didn't contact him or her directly. This often leads to insecurity, distrust, and lowered morale.

∇ Deliver feedback **immediately.** Feedback is like oatmeal—it doesn't go down as well when it's cold. To be effective, feedback should be given as soon after the event or situation as possible. Don't save it up for an annual performance review.

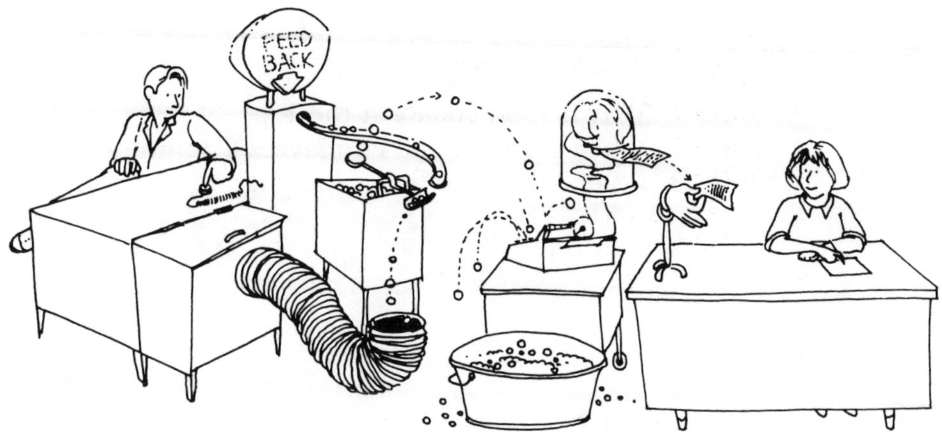

∇ Be **specific.** It is hard to improve performance based on generalized feedback. "You're doing a terrific job" helps employees feel good, but it doesn't tell them the specific strengths on which you want them to build. Likewise, "You really botched that one!" doesn't provide them with sufficient specific information to make constructive changes for the next time.

∇ Give feedback **honestly.** Whether the feedback is positive or negative, your employees can see through superficial or condescending feedback immediately. If it isn't honest, don't give it at all, for it will lessen your credibility for a time when feedback really matters.

Remember, too, that the purpose of feedback is to help change employee behavior in a way that improves performance. Feedback should only be given, therefore, concerning behavior over which the employee has some control. It only increases employees' frustration to be criticized for something they can't do anything about.

∇ Distribute feedback **equally.** Some managers use a feedback system that has come to be known as the LAZY model—*L*eave *A*lone, *Z*ap *Y*ou. Employees receive no feedback at all until they do something wrong, then the manager zaps them. The frequent result is employees' avoidance of the manager, once they realize that the appearance of the manager usually means bad news.

In Conclusion

Feedback can be considered a guidance system that helps employees know how closely their performance is matching your standards and expectations. By indicating areas of strength and weakness, it also helps them understand what they can do to improve performance. As with any guidance system, however, feedback functions best when it is accurate, timely, and on target.

∇ ***For additional information, see:***

Chapter 1. Why Is It So Lonely at the Top?
Chapter 2. When Manager and Employees Communicate
Chapter 3. If I'm Talking, Who's Listening?

Date ____________ **MANAGER**

∇ Giving Feedback Assessment

Directions: Place a square around a number to indicate how important you think that skill is for giving good feedback.
Place a circle around a number to indicate your estimation of your present skill level in giving feedback to your employees.

Suggestion: Have your employees fill out the "Employee" version. Place their averaged scores in the appropriate places and compare their perceptions with yours.

Scale: **High/Excellent - 5 4 3 2 1 - Low/Poor**

Skills		**Employees** □ O
1. Giving feedback that is accurate.	5 4 3 2 1	___ ___
2. Basing feedback on observed behavior.	5 4 3 2 1	___ ___
3. Giving feedback that is specific.	5 4 3 2 1	___ ___
4. Giving feedback that is objective.	5 4 3 2 1	___ ___
5. Giving feedback that is a balance between positive and negative.	5 4 3 2 1	___ ___
6. Giving feedback that is useful for making changes.	5 4 3 2 1	___ ___
7. Keeping the feedback confidential.	5 4 3 2 1	___ ___
8. Being timely in giving feedback.	5 4 3 2 1	___ ___
9. Providing the opportunity for responding to your feedback.	5 4 3 2 1	___ ___
10. Giving feedback in an appropriate mode: verbal, writing, images or kinesthetic.	5 4 3 2 1	___ ___
11. Giving feedback that is honest.	5 4 3 2 1	___ ___
12. Giving feedback directly--not second-hand or roundabout.	5 4 3 2 1	___ ___

Overall rating of the quality of your feedback to your employees:

Very high - 10 9 8 7 6 5 4 3 2 1 - Very low (circle one)

Your employees' averaged rating: __________

Note: Circled items in the 1-2 area may require immediate attention to improve your feedback skills. Also, give close attention to items in which the circle is two or more numbers to the right of the square, as this indicates a gap between importance and skill level.

Date ____________

EMPLOYEE

∇ Giving Feedback Assessment

Directions: Place a square around a number to indicate how important you think that skill is for giving good feedback.
Place a circle around a number to indicate your estimation of your manager's present skill level in giving feedback to employees.

Scale: **High/Excellent - 5 4 3 2 1 - Low/Poor**

Skills

1. Giving feedback that is accurate.	5 4 3 2 1
2. Basing feedback on observed behavior.	5 4 3 2 1
3. Giving feedback that is specific.	5 4 3 2 1
4. Giving feedback that is objective.	5 4 3 2 1
5. Giving feedback that is a balance between positive and negative.	5 4 3 2 1
6. Giving feedback that is useful for making changes.	5 4 3 2 1
7. Keeping the feedback confidential.	5 4 3 2 1
8. Being timely in giving feedback.	5 4 3 2 1
9. Providing the opportunity for responding to your feedback.	5 4 3 2 1
10. Giving feedback in an appropriate mode: verbal, writing, images or kinesthetic.	5 4 3 2 1
11. Giving feedback that is honest.	5 4 3 2 1
12. Giving feedback directly--not second-hand or roundabout.	5 4 3 2 1

Overall rating of the quality of your manager's feedback to employees:

Very high - 10 9 8 7 6 5 4 3 2 1 - Very low (circle one)

∇ 5. Growing the Corporate Culture

. . . and that's the way things are around here.
—*Steelworker, 1983*

Webster's defines *culture* as "the ideas, customs, skills, arts, etc. of a given people in a given period." This traditionally referred to large groups of people—nations, regions, or ethnic groups. More recently, astute managers have realized that an organization also has its own corporate culture. Social anthropologists are now as fascinated by corporate cultures as they once were by head-hunting tribes in Borneo.

Why is business now interested in areas once reserved for the Margaret Meads of social anthropology? The answer is simple—profitability. Research into organizational productivity indicates that the equation goes like this:

WORK CULTURE = PRODUCTIVITY = PROFITABILITY

If increased profitability is an organizational goal, one of the best places to start improvements is with an examination of the organization's work culture.

What do we mean by a work, or corporate, culture? Basically, it is the sum total of the formal and informal systems by which things happen in an organization. It is the information that precedes the statement ". . . and that's the way things are around here." The work culture reflects not only the organizational flowchart, but also who really has the power to make things happen, and how that power is used.

The strongest component of the work culture is the beliefs and attitudes of the employees, the people who make up the culture. If these cultural norms contains beliefs such as, "Around here, nobody dares make waves" or, "Do just enough to get by and people will leave you alone," the organization's performance will reflect those beliefs.

On the other hand, if the cultural belief system contains positive approaches, such as, "Winners are rewarded here" or, "People really care if you do a good job in this outfit," that also will be reflected in the organization's performance. No amount of high-sounding corporate slogans or mottoes will really influence bottom-line performance unless the employees' belief systems have created a productive culture that is in agreement with the organization's mission.

Influencing the Culture

What creates and influences the culture? There are several major factors:

∇ **The manager's behavior.** Studies indicate that the single greatest influence on the work culture is the manager. As Chrysler chairman Lee Iacocca says, "The speed of the boss is the speed of the team."

Employees soon realize that the best way to get ahead in an organization, while staying out of trouble, is to pay attention not so much to what the manager *says*, but to what the manager *does*. Actions, in fact, do speak louder than words. The belief system of the manager, as indicated by the manager's behavior, will usually be mirrored by a significant number of employees.

∇ **Employee selection.** Some of the major high-performance organizations, such as IBM, carefully select their employees to fit in with the existing corporate culture. They become "IBM-ers." Not everyone, of course, may want to work in such a uniform culture, but it does produce a highly productive organization, as well as very low employee turnover.

∇ **The nature of the business.** Some businesses have long-established cultures, either as individual organizations or as professions. For example, there are certain beliefs common to the newspaper business, whether you work for a small daily in rural Iowa or a large New York tabloid. The legal profession has a common culture, no matter which aspect of the law you practice. So do long-distance truck drivers, nurses, or jockeys. Most professionals bring a set of cultural beliefs with them, regardless of where they work.

The exception to this may be in new industries such as electronics, where neither the job roles nor the products even existed a few years ago. Firms in California's Silicon Valley, for example, literally had to build new corporate cultures since no models existed in their industry. According to consultant Robert Bly, this culture has developed into one of "high turnover, long work hours, intense enthusiasm for one's work, technology as king over marketing or the customer—and everyone's goal is to be an entrepreneur, not a vice-president."

This can create excessive employee stress and tension, and drug use, alcoholism, and divorce are reported to be higher than normal in those industries.

∇ **The external culture.** An organization's internal culture can be strongly influenced by the culture of the community that surrounds it. Americans who set up businesses abroad soon learn that they must respect the local cultural beliefs if they expect to have a smoothly functioning organization.

Improving the Culture

Since the nature and quality of the work culture seem to have a direct effect on organizational performance and profitability, managers understandably want to know how their work cultures can be improved. If this is an issue for you or your organization, here are some suggestions:

∇ **Establish a clear corporate mission.** It is amazing how many organizations can't state in simple terms the reasons for their existence. Try it for yourself by completing the statement, "This organization exists for the purpose of . . ." If this proves difficult, you have discovered a good place to start improving your work culture.

A clear and easily understood organizational mission statement makes it much easier for people within the organization to set priorities, make decisions, and determine values. It lets you know who you are as an organization. It helps everyone in the organization answer that most basic question, "What am I doing here?"

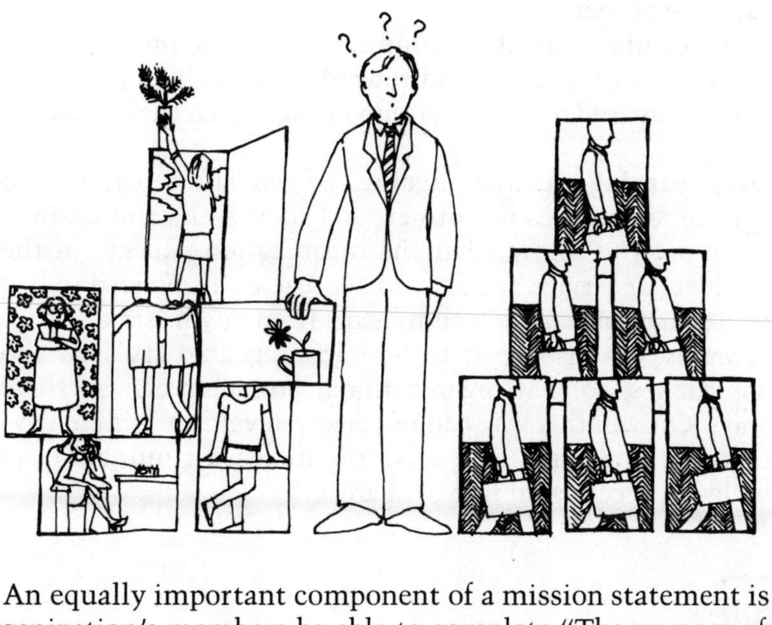

An equally important component of a mission statement is that all of the organization's members be able to complete "The purpose of this organization is . . ." and arrive at much the same answer as does upper management.

Many managers seem to assume that employees can do this, without ever really finding out.

Check it out for yourself: Have the members of your organization or work unit take a few minutes to complete the statement anonymously. Compare their statements with what you think is the purpose of your organization. The differences may astonish you.

It is imperative that managers clearly communicate to all members of the organization what the purpose of the organization really is. Without that understanding, employees do not feel that they are essential to the organization, its functions, or its future direction. They "just work there." The result can be mediocre job performance, absenteeism, low corporate loyalty, and high turnover. People only stay on a train as long as they have a clear idea of where it is going, and as long as its destination is the same as their own.

∇ **Keep the mission up front.** Once an organization's purpose has been clearly established, the manager must ensure that it is continually kept in front of the organization's members. These should be words that the organization lives by, not words stored in the janitor's closet, and they need frequent reiteration. It isn't enough to remind employees at the annual company picnic or the yearly sales meeting; it must be done on an ongoing basis. It would be hard to maintain a religion in a culture where everyone comes to church on only one religious holiday.

∇ **Managers must reflect the desired culture.** When an organization's mission and purpose have been made clear to all of its members, the manager must determine what behaviors are consistent with the desired culture and set an example of them.

For example, if clear communication is important, then it is up to managers to recognize and reward it, as well as practice it themselves. If positive attitudes and beliefs are needed, then they must come from the top.

∇ **Employee learning must be ongoing.** To generate a performance-oriented work culture, employees need to expand their skills and knowledge continually. They need to know what the organization expects in the way of quality products or service and how to achieve it. They need to be coached through new situations and helped to learn from any mistakes.

Employees also need to be encouraged to try new ideas, methods, or approaches, so that organizational problems can be solved in innovative ways. Only in this way can managers develop a sufficiently supportive work culture to imaginatively solve the increasing number of problems brought on by an accelerated rate of change.

In Conclusion

An organization's cultural norms are so all-pervasive that they are almost invisible, but if you would like to improve performance and profitability, norms are one of the first places to look. Ask yourself what employee beliefs or attitudes, including yours, relate to the question, "How are things done around here?" When you have the answers, you'll be on the track to understanding your own corporate culture and its relationship to organizational performance.

The successful manager cannot leave the development of a high-performance work culture to chance if the business is not to risk its very future. Fortunately, that needn't be the case. An alert manager can take the necessary steps to ensure that the quality of the work culture matches the quality of the organization's products or services.

The quality of the work culture and the quality of employee performance go hand-in-hand. It is up to the manager to determine along which path they'll walk.

∇ *For additional information, see:*

Chapter 1. Why Is It So Lonely at the Top?
Chapter 2. When Manager and Employees Communicate
Chapter 6. Managerial Styles—Plain and Fancy
Chapter 7. The Challenge of Change
Chapter 13. Creative Problem-Solving for Fun and Profit
Chapter 17. Team-Building for All Seasons
Chapter 22. Performance Appraisal: Who Needs It?
Chapter 23. Contrlling Qualitey Conttrol
Chapter 24. To Train, or Not to Train?

Date ____________ **MANAGER**

∇ Corporate Culture Assessment

Directions: Place a square around a number to indicate how important you think that item is in a positive corporate culture.
Place a circle around a number to indicate your estimation of the current situation in your organization's corporate culture.

Suggestion: Have your employees fill out the "Employee" version. Place their averaged scores in the appropriate places and compare their perceptions with yours.

Scale: **High/Excellent - 5 4 3 2 1 - Low/Poor**

Items		**Employees** □ O
1. Organizational mission clear to all employees.	5 4 3 2 1	___ ___
2. Positive level of group norms (widely-held beliefs of the employees as to "how things are done around here").	5 4 3 2 1	___ ___
3. Feedback on performance at all levels of the organization.	5 4 3 2 1	___ ___
4. The general level of corporate loyalty.	5 4 3 2 1	___ ___
5. Organizational awareness of need for balance between personal and organizational needs.	5 4 3 2 1	___ ___
6. The organization "practices what it preaches."	5 4 3 2 1	___ ___
7. Retention of good people in the organization.	5 4 3 2 1	___ ___
8. Organizational support for innovations.	5 4 3 2 1	___ ___
9. Consistent/predictable management practices.	5 4 3 2 1	___ ___
10. The organization develops good leader-managers.	5 4 3 2 1	___ ___
11. Creativity/innovation is rewarded.	5 4 3 2 1	___ ___
12. The quality of internal communications.	5 4 3 2 1	___ ___
13. People are treated fairly.	5 4 3 2 1	___ ___
14. The quality of fringe benefits.	5 4 3 2 1	___ ___
15. The organization encourages employee input.	5 4 3 2 1	___ ___

continued

Corporate Culture, continued.

16. Opportunities for employee involvement in organizational decision-making.	5 4 3 2 1 ___
17. Management adequate for its level of responsibilities.	5 4 3 2 1 ___
18. Organization responsive to employee input--there is follow-up.	5 4 3 2 1 ___
19. Quality of the physical facilities.	5 4 3 2 1 ___
20. Pay levels consistent with comparable work in other organizations.	5 4 3 2 1 ___
21. Rewards consistent with individual contributions.	5 4 3 2 1 ___
22. Support for professional development.	5 4 3 2 1 ___
23. Support for personal development.	5 4 3 2 1 ___
24. Adequate career development program.	5 4 3 2 1 ___
25. The organization consistently acts on the principle that <u>people</u> are its greatest asset.	5 4 3 2 1 ___
Other: ____________________	5 4 3 2 1 ___
Other: ____________________	5 4 3 2 1 ___

Your overall rating of this organization as "a good place to work":

<u>Very high</u> - 10 9 8 7 6 5 4 3 2 1 - <u>Very low</u> (circle one)

Your employees' averaged rating: __________

Note: <u>Circled</u> items in the 1-2 area can be problem areas that lower employee morale, motivation, and performance. They may need to be your highest priority for organizational change and development.

Also give close attention to items in which the circle is two or more numbers to the <u>right</u> of the square as this indicates a gap between <u>importance</u> and the <u>current situation</u>.

Date ______________

EMPLOYEE

∇ Corporate Culture Assessment

Directions: Place a square around a number to indicate how important you think that item is in a positive corporate culture.
Place a circle around a number to indicate your estimation of the current situation in your organization's corporate culture.

Scale: **High/Excellent - 5 4 3 2 1 - Low/Poor**

Items

1. Organizational mission clear to all employees.	5 4 3 2 1
2. Positive level of group norms (widely-held beliefs of the employees as to "how things are done around here").	5 4 3 2 1
3. Feedback on performance at all levels of the organization.	5 4 3 2 1
4. The general level of corporate loyalty.	5 4 3 2 1
5. Organizational awareness of need for balance between personal and organizational needs.	5 4 3 2 1
6. The organization "practices what it preaches."	5 4 3 2 1
7. Retention of good people in the organization.	5 4 3 2 1
8. Organizational support for innovations.	5 4 3 2 1
9. Consistent/predictable management practices.	5 4 3 2 1
10. The organization develops good leader-managers.	5 4 3 2 1
11. Creativity/innovation is rewarded.	5 4 3 2 1
12. The quality of internal communications.	5 4 3 2 1
13. People are treated fairly.	5 4 3 2 1
14. The quality of fringe benefits.	5 4 3 2 1
15. The organization encourages employee input.	5 4 3 2 1
16. Opportunities for employee involvement in organizational decision-making.	5 4 3 2 1
17. Management adequate for its level of responsibilities.	5 4 3 2 1
18. Organization responsive to employee input--there is follow-up.	5 4 3 2 1

continued

Corporate Culture, continued.

19. Quality of the physical facilities.	5 4 3 2 1
20. Pay levels consistent with comparable work in other organizations.	5 4 3 2 1
21. Rewards consistent with individual contributions.	5 4 3 2 1
22. Support for professional development.	5 4 3 2 1
23. Support for personal development.	5 4 3 2 1
24. Adequate career development program.	5 4 3 2 1
25. The organization consistently acts on the principle that people are its greatest asset.	5 4 3 2 1
Other: ______________________________	5 4 3 2 1
Other: ______________________________	5 4 3 2 1

Your overall rating of this organization as "a good place to work."

Very High - 10 9 8 7 6 5 4 3 2 1 - Very low (circle one)

Comments:

∇ 6. Managerial Styles—Plain and Fancy

Wherever managers gather, one topic almost guaranteed to start a vigorous debate is, "Which managerial style is best?" Each manager stoutly defends his or her own style and has the appropriate war stories to prove it. Why, after all this heated discussion, has one managerial style not emerged as clearly superior?

Basic Styles

To help answer that question, let's look at some of the basic managerial styles, along with their strengths and weaknesses.

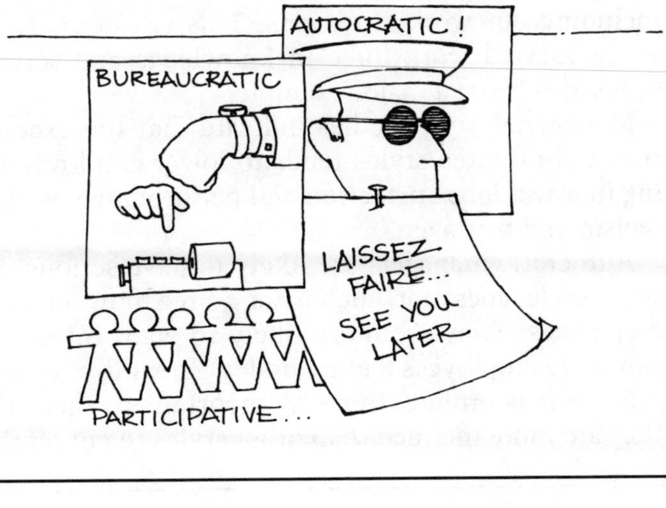

∇ **Bureaucratic.** A manager with this style is usually well-organized, does things by the numbers, and frequently makes decisions based on rules, regulations, and policies. It is a style best used when creative behavior by subordinates is unnecessary or would be disruptive, and where most of the problems to be solved remain the same over a period of time. It is often found in middle or lower management of large utilities, government agencies, old-line companies, or financial institutions.

It is least effective in situations of rapid change or where new problems frequently emerge, for it does not encourage creative problem-solving. It has been the source of serious problems in agencies or companies affected by deregulation, since this major change requires extensive readjustment and creative new approaches.

∇ **Laissez-faire.** This style is the most laid back of all the styles, letting things happen without a great deal of managerial interference. It is basically a nondirective approach, reactive rather than pro-active—it flows with the tide. You can find it in any organization but especially in creative arts-related organizations and volunteer groups.

This style is most effective with highly motivated, self-starting employees who do not need or want a great deal of supervision. It is least effective—even disastrous—in situations requiring quick decisions or highly specific directions and guidelines.

∇ **Autocratic.** This tell-oriented style features a "This is the way it is" approach. The word has come down from the mountain, and it is carved in stone. This style functions best in crisis situations, where quick decisions and prompt execution of commands are crucial. As the old foot soldiers' adage goes, "Ours not to question why, ours but to do or die."

Major organizational problems can occur around this style, however, when managers with few other managerial skills perpetuate crisis situations in order to justify the continued use of their autocratic style. This may happen unconsciously, but it is one of the first things to look for if a particular department or division seems to be constantly in crisis.

It is human nature for us to want some feeling of control over our lives, including our work situations. This is especially true in our increasingly well-educated work force in knowledge and service industries, high-tech industries being a major example.

Managerial style studies indicate that the excessive use of overly directive, tell-oriented styles tends to lower employee motivation, often resulting in lower job satisfaction and performance, with higher employee absenteeism and turnover.

Autocratic managers are likely to have serious information problems, as their style does not encourage a free flow of information upward from employees. They are more likely to want information on demand, which can leave employees feeling under a great deal of pressure.

Since it is often extremely important to them that things go their way, they are more inclined than other styles to cut off the head of the messenger with bad news. This further lowers the willingness of employees to give this style manager any unpleasant or unwelcome information; they are very likely to get only information that employees think they want to hear.

In short, authoritative or autocratic managers are the least likely to know what is really going on with their employees or organizations, although they may appear to know the most. When bad news finally breaks through, it may come as quite an unpleasant surprise to the autocratic manager.

∇ **Heroic.** As described in David Bradford and Allan Cohen's *Managing for Excellence* (Wiley, 1984), "heroic" managers tend to model themselves after the heroes of the Old West: superior to those needing to be helped or rescued in terms of knowledge, emotional control, coordination, and self-discipline—able to ride to the rescue on a moment's notice.

Their conscious or unconscious self-image is that they have technical or organizational skills superior to those of their subordinates, they are responsible for all outcomes, and they need to have a central role in their work units in order to carry out their responsibilities. They feel they must have both the answers and control of their subordinates.

This style is most useful when there are specific technical or coordination problems to be solved, and heroic managers can be a short-term solution. Unfortunately, their preference for riding in like the Lone Ranger, demonstrating their superiority, and riding off into the sunset does little to prepare the rescued to take care of the problem themselves the next time the Wayward Gang rides into town and heads for the bank.

Since heroic managers see themselves as the keepers of the keys, usually requiring that all information pass through them ("It's the only way I can know what's going on"), they also feel the necessity to make all final decisions. In complex situations this can lead to their making decisions in areas outside their expertise, sometimes with unfortunate results. It also demotivates subordinates. They soon learn that the heroic manager will have the final say anyway, so it's best not to get too heavily involved with the outcome. This does not result in fully committed employees.

Another problem with heroic managers can be their need to negate subordinates whose knowledge or skills approach or exceed theirs, since they feel their authority and position are based on superior abilities. It is hard to ride to the rescue unless the threatened victims are seen as helpless or incompetent.

Heroic managers may therefore view accomplished subordinates as threats to be kept in their place rather than as valuable resources. This is both demotivating to the employees directly involved and a message to other employees not to get better than the boss. In each case, the organization is wasting part of its most important resource, its people.

∇ **Democratic or participative.** Sometimes also known as the leader-manager style, this style recognizes that problems are solved and work accomplished by *people*, and therefore focuses on encouraging and developing subordinates. It emphasizes two-way feedback between manager and subordinates, coaching skills, employee participation in the strategic and decision-making process, and frequent positive rewards for high performance.

Managers in this style are less concerned with all information flowing through them than they are with subordinates solving problems at the lowest level possible. This helps them develop employees' skills, as well as leaving more time for higher-level problems or functions. Since they don't view subordinates as necessarily less competent than themselves, they feel less need to be personally involved with every facet of their operation or the decisions made at every level.

This style is most effective with mature, motivated employees in situations requiring creative responses to problems. It may be less effective in short-term crisis situations, or with some unskilled employees who may initially require close supervision and direction.

Management Styles and Organizations

To complicate things even further, there are also different types of organizations. In his book *The Dynamics of Management*, Waino Soujanen describes three basic categories of organizations:

1. Crisis-oriented, such as the military, police and fire departments.
2. Routine-oriented, dealing with similar problems and procedures day after day, such as some service organizations and many manufacturing facilities.
3. Knowledge-oriented, such as high-tech or scientific firms, and colleges or law offices.

Soujanen makes the point that each type of organization may require a different management style in order to be most effective. Using our management styles model, the authoritative style would generally function best in crisis-oriented organizations, the bureaucratic style would be more at home in a routine-oriented organization, and the leader-manager style is more conducive to employee development in knowledge-oriented organizations.

Which Is "Best"?

The best style ultimately depends on the work or problem situation, the makeup of the work force, and the type of organization. Studies indicate that the more directive styles work best in crisis situations and with employees who initially need more direction and guidance. The more participative styles seem to work best with motivated employees working in situations requiring independent action and creative problem-solving.

In Conclusion

In short, there is no "best" managerial style, for each can be productive in some situations, with some employees. Effective managers need to be aware of their own preferred style, able to read situations and predict what style is most likely to be successful, and then be versatile and skilled enough to use an appropriate style.

To the extent that managers can maintain this admittedly difficult style balance, they will also achieve the most effective environment for rewarding and productive work.

∇ ***For additional information, see:***

Chapter 4. Feedback Is Free
Chapter 7. The Challenge of Change
Chapter 9. Absentee Manager—Who's Minding the Store?
Chapter 17. Team-Building for All Seasons

∇ 7. The Challenge of Change

Life is either a daring adventure or nothing.
—*Helen Keller*

One of the primary factors in modern organizational life and planning is *change*. Because of its accelerating impact on organizations, successfully managing change has become a major part of the contemporary manager's responsibilities. For almost any organization, the question is not *if* major changes will strike the organization, but *how soon* and *how big*.

Effects of Change

Change affects people and organizations in many different ways and in different areas of their activities. For example, changes in marketing strategies may not cause significant upheavals in an organization, but changes in production techniques may be traumatic. An employee may have no trouble adjusting to a change in office location but be very threatened by the shift from a manual typewriter to an electronic word processor.

Here are some of the ways that both employees and organizations may feel or respond when significant change occurs:

Positive	Negative	Positive	Negative
Excited	Fearful	Delighted	Stressed
Stimulated	Paralyzed	Motivated	Angry
Rejuvenated	Threatened	Pleased	Procrastinating
Challenged	Avoiding	Anticipating	Rejecting
Rewarded	Punished	Accepting	Resenting

One of the reasons managers, employees, and organizations have such varied responses to change is that each has different tolerance levels for accommodating change. A small amount of change may produce positive effects, while increasing amounts or intensity of change may produce negative effects.

Change is such a complex phenomenon that there are no certain ways of knowing how any given change will affect any one employee or the organization as a whole. The effects of change are cumulative, and a small change may go by almost unnoticed, or be the straw that broke the camel's back. It requires a knowledge of the history of changes of a given employee or organization to make any sort of prediction as to the effect of the next change that comes along.

Change, Stress, and Burnout

Change is one of the major contributing causes of stress and, ultimately, of employee burnout. Whether the change is perceived as positive or negative, joyful or frightening, the shift of our physical or psychological equilibrium causes the body to prepare for fight or flight, the stress response.

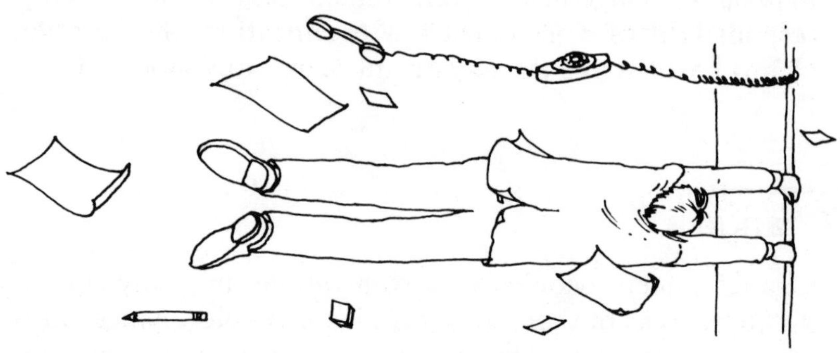

Adapting to change also requires *energy*, the single greatest nonproductive energy drain that we normally experience. Significant change can have a very inhibiting effect on creative thinking and innovative problem-solving. Creative energy, like the best cream, seems to come off the top of our available energy resources. If that energy is involved in adjusting to change, it isn't available for creative mental processes when it may be needed most. The constant energy drain of adapting to excessive change can lead to burnout.

Attempting to adjust to significant or sudden change is much like getting dumped into cold water: you're going to expend a lot of energy treading water and trying to keep warm, but you're not going to go very far in a new direction. Managers who want the maximum creative output need to walk a fine line between providing enough change to be challenging, and overwhelming with excessive change that can lead to employee burnout. It is not an easy line to walk.

Reactions to Excessive Change

Even though each person's tolerance level for change is unique, varying according to circumstances, some common reactions frequently occur when change becomes excessive. It's that point at which we say "Stop! That's enough! A little variety is fine, but this is ridiculous!" Following are some reactions to excessive change:

- *Denial:* "This can't be happening to us."
- *Avoidance:* "We don't have to deal with this yet."
- *Barely controlled panic:* "We've got to *do* something!"
- *Group-think:* "Let's form a committee to handle it."
- *Withdrawal:* "We won't participate."
- *Projection:* "If it weren't for *them,* it wouldn't be a problem."
- *Compulsiveness:* "We just have to work harder."
- *Guilt:* "It's all our fault. If only we hadn't . . ."
- *Regression:* "We must go back to basics."
- *Omnipotence:* "We'll have to handle this on our own—we're the only ones who can do it right."
- *Physical illness:* "*I* know how to get you out of this."

As a manager, watch for these reactions to change. It is your signal that change overload is occurring. If excessive change is allowed to continue, it is likely to have a negative impact on your work unit.

Problems with Change

Constructively managing change would be difficult enough if there were only one variety, but there are essentially two kinds of change that both individuals and organizations must be able to manage: initiated change and imposed change. The individual and collective reactions to each can be quite different.

∇ **Initiated change** is the change that occurs as a result of an individual's own decisions or actions: going back to college in middle age, getting married, accepting a new position, becoming a parent, retiring early. It can be frightening, uncertain, and stress-producing, but the reaction is usually not as severe as the reaction to imposed change.

∇ **Imposed change** is that change which comes uninvited, often without warning, and over which we feel we have little or no control: earthquakes or other twists of nature, inheriting unexpected money, our factory closing, a sudden promotion, financial recession, a new manager, failure of our bank, winning the state lottery, losing a loved one. Whether we perceive the change as positive or negative, it still creates a byproduct of additional stress while we adjust to the new situation.

If the imposed change has negative repercussions, it may leave us feeling victimized and out of control of our future. With these feelings of being the victim go feelings of loss—of control, options, power, self-confidence, security, and, in some cases, even self-esteem. The old, the familiar is gone, and the new is uncertain. Where will this lead . . . and when will it end? Can I cope with it, can I learn new ways fast enough? Will I need help . . . and if I do, will it be there? Will I be able to overcome my pride and ask for assistance? What of my expertise with the old—now that it's outdated, will people still respect me?

These feelings of loss generate one of the oldest and most common reactions on the planet: grief. No matter what the loss—lunch money or loved one—people everywhere have much the same five responses to grief:

- *Disbelief:* "I don't believe this is happening to me."
- *Anger:* "How *dare* this happen to me!"
- *Guilt:* "If only I hadn't . . . this wouldn't have happened."
- *Depression/self-pity:* "Why do these things always happen to me? I really don't care anymore."
- *Acceptance:* "It happened, but now it's time to get on with my life."

The first four symptoms may occur in any order, although the cycle usually starts with disbelief and concludes with acceptance. It is not unusual, however, for an individual to become stuck at one of the stages and have difficulty moving on to complete the cycle. It will be hard to take on new situations until the individual works through the cycle.

For example, imagine Sarah, unexpectedly passed over for promotion in favor of a newer and younger employee—an abrupt change in her relation to her manager, in the work unit, and in how she felt about herself. Her grief cycle lasted for months—anger, disbelief, guilt, depression—while her performance went straight downhill. It wasn't until professional counseling helped get her to the acceptance stage that she began to recover her old performance level.

Initiated change is not usually so traumatic. Since we have initiated it, we still retain feelings of control and direction, even if we launch ourselves into the unknown. There is an internal alignment between our purpose and the change. We have our vision to hang on to. The waters may be uncertain, but at least it's *our* ship and *our* journey. And if we arrive safely, it is *our* feeling of accomplishment.

The Manager's Problems with Change

Whether the change is perceived as positive or negative, initiated or imposed, the manager is going to run into the same basic problems:

∇ **Employee reactions.** Regardless of the nature of the change, employees are going to have questions, fears, arguments, rationalizations, doubts, and personal opinions. The manager must resolve as many of these as possible before performance-producing equilibrium can be restored to the work unit.

∇ **Establishment of new channels.** Any time change occurs in a system as complex as a functioning work unit, the channels for communication, power, and production may be disrupted. These need to be rebuilt to incorporate the change before full performance is again possible. An organization in constant flux may never realize its maximum performance potential.

∇ **Time and energy demands.** Any deviation from the normal rate of change (all organizations change, it is just that some change more slowly than others) will require the manager's additional time and energy to accommodate the change. No matter how positive the change may appear to outsiders, its time and energy demands can still be perceived as a threat, or worse, by the manager who must successfully implement it. The energy demands of implementing the change, as well as the ripple effect of the change itself through the organization, need to be taken into account in any organizational change decision.

∇ **Power shifts.** The delicate organizational balances of power and authority can be upset by change, especially if it is unexpected or unwelcome. Adjustments in the lines of authority take time and energy to rebuild or realign, and that energy must be subtracted from the time and energy available for moving the organization toward its goals. Managers need to allow for this energy drain in their performance expectations.

∇ **Flexibility.** Finally, in a change situation, the manager must be increasingly flexible. If the change is inevitable and irreversible, a manager's time and energy spent in attempting to hold on to the old dilutes the effort necessary to adapt to the new.

The Trailing Edge of Change

Much has been thought, discussed, and written about the leading edge of change. Unfortunately, little attention has been paid to what might be called the trailing edge of change—unfortunate, because that is where the manager's casualties occur.

Let's use the analogy of a ship moving through a troubled sea, an ongoing change process (see Figure 2 on the next page).

Watching kids play in a backyard pool provides quick evidence that most six-year-olds can design the bow of a ship, the leading edge. They know which end goes first, and what it needs to do.

What they probably won't realize without a nautical engineering degree and a sophisticated test tank is that the efficiency of a hull moving through water—an individual or organization moving through change—is largely

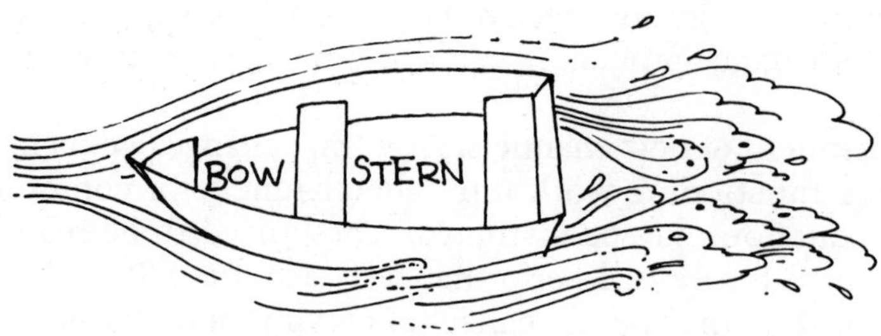

Figure 2. ***The trailing edge of change***

determined by what happens at the *stern*, the trailing edge of the hull.

It is the turbulence, the vacuum as the water leaves the ship's hull at the stern, that tends to hold it back, that can limit its performance. In other words, it is the water that is pushed aside by the leading edge that can impede the smooth passage of change.

It is the same with an individual or organization going through change; the "casualties" often occur in the backwash of the change, rather than at the leading edge. Those who get caught there can impede the progress of the entire organization. Who are they, these victims of change's trailing edge?

∇ **Older workers.** The generation gap consists of more than value differences between older and younger employees, although that can be a yawning chasm. It is also a difference in experience with handling an accelerating rate of change, speed in adapting to the new and different, and tolerance for ambiguity while change is taking place.

An engineer friend recently returned from England's Cambridge University tells of his mounting puzzlement as each day on his way to the campus he watched an old metal latticework bridge being painted. An elderly worker with a two-inch brush was painstakingly painting each lattice by hand, a process that my efficiency-minded friend estimated would take at least a month.

"Why," he finally asked one of his English colleagues in exasperation, "don't they use a power sprayer to paint that bridge? You'd have it done in half a day." "True," replied his English host, "but then what would we do with old 'enry?"

What *will* we do with "old 'enry"? Rapid technological changes can leave the older worker in the backwash, feeling outdated and obsolete as years of training and experience become useless. Any manager with older workers needs to realize that probably nothing is more frightening for them than this. Training, patience, and careful job planning are called for if the manager is not to lose years of very valuable experience.

It is not a fear that the younger generation of employees easily understands. Time is on their side.

∇ **The untrained.** As the marketplace rapidly changes and the need for more sophisticated technical and interpersonal skills increases, a growing stagnant pool of untrained workers is created. Some don't have the opportunity for training, others lack the ability, while others have already given up: future shock's first victims.

Ultimately the choices for organizations will narrow down to one of two options: either train them for productive jobs in a changed workplace or support them. They will not just go away.

∇ **The cautious and conservative.** Older employees do not hold all the patents on feeling uncomfortable with change. Many younger employees also would like to move more slowly than rapidly changing circumstances permit.

Some come from a very narrow range of life experiences, either by choice or geographical accident. Others have had painful learning experiences during their developing years and dread the necessity for relearning that change entails.

Whatever the cause, slow-to-adapt employees caught up in the wake of swiftly moving events, may be forced either to reposition themselves in a work environment of slower changes, or to reconsider their career paths. Despite a manager's best efforts with coaching, training, and supporting, some of these employees will still become victims of rapid change, overstressed and lacking the sense of job fulfillment that rewards their more adaptable co-workers.

∇ **Those with one-dimensional jobs.** Greg had worked in a Detroit-area automobile factory since high school as an assembly-line arc welder, a good one. Late one recent summer, during the annual shutdown for new-model changes, Greg was replaced by a computerized arc-welding robot. Each of the robot's twenty-eight arms could weld three times as accurately and eight times as fast as Greg could on even his best days.

Arc welding is *only* arc welding, a one-dimensional job—the skill isn't transferable—and neither Greg nor his manager had given much thought to preparing Greg for a lateral or vertical career shift when robots took up arc welding. Left bobbing in the wake of a changing technology with a one-dimensional job skill, Greg finds his options are extremely limited: either find a quiet tidewater job environment not yet invaded by arc-welding robots, or change career directions and start over. Because Greg has a wife and three young children, neither option is going to be easy.

Managers with employees in one-dimensional jobs need to be especially conscientious about encouraging them to do at least basic career planning. In this case, planning would have retained a hardworking employee within the organization.

∇ **The nonassertive.** The tidal wave of rapid change washes over the nonassertive employee or organization like an ocean breaker over mud flats at low tide. The first victims of change are those without the self-confidence or assertiveness to attempt to swim out of change's turbulent backwash. The organization or manager who does not do everything possible to build employees' self-confidence leaves the way open for either high rates of employee turnover or low job performance once change begins to ripple through the organization.

For the manager who feels, "My people have plenty of self-confidence," an analysis of that self-confidence is helpful. Is it based on their ability to adapt quickly to new and changing situations, or is it based on their expertise with one-dimensional job skills? If it is the latter, which is more typical, they are still extremely vulnerable. Ensuring a work force with solidly based self-confidence requires that the manager encourage and provide the opportunity for employees to acquire as broad a variety of skills and job experiences as possible.

Skills for Handling Change

If change is such a problem, what can be done about it? What are the skills that enable one individual or organization to take advantage of change, while others drown in its wake? Following are some of the skills that help contemporary managers and employees to weather change. Observe people whom you consider to have good change management skills and you may discover other traits to add to this list.

∇ **The hardiness factors.** Stress and change researchers had long been puzzled by the fact that some people and organizations were greatly stressed by change, whereas others seemed to thrive on it. Are there any attributes or skills the "thrivers" have in common? Current research seems to indicate that there are.

In some of the most important work done to date, Suzanne Kobasa and Salvatore Maddi of the University of Chicago conducted a stress study of high-level business executives. They discovered four factors that those executives who were least physically affected by stress and change had in common, now known as "the hardiness factors":

1. They viewed change as a challenge, rather than a threat; their stance regarding change was pro-active, rather than reactive.
2. They made commitments to life and to themselves; they engaged life rather than avoided it.
3. Their goals, values, and priorities tended to be well-defined; they had a clear sense of mission.
4. They had a strong sense of control, both over their own lives and over external events; they felt in command, rather than victimized.

To the extent that a manager can incorporate these four hardiness factors into his or her work unit, both the work team and the individuals in it will be better able to resist the debilitating effects of change.

∇ **Curiosity.** It may have had fatal results for the cat, but a healthy curiosity seems to be an attribute of those who can handle change. A manager's desire to see what's coming next makes change much more appealing and less threatening.

∇ **Positive view of the future.** It probably comes as no surprise that studies indicate that those who have a positive outlook about the world's future seem better able to handle change than those who are more pessimistic. It is hard to accept *any* change if it is seen as another bit of grease on the planetary skids.

∇ **Letting go.** Some of us aren't very good at this. We want to hang on to everything from old flames to old clothes. Since change is often regarded as the loss of the known and familiar, being unable to let go can leave us wallowing in the grieving process. There's an old saying in the theater, "Any fool can make an entrance, but it takes a professional to make an exit." The same is true of letting go in the face of change.

∇ **Self-confidence.** Change often dictates that, like it or not, we suddenly switch from the role of expert to that of neophyte. If our self-confidence is built solely on expertise, we're in trouble. Much better to face change with self-confidence in our ability to adapt quickly to new situations, learn new rules, and accept new realities. Given that brand of self-confidence, we don't panic if we suddenly find ourselves in Rome—we know we'll soon be doing it like a bona fide Roman.

∇ **Future shock antidotes.** Alvin Toffler says future shock is caused by accelerating rates of change—the future arrives before we're ready for it. He recommends three important skills as antidotes:

1. *Learning to learn* is an absolutely vital skill in a world where the amount of information increases exponentially, while at the same time most school systems exclude students from the *how* of the learning process.
2. *Learning to choose*—decision-making—is another vital skill when the change process brings us decision points in a dizzying, accelerating procession, like alien spaceships in some hyped-up video game.
3. *Learning to relate* becomes increasingly necessary as change scatters families across the land and often puts together new work teams for each new project. Gone forever are the days when your twenty-five-year pin was probably awarded by the same manager who hired you.

∇ **Self-awareness.** In a rapidly changing work environment, it becomes even more important that both managers and employees remain aware of their own performance goals and criteria, and how they are perceived by others in the pursuit of those goals. When the work environment was more static, it was not necessary to check the pulse of individual and team performance as often. You don't need to check your map as often if you're traveling by bicycle as you do if you're covering the same territory in a GT Ferrari—the landscape doesn't go by nearly as fast.

∇ **Ability to ask for help.** I say "ability" to ask for help because not everyone is able to do it. For example, we've all ridden with drivers who wouldn't ask for directions if they were looking for Minneapolis on a road lined with palm trees!

In an era of accelerating change, this "press on regardless" attitude is as guaranteed to get you into trouble as telling a burly Scotsman, "Real men don't wear skirts." Rapid change means that most of us will need help much of the time, and the manager or employee who, for whatever reason, is somehow unable to ask for help will be in a continuous struggle with the effects of change and the resultant stress.

A self-confident "I have a problem, and I need your help" is one of the best counterirritants for change currently available. No prescription necessary.

The Manager's Role

When it comes to managing change, setting an example for employees is extremely important for the manager. It is an unsettling time for many employees, and they will be looking to you for leadership and guidance. When there is uncertainty in the air, employees' antennas are extended full length, and you will be closely monitored to see if you "Walk your talk." Your example of handling change will be subsequently mirrored by many of your employees.

So what *is* your role in managing change? What can you reasonably be expected to do when the future arrives, ready or not? Here are ideas which many managers have found helpful:

∇ **Prepare your employees.** Announce changes as far in advance as possible. Typically, many of your employees don't like surprises—of any kind. Many otherwise quite normal people don't even like surprise birthday parties. Imagine how they'll feel when you announce in a hastily called staff meeting that starting next Tuesday the paper system installed during World War II will be replaced with a new electronic system, and that the computer orientation classes will begin tomorrow morning at eight-thirty.

You'll get about the same enthusiastic response you'd get after telling a teenager that all radio stations had just been ordered to play only Bach, Brahms, and Beethoven.

Most of us need a core of predictable events and relationships that we can hang on to if we are to weather change successfully. Constant surprises, even pleasant ones, make it hard to retain our balance. In other words, keep work unit surprises to a minimum.

∇ **Make contingency plans.** This is another important aspect of preparing your employees for change. Not only does it help prepare you and your work unit for a variety of change situations, but it also lets employees know that you have as much control as possible of an uncertain situation. Remember that in time of change, many employees will look to you as a stabilizing influence. If you appear to be out of control, they will feel that their worst fears are realized, and that everything is up for grabs.

If your response to preparing your employees for change is, "I'm too busy, I don't have time," then future shock may have already caught up with you.

∇ **Fully explain changes to your employees.** Typically, a change announcement and explanation process follows a specific route: The people at the top know all about the change, in elaborate detail, while the people at the lower end of the chain—the ones most affected and who must carry it out—know the least. A change that started with upper management as, "What if we . . .?" ends up at the employee level as, "Now listen up. From now on . . ."

As a manager announcing change, remember that:

- You probably knew about the change before the employees (unless there's a good employee rumor mill), and have had more time to adjust to it. When you announce it, they will feel and think much the way you did when you first heard it. They will probably get the announced change in the middle of their other duties, with little time to digest it fully.
- You should try to ensure that all questions, doubts, and uncertainties are answered, or what is left unspoken and unasked will have a negative effect on morale and performance just beneath the work unit's surface. This does not mean that you have to agree with those who may be opposed to the change. The important thing is for each employee to feel that his or her point of view has at least been expressed, without negative repercussions.

In short, when announcing a change is no time for the manager to practice "seagull management": fly in out of the blue, make a lot of noise, dump on everyone, and fly off.

∇ **Allow for change's impact on performance.** The impact that adjusting to the change will have on your employees' job performance is in direct proportion to the magnitude of the change. If the change is a significant one, assume that job activities will not proceed at their normal pace until the effects of the change on the work unit are assimilated. Allow for this slowing process in your production expectations and scheduling—it will happen anyway, whether you've adjusted for it or not. When you throw a rock in the pond, it takes time for the ripples to subside.

∇ **Encourage employee input whenever possible.** Try to convert imposed change to initiated change by letting employees in on the change process at every opportunity. Most of us have a need to feel in control of at least some things that affect us, and the negative impact of even unpleasant change is much less if employees feel that they've had some say in how the change is to be implemented and what its effects will be. Any change is much more likely to be accepted and smoothly implemented if all concerned have had a chance to "buy in" at the earliest stage possible. With some changes, employees can be shown personal or individual benefits that help them positively anticipate the change.

∇ **Incorporate the hardiness factors.** Help your employees put the four factors into practice, using the change as a vehicle:

1. *View change as a challenge.* Help them reposition the change as an opportunity for growth, rather than a threat.
2. *Make commitments.* Announcing a change as though it were a fact is actually an act of faith, for it assumes that everyone within earshot of the announcement will agree to carry it out or abide by it. However, with the exception of a few penitentiaries and military organizations, that is seldom the case unless there is also a firm commitment from all concerned to implement the change.

   Once the change is fully explained by the manager and understood by the employees, the manager's next step is to make action plans for implementation to which all members of the work unit can make an honest commitment. If they can't make a commitment to implementing the change, it is unlikely to happen in the way that it was intended.
3. *Redefine goals, values, and priorities* in light of the change. Reemphasize the organization's mission and goals, showing how the change fits into that mission. (If it doesn't, don't paper it over—decide if alterations need to be made in your mission statement or goals in light of the change.)

   Check to see if individual employee values, goals, and personal missions are still in agreement with those of the organization. If the change is big enough, and the change in organizational direction and goals is large enough, this is where you are most likely to suffer casualties.
4. *Provide a sense of control.* Neither you nor your work unit is usually in a position to determine what changes will occur, but you can often have an impact on how they will be implemented. Employees need this sense of having some control over events that have an impact on them and their work lives.

∇ **Provide appropriate training and coaching.** Employees will be less threatened by a change if they realize that the necessary training and coaching will go along with it. Losing expertise is very unsettling for some employees, and depending on the nature of the change, the restoration of expertise as quickly as possible will make the change transition much smoother.

Assume that during a change period, people will make mistakes. This is a result both of the shift in the ways of thinking and doing things, and of the added stress instigated by the change itself. As a manager, this will require added patience and coaching skills on your part.

∇ **Encourage self-management and burnout prevention.** Since change and stress go hand-in-hand, encourage your employees to be especially aware of good self-management practices during a difficult change situation. Unfortunately, the tendency during a period of stress/change is to do all the wrong things in an effort to reduce the tension, such as activating the three "mores": Smoke more, drink more, and eat more. Coupled with less exercise, rest, and outside activities, these can greatly increase the negative physical and emotional impact of change.

Ideally, managers and employees would go into training for a major organizational change with the same professional outlook that an athlete takes into training for a major event. If the outcomes are of equal importance, then the training needs to be of equal intensity.

∇ **Give additional feedback.** Employees in changed and uncertain situations need more feedback than usual. They are not as sure of themselves as they were before the change, they're making more mistakes, things are going slower than they'd like, and they're concerned about their performance.

Reassure them. Notice things they're doing right. Give them plenty of positive feedback through the transition period.

∇ **Prepare for casualties.** Not that organizational change has to resemble M*A*S*H, but be mentally and emotionally prepared for the fact that despite your best managerial efforts, if the change is large or significant enough, you may lose some people. To be ready:

- Have replacement strategies in place *before* it happens.
- Get people cross-trained to fill in during emergencies—every team needs utility infielders and pinch-hitters.
- Alert any support resources that a major change is imminent and you may need their help.
- Prepare yourself for the feeling of failure that goes with losing people, even though the change was beyond your control. Neither you nor anyone else can win them all.

∇ **Facilitate the grieving process.** You may not want to call it that, but if the change is negative or difficult you nonetheless need to help employees through the five phases and the accompanying feelings: disbelief, anger, guilt, depression, and, finally, acceptance.

Does this mean that you need to be a licensed counselor to accomplish an organizational change? Certainly not. The important thing is to allow and encourage the expression of employees' feelings that accompany the change process. Be up-front with your employees: tell them of the change and let them know that you realize that they may feel disbelief, anger, guilt, or even depression about it. Assure them that those feelings are normal, human—and O.K.

Realize that if employee anger seems directed at you, you are not the real object—*change* is. You just happen to be the closest available target.

In Conclusion

No matter how unexpected or difficult the change, reassure your employees that on the other side of their feelings is acceptance of the new reality and the moving on into the future. If you will allow those feelings to be expressed, you may be surprised at how quickly the storm of change passes.

∇ ***For additional information, see:***

Chapter 2. When Manager and Employees Communicate
Chapter 5. Growing the Corporate Culture

∇ Change Worksheet

With regard to the possible or coming change:

1. Upon whom will it have the most impact? ______________________________

   What is that impact? ______________________________

   ____

2. For whom will it be the most difficult? ______________________________

   What are those difficulties? ______________________________

   ____

3. For whom will it present the most exciting challenges? ______________________________

   What are those challenges? ______________________________

   ____

4. For whom will it have the most benefits? ______________________________

   What are those benefits? ______________________________

   ____

5. Who or what is most likely to attempt to block this change? ______________________________

   ____

6. Who or what is most likely to attempt to sabotage the change if/when it is implemented?

   ____

7. What can you do to help those for whom the change will be the most difficult? __________

   ____

8. What are your rewards for helping the change go smoothly? ______________________________

   ____

∇ Managing Change Self-Assessment

Directions: Place a square around a number to indicate how important you think that skill is for good change management.
Place a circle around a number to indicate your estimation of your present skill level in managing change.

Suggestion: Have your employees fill out the "Employee" version. Place their averaged scores in the appropriate places and compare their perceptions with yours.

Scale: **High/Excellent - 5 4 3 2 1 - Low/Poor**

Skills		**Employees** □ O
1. Viewing change as a challenge, rather than as a threat.	5 4 3 2 1	___ ___
2. Maintaining a high level of self-confidence.	5 4 3 2 1	___ ___
3. Decision-making when change occurs.	5 4 3 2 1	___ ___
4. Letting go of the old when change occurs.	5 4 3 2 1	___ ___
5. Preparing contingency plans in case of change.	5 4 3 2 1	___ ___
6. Asking for appropriate help when change occurs.	5 4 3 2 1	___ ___
7. Preparing employees for an upcoming change.	5 4 3 2 1	___ ___
8. Explaining all aspects of change when it occurs.	5 4 3 2 1	___ ___
9. Allowing for impact of change on work unit's production.	5 4 3 2 1	___ ___
10. Encouraging employee input regarding change.	5 4 3 2 1	___ ___
11. Providing appropriate training/coaching to accommodate changed situation.	5 4 3 2 1	___ ___
12. Giving employees additional feedback and support during transition periods.	5 4 3 2 1	___ ___

Overall rating of the quality of your change management skills:

Very high - 10 9 8 7 6 5 4 3 2 1 - Very low (circle one)

Your employees' averaged rating: __________

Note: Circled items in the 1-2 area may require immediate attention to improve your change management skills. Also, give close attention to items in which the circle is two or more numbers to the right of the square, as this indicates a gap between importance and skill level.

Date ______________

∇ Managing Change Assessment

Directions: Place a <u>square</u> around a number to indicate how <u>important</u> you think that skill is for good change management.
Place a <u>circle</u> around a number to indicate your estimation of your manager's present <u>skill level</u> in managing change.

Scale: **High/Excellent - 5 4 3 2 1 - Low/Poor**

Skills

1. Viewing change as a challenge, rather than as a threat.	5 4 3 2 1
2. Maintaining a high level of self-confidence.	5 4 3 2 1
3. Decision-making when change occurs.	5 4 3 2 1
4. Letting go of the old when change occurs.	5 4 3 2 1
5. Preparing contingency plans in case of change.	5 4 3 2 1
6. Asking for appropriate help when change occurs.	5 4 3 2 1
7. Preparing employees for an upcoming change.	5 4 3 2 1
8. Explaining all aspects of change when it occurs.	5 4 3 2 1
9. Allowing for impact of change on work unit's production.	5 4 3 2 1
10. Encouraging employee input regarding change.	5 4 3 2 1
11. Providing appropriate training/coaching to accommodate changed situation.	5 4 3 2 1
12. Giving employees additional feedback and support during transition periods.	5 4 3 2 1

Overall rating of the quality of your manager's change management skills:

<u>Very high</u> - 10 9 8 7 6 5 4 3 2 1 - <u>Very low</u> (circle one)

∇ 8. Delegating—The Ultimate Skill

There is an old saying, usually attributed to grandmothers, that has probably led to more coronaries, high blood pressure, and managerial stress than any other ten words in the English language. This venerable maxim is also at least partly responsible for underdeveloped employees, overworked managers, and limited organizational performance. The ten deadly words? "If you want it done right, dear, do it yourself."

Before I unduly antagonize grandmothers, let me quickly add that I'm sure this advice was never intended to be deadly. It is just that strategies that may have been adequate in our grandparents' era are no longer appropriate in the managerial world of the 1980s.

The major curse of this old adage is that managers who bought into it—and I'm as guilty as anyone—may never have developed what many management experts believe to be the ultimate managerial skill: *delegating,* the skill of passing on to an employee the responsibility for a given task, as well as the authority to carry it out.

Note that true delegating can only be to people who report to you. For example, you can delegate a project to your assistant, but you can't delegate that same project to a fellow manager. You can ask, barter, plead, negotiate, or cajole, but you can't delegate, as there is no reporting relationship.

Benefits of Delegating

Good delegating skills have several payoffs for the modern manager. First, delegating routine tasks gives managers time to do what many experts consider the primary managerial functions—planning, coordinating, controlling, and developing your employees. Some management specialists go so far as to contend that four out of every five tasks that cross a manager's desk should be delegated.

Stan Kossen, in his book *The Human Side of Management,* refers to the "exception principle." This managerial concept contends that "regular, recurring activities and decisions should routinely be delegated to and handled by subordinates, and that unusual, non-reoccurring decisions should be referred to a higher level."

What does the exception principle leave for the manager to do? Planning, controlling, coordinating, creative problem-solving . . . and time for his or her people.

A second, and perhaps even more important, benefit of good delegating skills can be employee development and job enrichment. Robert Townsend, author of *Further Up the Organization,* states that the wise manager "delegates as many important matters as he can because that creates a climate in which people grow." Employees who are given important work to do are more likely to develop into important employees.

But if delegating is such a valuable managerial skill, why don't more managers consistently use it? There are about as many reasons as there are managers. I've found one of the major reasons is a hidden concern that if given the chance, subordinates might outperform the manager and be given the manager's job. If a manager is that insecure, then the subordinate probably *should* have the job.

I also hear managers, defending the grandmother's adage approach to delegating, say, "It takes longer to show someone else how to do it than to do it myself." That's true—the first time. Or perhaps even the second or third time. At some point, however, your coaching skills will have helped an employee gain a new skill, while you will have gained valuable time. It's a question of short-term gain—you do it—versus long-term gain and employee growth—you show your employee how to do it.

Another reason for hesitating to delegate can be the fear that subordinates will somehow botch the job, and the manager will be held responsible. This fear usually leads to the "Do it yourself" syndrome. There is, however, only a finite amount of important work that any one manager can do. The manager's failure to delegate effectively can place a self-imposed limit on the performance of the manager and, ultimately, the manager's work unit. A group's low performance may be masked by a number of other factors, but if you look beyond those factors, you'll often find that a manager's fear of delegating is at the root of the performance problem.

Largely because of the emotional components mentioned above, delegating is one of those managerial skills that is easy to understand but harder to carry out. In theory, it is as easy as A-B-C-D.

A. Appropriate authority should always be given to employees along with the delegated responsibility. Nothing is more frustrating to a willing employee than to be delegated a task, but then to have to check back with the manager continually for the authority to carry it out successfully. Delegating responsibility without authority is neither an efficient use of the manager's time nor a growth-producing experience for employees. Additionally, if you can delegate the entire task, employees will get a greater sense of accomplishment when it is completed.

For example, Susanne calls in her administrative assistant to delegate the completion of an important project proposal: "Gabrielle, I'm headed for a conference in Bangor, and I want you to finish up this proposal for me while I'm gone. I take it to the planning committee Wednesday morning. I'll be back early Tuesday afternoon, so have it on my desk for signing by Tuesday noon, O.K.? If you need anything, call me." And Susanne is off to the delights of Bangor, leaving Gabrielle to soldier on with the proposal.

When poor Gabrielle gets into the proposal, she finds what she may need most is aspirin. Getting it done on that time schedule will require some overtime work by data processing, at least two temporary typists, subcontracting the photocopying, and a free-lance artist. Not to mention the aspirin. And Gabrielle doesn't normally have the authority to request any of those services on her own.

After a flurry of long-distance calls back and forth to Bangor, several very late nights, and more aspirin than her doctor should know about, Gabrielle delivers the proposal at two on Tuesday—only a couple of hours late. She then goes home "sick" for the rest of the day.

Sound familiar? It would have gone much more smoothly for all concerned if Susanne had simply given Gabrielle the necessary authority before she left—a couple of phone calls or memos to the appropriate departments—or made arrangements with the departments herself for Gabrielle to get extra help in her absence.

Also, if Gabrielle had been in on the beginning of the proposal, instead of receiving it cold, she would have known what would be needed to complete it and the time schedule, so that she could set priorities for her other work. She would also have had a greater sense of accomplishment when the proposal was finished.

B. Build into the delegated task the following:

- Standards—how well it needs to be done.
- Structure—how it is to be done, and checkpoints or progress reports along the way.
- Support—available help and resources.

For example, Susanne should also have added, "Gabrielle, this proposal is going to have quite an effect on next year's budget, so it needs to be done really well. Put it in our usual proposal form, with a little fancier cover, and call me Monday morning to let me know how it's going. I've made arrangements for additional help if you need it."

C. Clarify communications, preferably in writing, to be sure that the task is clearly understood and that the rewards to both the employee and the organization are evident. It is important for the employee to realize that each task, no matter how small or mundane, is part of a larger organizational mission or goal.

D. Debrief the employee once the job is completed. This gives you the opportunity to praise the employee's performance, as well as to do any necessary coaching for the next time the job comes up. It also lets employees know that you were interested in the outcome and helps them become more responsible for their performance.

For instance, upon her return Susanne might have told Gabrielle, "I really appreciate your extra effort on this thing—it's going to make a big difference to the department. How do you feel about the way it went?"

In Conclusion

If you want to free up more of your own time and also improve the level of employee performance, delegate some of the important jobs—let your employees show you what they can do.

∇ ***For additional information, see:***

Chapter 9. Absentee Manager—Who's Minding the Store?
Chapter 20. About Time for Time Management?
Chapter 25. Managerial Stress Management

Date ____________

∇ Delegating Skills Assessment

Directions: Place a square around a number to indicate how important you think that skill is for good delegating.
Place a circle around a number to indicate your estimation of your present skill level in delegating to your employees.

Suggestion: Have your employees fill out the "Employee" version. Place their averaged scores in the appropriate places and compare their perception of your skills with yours.

Scale: **High/Excellent - 5 4 3 2 1 - Low/Poor**

Skills		**Employees** □	**Employees** O
1. Delegating necessary authority with task responsibility.	5 4 3 2 1	___	___
2. Setting reasonable timelines for delegated tasks.	5 4 3 2 1	___	___
3. Delegating worthwhile projects, rather than just grunt work.	5 4 3 2 1	___	___
4. Providing sufficient resources to accomplish the delegated tasks.	5 4 3 2 1	___	___
5. Providing adequate guidelines and boundaries for the task.	5 4 3 2 1	___	___
6. Giving sufficient instructions for the task.	5 4 3 2 1	___	___
7. Providing coaching, if the task is new or unfamiliar.	5 4 3 2 1	___	___
8. Providing follow-up during the task.	5 4 3 2 1	___	___
9. Giving feedback on the performance of the delegated task, once it has been completed.	5 4 3 2 1	___	___
10. My employees' willingness to accept delegated tasks.	5 4 3 2 1	___	___

The overall amount of work and projects you delegate to your employees:

Too much - 10 9 8 7 6 5 4 3 2 1 - Not enough (circle one)
Just right

Your employees' averaged rating: ____________

NOTE: Circled items in the 1-2 area may require immediate attention, as they can be causing problems with your delegating process. Also pay attention to those items in which the circle is two or more numbers to the right of the square, as these indicate gaps between what you want to happen and what is happening.

Date _____________ **EMPLOYEE**

∇ Delegating Skills Assessment

Directions: Place a square around a number to indicate how important you think that skill is for good delegating.
Place a circle around a number to indicate your estimation of your manager's present skill level in delegating to employees.

Scale: **High/Excellent - 5 4 3 2 1 - Low/Poor**

Skills

1. Delegating necessary authority with task responsibility.	5 4 3 2 1
2. Setting reasonable timelines for delegated tasks.	5 4 3 2 1
3. Delegating worthwhile projects, rather than just grunt work.	5 4 3 2 1
4. Providing sufficient resources to accomplish the delegated tasks.	5 4 3 2 1
5. Providing adequate guidelines and boundaries for the task.	5 4 3 2 1
6. Giving sufficient instructions for the task.	5 4 3 2 1
7. Providing coaching, if the task is new or unfamiliar.	5 4 3 2 1
8. Providing follow-up during the task.	5 4 3 2 1
9. Giving feedback on the performance of the delegated task, once it has been completed.	5 4 3 2 1
10. My willingness to accept delegated tasks.	5 4 3 2 1

The overall amount of work and projects delegated to you by your manager:

Too much - 10 9 8 7 6 5 4 3 2 1 - Not enough (circle one)
Just right

∇ 9. Absentee Manager—Who's Minding the Store?

An old truism in management circles states, "Managers can be judged not so much by what happens when they are there, but what happens when they're *gone*." The demands of contemporary business practices—frequent regional meetings, sprawling sales territories, widespread organizations, and business conferences, among others—have created an increasing number of opportunities to judge managers by what happens when they're gone. The absentee manager has become a reality in the operation of many, many businesses.

Are absentee managers really a problem? Apparently they can be. Businesses report some of these counterproductive situations relative to frequently absent managers:

∇ "While the cat's away," the employees may tend to behave like the proverbial mice. This is especially true if the absent manager's style has trained employees to work more by authoritative pressure than as a result of creative leadership and self-motivation. Managers who have not built an autonomous work force can expect a decline in productivity almost as soon as they're out the door.

∇ Absent managers may adopt a "nothing has changed" attitude upon their return, as though time had somehow stopped in the interim. Not so. People have worked, made decisions, carried out instructions, and generally soldiered on while the boss was away. It is only human nature to want and expect some recognition of this from the returned manager.

∇ Tasks were delegated, but insufficient authority was given to employees for effective implementation, so the tasks remain undone or incomplete.

∇ The decision-making process for the period during the manager's absence was not clearly spelled out prior to departure, so either the absent manager was constantly bothered long-distance with routine decisions, or major decisions were made by the wrong person. Both can prove to be very expensive.

Making the Best of It

What can an absentee manager do to make the best of a difficult though necessary situation? These are several suggestions that other organizations have found to be effective:

Prior to leaving

∇ If you delegate tasks to be accomplished while you're gone, be sure that you also delegate adequate authority to carry them out. Some managers resist delegating authority because they are afraid things might go so well that they will be seen as unnecessary. Other managers are afraid that delegated tasks won't go well, and they will be held responsible. Both attitudes can cause a significant slowdown in work while the manager is gone.

∇ Be sure that assigned tasks are clearly understood, adequate resources are accessible, and assistance is available if needed.

∇ Establish a decision-making hierarchy, so that employees know what decisions they can make on their own, and which need to be communicated to you.

Some managers use an A-B-C-D system:

A = Decisions that need to be made by the manager.
B = Decisions that can be made by the employee, in conjunction with the manager.
C = Decisions that are to be made by the employee and reported to the manager.
D = Decisions that are to be made solely by the employee, with no report necessary.

∇ Set up a communication plan to convey necessary information while you're away, including who will be the contact person and contingency plans for emergencies. Leave your itinerary and where you can be reached at all times with your secretary, assistant, or receptionist.

∇ If possible, establish a time with your work unit when you'll be in contact. This allows employees to have the necessary information on hand to discuss with you, making the most efficient use of both your time and theirs.

While you're away

∇ Above all, stick to your communications plan! There's nothing more frustrating for the people left behind than to be told, "Call me if you need me"—and then not to be able to reach you. If you have a prearranged time to call, be sure to do it.

∇ Talk to as many people in your work unit as possible, especially if you are away for some time. This has nothing to do with transmitting information, but rather with psychological support. Think of who in your unit may need special support for either a job-related or a personal situation.

∇ The excitement adrenalin usually pumps higher for those out in the field than for those left behind in office routines. To keep up your work unit's morale, don't wait to get back to tell them any good news—share it with them as you go along.

Upon your return

∇ Handle your hot issues immediately, for they're the ones that have been keeping your people on edge.

∇ As soon as possible, acknowledge employees appropriately for responsibilities that were carried out while you were away.

∇ Finally, debrief with any people necessary, both to be sure that you're up-to-date on all pertinent information and to reassure them that you realize things *do* happen while you are gone.

In Conclusion

Being an absentee manager isn't easy for manager or for employees, but acknowledging the situation and taking basic steps to prepare for it will minimize the problem and help answer the question, "Who's minding the store?"

Date ______________

∇ Absentee Management Assessment

Directions: Place a square around a number to indicate how important you think that item is relative to effective absentee management.
Place a circle around a number to indicate your estimation of your present skill level in absentee management.

Suggestion: Have your employees fill out the "Employee" version. Place their averaged scores in the appropriate places and compare their perceptions with yours.

Scale: **High/Excellent - 5 4 3 2 1 - Low/Poor**

Items		**Employees** □ O
1. The general impact on my work unit of my being absent. (5 = no problem ----- 1 = very detrimental)	5 4 3 2 1	___ ___
2. The frequency of communications while I'm away.	5 4 3 2 1	___ ___
3. The quality of communications while I'm away.	5 4 3 2 1	___ ___
4. Communicating on an established schedule while I'm away.	5 4 3 2 1	___ ___
5. The frequency of my absences.	5 4 3 2 1	___ ___
6. The duration of my absences.	5 4 3 2 1	___ ___
7. Upon my return, giving appropriate praise for holding the fort while I was gone.	5 4 3 2 1	___ ___
8. The quality of my delegating before I leave.	5 4 3 2 1	___ ___
9. Ease of locating me if necessary while I'm gone.	5 4 3 2 1	___ ___
10. The level of my "I'm the boss again" attitude when I return.	5 4 3 2 1	___ ___

Overall rating of the quality of your absentee management skills:

Very high - 10 9 8 7 6 5 4 3 2 1 - Very low (circle one)

Your employees' averaged rating: ___________

Note: Circled items in the 1-2 area may require your immediate attention, as they can be detrimental to the productive functioning of your work unit while you're away. Also give attention to items in which the circle is two or more numbers to the right of the square, as this indicates a gap between importance and skill level.

Date ______________ EMPLOYEE

∇ Absentee Management Assessment

Directions: Place a square around a number to indicate how important you think that item is relative to effective absentee management.
Place a circle around a number to indicate your estimation of your manager's present skill level in absentee management.

Scale: **High/Excellent - 5 4 3 2 1 - Low/Poor**

Items

1. The general impact on my work unit of my manager's absences. (5 = no problem --- 1 = very detrimental)	5 4 3 2 1
2. The frequency of communications while he or she is away.	5 4 3 2 1
3. The quality of communications while he or she is away.	5 4 3 2 1
4. Communicating on an established schedule while he or she is away.	5 4 3 2 1
5. The frequency of my manager's absences.	5 4 3 2 1
6. The duration of my manager's absences.	5 4 3 2 1
7. Upon return, giving appropriae praise for holding the fort while he or she was gone.	5 4 3 2 1
8. The quality of his or her delegating before leaving.	5 4 3 2 1
9. Ease of locating him or her if necessary while away.	5 4 3 2 1
10. The level of an "I'm the Boss again" attitude when he or she returns. (5 = no problem ----- 1 = very detrimental)	5 4 3 2 1

Overall rating of the quality of your manager's absentee management skills:

Very high - 10 9 8 7 6 5 4 3 2 1 - Very low (circle one)

∇ 10. Helping the Problem Employee

Helping the problem employee may be one of the most difficult tasks faced by many managers. It's only human nature to want things to go well, and when employees are problems, managers may run the gamut from concerned to furious.

What do we mean by problem employee? A problem employee is generally an employee who requires the manager's attention on a regular basis to deal with problems that don't have a direct relationship with the work unit's main function.

This is a lengthy way of describing employees who border on being more managerial trouble than they're worth. (If they cross over that border, you may need to refer to Chapter 11.)

But why help them? If they're a problem, and they can't shape up, why not just let them go? There may be several reasons:

- They have useful skills. If they don't, why were they hired in the first place? Do hiring practices need to be given as much attention as the problem employee?
- The problem behavior may be recent enough that it can be changed, if it is dealt with before it becomes significant enough to require termination.
- Working with problem employees sharpens the manager's coaching skills.
- Not giving up on problem employees sends a morale-boosting message to all employees that "this company cares."

Still, isn't it easier just to fire the problem employee? In an era distinguished by legal decisions that are intended to protect employees from shaky management practices, it is seldom easy to fire an employee, and it can often be expensive. (See Chapter 11.)

Types of Problem Employees

How do we know problem employees if we see them? What do they do that distinguishes them from your other employees? There seem to be three general types of behavior that employees at any level engage in that earns them the label of "problem employee":

Type 1—job performance problems
Type 2—on-the-job interpersonal problems
Type 3—dysfunctional behavior problems

Some employees will exhibit all three types of problems, while others will be limited to one or two. The first step for the manager confronted with a problem employee is to determine which type of problem it is, for there are differences in the way that each type may need to be handled.

Let's take a closer look at each type:

∇ **Type 1—job performance problems.** Here we see behavior that is directly related to the employee's performing specific job functions. In some ways it is the easiest type to deal with, for job skills are usually the most recently learned and have the fewest emotional components of the three types of behaviors, often making them the easiest to change.

Managers need to look at these behaviors carefully, for at first glance it may be difficult to tell if the problem is a result of inadequate skills or of insufficient motivation.

If inadequate skills is the problem, the manager needs to decide whether the inadequacy is a result of a lack of training or the employee's inability to learn. Additional training may solve one need, but if the employee is incapable of learning the skills necessary, a transfer to a simpler job may be in order.

If you determine that the problem is one of *will not* rather than *can not*—a motivational problem—the solution may be more complex, because you'll then need to find out if the performance problem is the result of long-standing attitudes and personal value systems or current situations within the work environment.

For example, if low motivation is caused by being passed over for an important assignment, it can be handled more easily than if it is caused by "having to take orders from a woman." The first may be resolved with a frank discussion, while the second may require a transfer or even termination.

∇ **Type 2—on-the-job interpersonal problems.** These employees have ongoing interpersonal relationship problems with fellow employees—authority figures, the opposite sex, subordinates, a particular ethnic group, and so forth, or it may be an across-the-board problem. Depending on the nature of the employee's work, it may not directly interfere with his or her job performance, but it may make it difficult for co-workers to get *their* jobs done. High team performance does not occur in a social vacuum.

In this case, your first step is usually to point out to the employee the effect his or her behavior is having on other work unit members. If that doesn't solve the problem, you may want to recommend specific human relations training, depending on the nature of the problem. The last step would be to set up a "consequences session," as outlined later in this section.

∇ **Type 3—dysfunctional behavior problems.** Employee behaviors such as sexual harassment, unacceptable dress, petty theft, working under the influence of alcohol, and chemical dependencies are called dysfunctional for they can create serious performance and social problems for the employee, co-workers, and the manager. The behaviors "don't work." These employees can be highly skilled and generally socially acceptable, yet a specific aspect of their behavior causes ongoing problems for the organization and the overall work culture.

Fortunately, these employees are in the minority in most work units, although drugs and alcohol are becoming an increasing problem. For example, one study of approximately six hundred job applicants found that one in three had used drugs within the previous seventy-two hours.

Dysfunctional problems are often serious enough to require specific professional counseling help and application of your organization's due process machinery. Depending on both the nature and seriousness of the problem, you as manager must decide what will need to be done. Only one thing is certain: managerial procrastination will not work. Most type 3 problems do not go away of their own accord—they usually get worse.

Problem Causes

Another way of examining the problem employee's behavior is to determine if the causes of the behavior seem to be internal or external, since this will also have a bearing on your course of corrective help. (Also see Chapter 18 for a discussion of poor performance.) Here are several causes in each area:

Problem Causes

Internal	External
Personality factors	Cultural background
Personal habits	Work environment
Inadequate skills	Lack of resources
Learning potential	Sex-role stereotypes
Low motivation	Available training
Age: maturity	Age: generation gap

Internal causes

The skills and motivation issues are discussed in Chapters 16 and 18, but let's look at the others on the list:

∇ **Personality factors.** Personality means different things to different managers, but let's use it here to denote such personal traits as assertiveness, personal warmth, task or relationship orientation, shyness, and self-motivation. Any extreme of such personality factors will often cause interpersonal difficulties with managers and co-workers. If high organizational performance relies on teamwork—and it usually does—then managers must take into account employees' abrasive or dysfunctional personality factors.

∇ **Personal habits.** Although it might not have been a problem for your great-grandparent in the 1880s if your sharpest, most socially affable employee is sitting in your office spitting tobacco juice into your wastebasket, it would likely be considered a problem in most contemporary work units.

Other personal habits, including smoking, can be considered offensive or annoying by members of your work unit and will require your attention. To ignore them sends signals to your employees that you are either not concerned with the social environment or that you are unwilling to confront employees' problem behaviors. Even the loud, off-key perpetual whistler can eventually drive some co-workers to earplugs and then the aspirin bottle.

∇ **Age: maturity.** Maturity is not always a function of age, but it is generally true that younger employees may not have the judgment and social skills of their older contemporaries. This is especially true if they are on their first job. If they are not to be seen as a problem, they may need a much more thorough orientation program than that provided for more experienced new employees.

A lack of maturity also requires that you give closer than normal supervision and shift your management style toward a more directive approach. Simply telling an immature employee, no matter what the chronological age, to "grow up!" doesn't solve the problem. They usually require the manager demonstrating what grown-up behavior means in your working environment.

External causes

Whereas most of the internal causes are under the employee's control, some of the external causes of problem behaviors are under your control as manager. Some of them are also beyond the direct control of anyone in your organization and simply must be adapted to as painlessly as possible.

∇ **Cultural background.** There are parts of the country where local businesses or organizations might as well shut down when the deer/trout/duck/elk season opens, or when there's harvesting to be done on the family farm. If there is a clash between the cultural values of manager and employee—for example, between a native American's need to hunt deer, as his family has done for generations, and his manager's need to support the Protestant work ethic—the work unit suddenly has a problem employee.

Such differences in cultural value systems can usually be resolved if both the organization and employees are willing to take these steps:

- Become consciously aware of their respective value systems and how they impact on organizational performance and the social work environment. This involves both manager and employee realizing that alternative cultural value systems aren't right or wrong, just different.
- Negotiate work arrangements that can accommodate those value differences. For example, American businesses traditionally close for Christian holidays, yet there are other cultural customs and values that are equally significant to other segments of the work force.

The organization that consistently approaches legitimate cultural differences with a "Do it our way or else!" attitude will continue to have problem employees.

∇ **Work environment.** The work environment, both physical and psychological, can be instrumental in creating problem employee situations.

For example, some employees are very susceptible to auditory or visual distractions, variations in heat and cold, or other physical environmental factors. If these are not taken into account in their working space, their performance suffers, and they become another problem employee.

This is equally true for the psychological work environment. Employees who need frequent feedback on their work to maintain high performance may become problem employees in the eyes of the new manager who doesn't believe in giving feedback. In such a situation, some employees may feel unsupported and suffer a drop in performance, while the co-worker across the aisle is relieved to "finally get the boss off my neck" and improves in performance.

∇ **Lack of resources.** Employees' performance can drop to the problem level if they feel they are not given the resources necessary to carry out their jobs as efficiently as possible. The performance-conscious secretary who must spend endless hours typing repetitive documents even though it would be significantly faster, easier, and more accurate to use a memory typewriter or word processor will likely become a problem employee—coming in late in the morning, taking more sick days, taking long lunch hours, or making excessive personal phone calls.

One of the problems that occurs in small businesses is that they are either undercapitalized or can't justify the purchase of the latest in labor-saving devices. This can leave them at a competitive disadvantage and with disgruntled employees. It is best to be up-front about it and share the plans to get more up-to-date equipment as revenues expand.

∇ **Sex-role stereotypes.** Organizations whose own cultural values are still tied to sex-role stereotypes can create a number of problem employee situations.

For example, a predominantly male engineering firm might subscribe to unspoken, unwritten cultural norms that men are assertive, task-oriented, technically expert, fast-paced, and seldom talk about personal issues on the job. On the other hand, women (mostly clerks and secretaries, in this case) are seen as passive, people-oriented, technically naive, gently paced, supportive of male activities, and frequently relating personal news to coworkers—they make great cheerleaders.

Imagine the consternation in that sex-role stereotyping culture when they hired a bright, attractive, young female engineer—who turned out to embody all the "male" attributes. She was considered a problem employee from the first day she declined to make the coffee! ("We didn't have a course in that at Purdue," she replied, as tactfully as possible.)

Before attaching a problem employee label, be sure that you understand the values of both the employee and whoever is doing the labeling.

Managers who want to improve the sex-role stereotyping situation in the work unit can take these steps:

- Raise their own consciousness of sex-role issues, including language, behavior, and their own attitudes and beliefs.
- Ask men and women how they feel about certain behavior and make appropriate changes. For example, most women heartily resent being called "girl," or pseudo-affectionate nicknames (Honey, Toots, Sweet-

heart), yet may not feel in a politically secure enough position to say anything about it—especially to a male manager.

Male managers typically don't see sex-role stereotyping as a big issue. This is to be expected, however, as stereotyping behavior is usually invisible to the dominant group in any culture. The corporate culture is no exception.

∇ **Available training.** Given the rapid changes occurring in most fields, the employee who does not have access to sufficient training to maintain adequate professional development may become a problem employee. This is especially true in many technical areas, where entire college educations are technically out-of-date within a few years. If the organization will not provide adequate training, the employee is not only frustrated by the specter of a career going stale, but also may fear—sometimes with good reason—that the organizational strategy may be to scrimp on training and then replace current staff members with cheaper new recruits from schools or competitors.

This situation can be resolved by providing the opportunity for professional training on a regular basis. This sends a message to employees that their skills are valuable and worthy of keeping sharp. It is also usually less expensive in the long run to improve the skills of present good employees than to hire new ones.

∇ **Age: generation gap.** The so-called generation gap is really a values gap that is most evident between those born during or shortly after the Depression and those born during or after World War II. Better educated, and growing up surrounded by an affluence not experienced by any other nation in the history of the planet, the post–World War II generations have entirely different views on the nature of work, the responsibilities of organizations to their employees, and the relative balance between corporate and personal life.

To those who experienced the Great Depression, the new values can seem to be heresy of the highest order. The managerial "You should be thankful you even *have* a job!" is a long way from an employee's "I want challenging work with just compensation and results that will make this world a better place to live."

As the luck of historical sequence would have it, the former is most likely to be the Depression-oriented manager, while the latter is the affluent age new employee. As far as the manager is concerned, given the personal values difference, the organization just *hired* a problem employee!

The generation gap is best handled by the manager who gets each side of the gap to become more fully aware of the values of the other, as well as their own. Once such value systems can be fully articulated, significant discussions and accommodation can occur, with each learning from the other. The manager must take a firm lead in the process because it is not one that will usually occur on its own.

Face-to-Face Encounters

What if the manager's analysis of the problem situation is thorough and on target, the problem behaviors have been pointed out to the employee, and the employee chooses to continue with the offending behaviors? What then? The next step can be a "consequences session."

The consequences session is a face-to-face session between manager and the problem employee. Sometimes known as a change interview, the consequences session has the primary purpose of helping the employee be fully aware of the consequences of continuing to choose the present troublesome behaviors, and then helping the employee plan a remedial course of action.

Since an employee's future with the organization can hinge on the successful outcome of such a meeting, it should be carefully planned by all concerned. Here are a few guidelines for such a meeting:

∇ **Provide privacy.** The consequences session needs to be held in a location ensuring privacy, so that the discussion is confidential and free of distractions. Confidentiality is very important in this kind of situation to instill trust and indicate your good faith.

∇ **Have appropriate consequences in mind.** The purpose of the consequences session is to spell out for the employee the consequences of continuing the present problem behavior. This allows the employee to make choices and take responsibility for actions. If the employee's choice is to attempt to change the problem behaviors, then your role as manager is to assist in the development of a mutual plan to accomplish the desired change.

To carry this out, you'll need to have specific consequences in mind if the employee chooses not to change. "You're going to be in big trouble!" isn't sufficiently specific to leverage a significant behavior change. Make the consequences as vivid and literal as possible—paint a verbal picture, just as a good salesperson would. It's the strongest way to get your point across.

∇ **Cover one point at a time.** No matter how many points or events may be pertinent to the discussion, handle them one at a time. The manager's tendency is to dump everything on the employee at once, creating a sense of futility, anger, and defensiveness in the employee. Remember that this is a problem-solving meeting, not an inquisition, and that your mutual goal is to remove the barriers that stand in the way of the employee's satisfactory performance.

∇ **Give specific examples.** "You're doing a lousy job, Chris!" doesn't really tell the employee the gap between the behavior you want and the current behavior. It doesn't define the *why* of the problem employee label.

It also doesn't help the problem-solving process to rationalize that "Well, they *know* what the problem is. I'll just tell them to stop it." Be specific.

Otherwise employees have good reason to suspect that you're not being up-front with them about what the real problem is. If that is in fact the case, then you're not ready to have a consequences session. Hold off until you have your facts in order.

∇ **Focus on the problem, not the person.** It is very important that you keep the meeting focused on the specific behaviors that are causing the problem. It is those behaviors that are the problem, not the person.

I can't overemphasize how important the distinction is between behavior and person any time you're attempting to change a behavior, on or off the job. If employees—or child, spouse, or friend—feel that you are challenging them as persons, rather than challenging a specific behavior, they will go on the defensive to protect their self-worth as human beings. That's only natural. Once they're on the defensive, problem-solving stops.

∇ **Don't bluff.** As in any sincere negotiations, there's no point in bluffing. If you say something, mean it!

The Session

There are four basic steps to follow in the consequences session itself. You can of course adjust these to the situation, but these are the four things that need to happen:

1. Present documented evidence of the problem behavior to the employee. Spell out the specific differences between satisfactory behavior and the current behavior, and present the specific consequences of continuing that behavior. Let the employee know that he or she is of value to the organization, or you would not invest the time in such a meeting.
2. Ask for the employee's version of the problem and what he or she thinks are the barriers to improving the situation. Accept reasons, but do not accept excuses or blaming others. Draw out the employee's feelings about the present situation and the possible consequences.
3. If the employee chooses to attempt to change the problem behaviors, establish a remediation plan. Let the employee take the lead, suggesting solutions, plans, and the necessary benchmarks along the way. Most of us know what we need to do to change unwanted behaviors, we just need reinforcement in doing it. The possible loss of a job can often act as a very powerful reinforcer.

   Help the employee focus the remediation plan on the employee's *positive* strengths and assets, for new behaviors are built on strengths, not weaknesses. Keep the focus on what you mutually want to have happen in the future, not what has happened in the past.

   If the employee chooses not to attempt to change the problem behaviors, then you must be prepared to implement the consequences.

4. Set specific dates when you both will check the plan's progress and readjust it, if necessary. This is the step that tests the manager, for inadequate follow-up sends the message to your employees that you were really not serious about the behavior change. In short, the consequences session is important, but the follow-up is crucial.

Off-the-Job Employee Problems

An employee whose personal problems are brought to the workplace presents a special challenge for the conscientious manager. When things go wrong for an employee personally, how can the manager maintain an appropriate professional distance, yet help the affected employee maintain performance at the same time? It is a difficult, yet essential, balancing act.

One manager's adage was, "I just tell my people to leave their personal problems at home, where they belong." That is simple, but not very realistic. The manager might just as well tell employees to leave their sneezing at home if they come down with a cold.

No matter how strongly managers may wish otherwise, employees' personal problems come along to work with them just as the tail follows the dog. Off-the-job worries, anxieties, anger, and other strong negative emotions produce physical stress responses that cannot be shed like an old sweater at the organizational coat rack. Problems are problems, and most of us can't put them out of mind just because we've punched a time clock.

This crossover effect of personal problems and issues into the workplace can have a very debilitating effect on the employee's job performance, interpersonal relationships in the work unit, and work unit morale—not to mention the manager's piece of mind. Without playing psychologist, what can the concerned manager do?

When to Counsel, When to Refer

Unfortunately, there are no hard and fast rules as to when a manager should attempt to counsel an employee with off-the-job problems, and when the manager should refer the employee to other resources. I strongly recommend, however, that as a manager your basic rule should be: *Refer off-the-job problems to appropriate professional resources.*

While this might at first seem to be a noncaring approach, there are several good reasons for that recommendation:

∇ No matter how much you care and want to help, unless you are a trained counselor, you won't be able to help as much as a professional. Attempting to counsel employees yourself may only delay their getting the in-depth help they need.

- Counseling significantly changes the manager-employee roles in ways that may inhibit the effectiveness of your management functions. It would be almost impossible to successfully mix your responsibility for maintaining employee performance with that of counselor. Even professional counselors resist the temptation to counsel personal friends.

- Attempting to counsel an employee with off-the-job problems can raise all sorts of difficult legal problems for you and your organization if the employee subsequently is dismissed for inadequate performance, or if the employee's problem is such that it ends up in court.

  In short, let the professionals handle it!

A Special Problem—The Stress Junkie

A problem that often puzzles managers is the one work unit where things always seem to be in turmoil. Work may get done on time, but it usually seems to be finished in a state of panic. It is the unit that runs up outrageous bills for overnight delivery, has the highest turnover, and has employees who usually look as if they know Armageddon is just around the corner.

If this seems to be a problem in your work unit, look first for a "stress junkie."

The stress junkie is not using recreational drugs on the job, but may be suffering from what is becoming known as stress addiction. Basically, it is a behavioral and chemical addiction to the body's stress response. As the stress level rises in many organizations, stress addiction is becoming a more significant factor adversely influencing work unit performance.

The addiction occurs as a result of the body's fight-or-flight response, preparing the body to take action for survival in time of physical or psychological danger. This orchestrates a powerful set of chemical and physical changes in the body, giving the body quite a jolt. It takes only seconds to occur, but much longer to wear off.

Adrenalin is one of the most powerful hormones in this reaction. It is also chemically very close to amphetamines. Depending on the individual's metabolism and physical makeup, it can be every bit as potent for some people as the less legal products bought in parking lots, drive-ins, and public restrooms.

If you think that you may have a stress junkie problem in your work unit, there are several things you can watch for:

- **Constant crisis situations.** The true stress addict usually develops a pattern of crisis-related situations, both on and off the job. If the employee's or manager's personal life is usually in crisis, and the situation in the work unit is also crisis-ridden, you have good reason to be suspicious.

- **Procrastinate-rush cycle.** Be aware of a pattern of procrastinating, then rushing to get work out on time. See who depends most on overnight delivery services or frequently requires overtime help. This will not only give you clues as to possible stress addiction in your work unit, but will also point the way to cutting your overhead costs.

∇ **Last-minute changes.** One way to throw an otherwise well-planned operation into an adrenalin-producing crisis is to change something at the last minute. This isn't changing something that was found to be faulty "just in the nick"—that can happen occasionally even in the most organized operation—but for the stress addict it is more often the result of having "a better idea." You can be justifiably suspicious of a consistent pattern of "better ideas" that come later, rather than sooner.

∇ **Thriving on crisis.** Stress addicts are drawn to stress and crisis like flies to ice cream. They are the ones who go laughing into combat, high on their own adrenalin, while the bodies pile up around them. What's more, if they are in a position of authority, they may also have started the war.

∇ **Avoiding responsibility for damage.** The major problem in working with any addiction is to get the addict to admit to the problem. Stress addicts, for example, are likely to respond with "Who, me?" if confronted with their behavior pattern.

Stress addicts are often unable or unwilling to realize or admit the problems their crisis-producing behaviors have caused. To do so would be to admit the overall addiction problem and the necessity for solving it—both painful. This is especially true if it runs counter to their self-image as a dedicated worker or manager. Few of us want to admit that we're causing more problems than we're solving.

∇ **Seeking the new and different.** The stress addict usually prefers to seek out the new and the different, rather than refine the existing. They may be easily bored, and the new provides much more excitement than the old. This pattern of constant change may be reflected in both personal and professional life situations. What they consider terrific today is likely to be forgotten tomorrow.

∇ **Management style.** The management style best suited to crisis situations is autocratic—"There's no time to ask questions, just do as I say!" If the suspected stress addict is a manager, observe which management style he or she uses in a crisis. Often a manager who is most comfortable with the authoritative, crisis-management style will continue consciously or unconsciously to generate one crisis after another in order to use it.

∇ **High turnover.** Co-workers and employees of the stress junkie often feel like victims of the procrastinate-rush cycle and last-minute changes, and will bail out when they can't stand it anymore. As a result, the organization loses some good people, and the addict is left to wreak equal havoc on the new replacements.

Helping the Problem

If stress addiction appears to be a problem in your work unit, there are several things that can be done:

∇ **Self-awareness.** One of the greatest problems in helping any addiction is getting the addict to recognize and admit to the problem. This is not easy to accomplish—witness the number of alcoholics still without treatment. Until addicts recognize the effect of their dysfunctional behavior on relationships, job performance, and others in the work unit, there is little possibility of significant change.

In short, the stress addict needs to answer honestly these two questions:

1. How many stressful events in my life are caused by my own behavior and choices?
2. What is the effect on those around me of my behavior and choices?

Until the addict can face up to the answers to those two questions, there is little likelihood of change.

∇ **Examine the diet.** The stress addict often reinforces the addiction with poor eating habits: excessive stimulants, sweets, junk food, and irregular eating schedules ("I'm just too busy"). It's also a safe bet that the stress addict usually doesn't eat breakfast.

∇ **Respect other's choices.** Stress addicts need to realize that not everyone wants to get high on stress-induced adrenalin. The effect on the work unit of the manager who assumes the rest of the work unit gets the same high from crisis situations as he or she does is similar to the alcoholic parents who encourage the children to drink with them—it isn't long before the whole family system comes apart. Either the children also become dependent on alcohol or they revolt and leave.

What also often happens in such a family is that one of the children, out of the necessity to keep things running, takes over the role of parent. The same thing happens in the work unit "family" of an addicted manager. In one way or another, someone in the work unit takes responsibility for attempting to keep things under control and functioning as smoothly as possible. Because of the added frustration and stress such a situation causes, however, that employee may not remain in the work unit very long.

∇ **Stop enabling the addiction.** Every type of addict who doesn't live on a desert island or in a lighthouse requires people around him or her who somehow put up with the addiction—the "enablers." They make up excuses, cover up to others, look the other way, rationalize ("But he's such a good father when he's sober"), pick up the pieces, or in some other way enable the addictive behavior to continue.

For a stress-addicted manager or employee, negotiating a "nonenabling contract" with co-workers can be helpful. Such a "contract" can include having the stress addict:

- Plan ahead—and carry out the plan.
- Be on time to committed appointments.
- Make no last-minute changes—"Don't fix it if it ain't broke."
- Avoid daily "Emergency—drop everything!" requests or meetings.
- Clean up the diet, and don't mooch stimulants from others.

If the addict can get others to help reinforce even a few of these, the situation in the work unit should start to calm down and morale and productivity go up.

∇ **The switch.** Even if the stress addict doesn't choose to work on the addiction, the situation in the work unit can often be improved by the switch: the addict finds an activity outside of work that provides the necessary adrenalin "hit." The surgeon who races sports cars on weekends, the hang-gliding accountant, the executive secretary who whitewater rafts on vacation—all have figured out a way to get a natural high without stirring up their work situation.

∇ **Professional help.** If the addict's job is at stake, or other attempts to change behavior haven't worked, then professional counseling may be needed. For progressive organizations with employee assistance programs, this is the first step. Often enrollment in an organization's "wellness" program is sufficient. For those who suspect that diet is part of the problem, a visit to a good nutritionist can help.

As more emphasis is placed on high performance and innovative work units, managers of such units will need to become increasingly aware of the negative impact the stress addict can have on team performance, as well as monitoring themselves for stress addiction tendencies.

Managerial Self-Awareness

No matter how objective we attempt to be as managers about the problem employee, any such labeling process is at least in part subjective: our judgmental forces are at work. This is especially true when we consider our employees. Here are several questions managers have found helpful to ask themselves as part of problem employee situations:

∇ Am I labeling this a problem simply because the employee's behavior makes me feel uncomfortable? Does the behavior impair the performance of the individual employee, the work unit, or the organization? If not, what would it take to help me become more comfortable?

∇ Can I make this a win/win situation for employee, myself, the work unit, and the organization? If that is not my goal, what are my real motives? Have I fallen into a "Don't get mad, get even" trap?

∇ Have I avoided or procrastinated confronting the employee with the problem behaviors? If so, was it because I want to be liked? Have I forgotten that the manager's job is to raise the tough issues . . . not necessarily to be liked, but to be competent?

In Conclusion

Problem employee situations are some of the toughest facing any manager. Handling them both effectively and humanely can often be what separates good managers from the also-rans.

One of the major differences seems to be that the good managers regard problem behaviors as a challenge, while less effective managers regard them as a problem. If you can approach the problem employee with the same creative zest and spirit with which you approach other managerial challenges, you will find that both you and your employees will benefit.

∇ ***For additional information, see:***

Chapter 5. Growing the Corporate Culture
Chapter 11. Firing Is Never Easy
Chapter 18. Poor Performance Comes In for Analysis
Chapter 22. Performance Appraisal—Who Needs It?
Chapter 25. Managerial Stress Management

Date ____________ MANAGER

∇ Stress Addiction Self-Assessment

Directions: Place a circle around a number to indicate your estimation of the frequency of each behavior.

Suggestion: Have your employees fill out the "Employee" version. Place their averaged scores in the appropriate places and compare their perceptions with yours.

Scale: **5-Never 4-Seldom 3-Occasionally 2-Usually 1-Always** (circle one)

Items		**Employees**
1. I get most things done at the last minute.	5 4 3 2 1	___
2. I enjoy a very hectic pace during the work day.	5 4 3 2 1	___
3. I call meetings on the spur of the moment.	5 4 3 2 1	___
4. I like juggling many things at the same time.	5 4 3 2 1	___
5. I expect employees to maintain as rapid a pace as I do.	5 4 3 2 1	___
6. I get bored if things slow down.	5 4 3 2 1	___
7. I change things when they are near completion because I suddenly get a better idea.	5 4 3 2 1	___
8. Change excites me.	5 4 3 2 1	___
9. Some people think of me as a daredevil.	5 4 3 2 1	
10. My personal life could be considered hectic or complex.	5 4 3 2 1	
11. There are many hellos and goodbyes to people in my life.	5 4 3 2 1	
12. I am or have been involved in sports or hobbies that could be considered dangerous.	5 4 3 2 1	

Overall rating of the quality of your stress addiction behavior:

Very high - 10 9 8 7 6 5 4 3 2 1 - Very Low (circle one)

Your employees' averaged rating: ___________

Note: Circled items in the 1-2 area may warrant your closer attention, as they can be indicative of a potential problem with needing excessive stress. This is especially true if you have circled several items in this area, or if there are major differences in the way you perceive yourself and the way you are perceived by others.

Date ____________

EMPLOYEE

∇ Stress Addiction Assessment

Directions: Place a circle around a number to indicate your estimation of the frequency of the following behavior by your manager.

Scale: **5-Never** **4-Seldom** **3-Occasionally** **2-Usually** **1-Always** (circle one)

Items

1. Gets most things done at the last minute.	5 4 3 2 1
2. Enjoys a very hectic pace during the workday.	5 4 3 2 1
3. Calls meetings on the spur of the moment.	5 4 3 2 1
4. Likes juggling many things at the same time.	5 4 3 2 1
5. Expects employees to maintain his or her pace.	5 4 3 2 1
6. Gets bored if things slow down.	5 4 3 2 1
7. Changes things when they are near completion because he or she suddenly gets a better idea.	5 4 3 2 1
8. Change excites her or him.	5 4 3 2 1

The overall rating of the quality of your manager's stress addiction behavior:

Very high - 10 9 8 7 6 5 4 3 2 1 - Very low (circle one)

∇ 11 Firing Is Never Easy

Perhaps the most difficult job a manager faces is firing an employee. It is a process that has "failure" written all over it: failure of the organization, failure of the manager, and failure of the fired employee. With that many failures involved, no wonder firing is usually the most dreaded managerial function. Divorce is tough on everybody.

Let's look more closely at the failure aspect, since if some of the failures can be avoided, so can some of the firings.

Failure of the Organization

As we begin to get a better understanding of the impact on job performance of corporate culture—the system of beliefs, values, and behavior that form the workplace environment—we can also better understand how the organization may contribute to what was once considered only the employee's failure. Several basic factors under the organization's control can lead to an employee's being fired:

∇ **Selection process.** An inadequate selection process at the hiring stage can lead to firing down the line: the organization hires the wrong person in the first place. The process for hiring in some organizations almost guarantees problems: "I met this terrific guy at a gallery opening. He'll start Monday as your new assistant." Or "Charlie's daughter is getting a divorce and really needs a job. I'm putting her in your department." Or "You *know* we need someone from this ethnic group for balance. Do what you can for him."

Other managers tend to hire people they think will like them, who won't challenge their authority, or whose looks will grace the work environment. Unfortunately, none of those traits is a good substitute for competence.

Some of these situations turn out surprisingly well. When they do, however, it is usually with no thanks to the organization that created an awkward position to start with, but rather the result of good managing and a self-motivated employee. Inadequate hiring practices are not fair to anyone: the organization, the individual manager, or the employee.

Of course, even the best selection process lets through a few unfortunate surprises. However, when an organization discovers that it is having to push an inordinate number of employees out the back door, it needs to look at how it is bringing them in through the front.

∇ **Supportive environment.** Once an employee is hired, does the organization make the newcomer welcome, with an adequate orientation and a carefully managed trial period, or does it seem to regard people as interchangeable parts in a machine, who can attain peak performance as soon as they are slotted into place?

Even organizations that start new employees well often haven't thought through the necessary steps to help employees maintain adequate performance. The employee's work environment needs to be not only receptive but also supportive.

∇ **Unrealistic expectations.** The organization, in an effort to lure an attractive job candidate, may have intentionally or accidentally set up unrealistic expectations about the future opportunities and rewards. If the employee is not able to realize those expectations once on the job, disillusionment and resentment set in, often accompanied by a decline in performance. In the long run, making unrealistic promises at the hiring stage doesn't do anyone any favors.

∇ **Insufficient training.** In a culture where technology and job roles change rapidly, an organization that does not supply adequate training is not only assembling an outmoded labor force, but will also have difficulty retaining its best employees. This puts an added strain on manager and employee alike, for both know that an outmoded *anything* has a very limited future in a rapidly changing workplace and that dismissal from the organization may be just around the corner.

∇ **Inadequate remediation procedures.** The organization needs to have effective remediation procedures once inadequate employee performance becomes evident. Neither organizational wishful thinking nor "Do better or else!" directives have proven effective in raising employee performance or changing behaviors. A manager's hands are tied without adequate remedial procedures available to help employees with performance or behavior problems.

Failure of the Manager

A fired employee can also be considered a managerial failure. If one of the manager's primary jobs is to remove the barriers to employee high performance, an employee who doesn't measure up to minimum performance criteria is a symptom that the managerial process wasn't successful.

This, of course, is not to put all the responsibility for employee performance or behavior on the manager. There are obviously both organizational and employee performance barriers over which the manager has no direct control. On the other hand, several factors under the manager's control can have a direct impact on an employee's ultimately getting fired:

∇ **Feedback.** Feedback about how an employee's performance is measuring up against the required criteria is primarily the responsibility of the employee's direct supervisor.

Employees who, when asked how they're doing, respond, "I must be doing all right, nobody's yelled at me lately," obviously aren't getting the level of managerial feedback necessary to generate high performance. Such feedback needs to be timely, specific, and balanced between good news and bad. Failing to provide feedback with these three dimensions can lead to employees being unaware of the gap between their performance and what their job requires.

To avoid their discomfort with giving employees feedback, many managers will contend, "They already know how well they're doing." This managerial rationalization may let managers off their personal hook about giving feedback, but isn't borne out by experience in the workplace. The marginal employee, in danger of being let go, is in even greater need of specific, timely, and balanced feedback on performance.

In short, *firing should never come as a surprise!*

∇ **Coaching skills.** The manager with inadequate coaching skills may not be able to help employees bring performance up to satisfactory levels even after problems are identified. In the complex and time-pressured settings of contemporary organizations, managerial coaching skills are becoming an absolute necessity. If an employee has inadequate skills, is the problem an employee who can't learn, or a manager who can't teach? If a professional sports team doesn't perform up to expectations, the organization usually fires the manager, not the players.

- ∇ **Employee burnout.** Burnout is such a complex hazard that no one person may be totally responsible for its onset. The manager who ignores, or even encourages, some of the basic causes of burnout—workaholism, perfectionism, social isolation, unrealistic goals and expectations—may inadvertently play a role in the ultimate performance decline that leads to an employee's dismissal.

- ∇ **Personality problems.** Sometimes two personalities just can't relate well enough to each other to get the job done. But that's rare. More often it's an unwillingness on the part of one or both to communicate the fact that "I'm uncomfortable around you," and then work out their differences.

  Managers in such situations, having the authority, tend to think that employees should adjust to *their* personalities. That feels very much like a one-way street to employees, and can build resentment and a further polarization of the situation. If adjustments need to be made, it's up to the manager to model the process.

- ∇ **Job descriptions and performance criteria.** It is definitely the manager's responsibility to be certain that employees fully understand not only what they are to do—their job description—but also how they are to do it, and how well. In other words, it isn't enough just to provide employees with a job description. They also need specific performance criteria against which to measure themselves. It's impossible to tell how well you're playing the game if no one has told you how to keep score. And knowing the score determines what strategy you'll use to play the game.

- ∇ **Consequences.** It is also up to the manager to inform marginal performance employees of the likely consequences of a failure to change substandard behavior. Not only does this increase the probability of change, but it also places the responsibility for behavioral choice where it belongs—on the employee.

  Once again: Firing should come as no surprise.

Failure of the Employee

Traditionally, firing was *always* the fault of the employee—the king was always right, the peasants were always wrong—but that has changed as we get a better understanding of job performance. Even so, there are still a number of areas in which the employee's choices may lead to a dismissal. Here are several of the most significant:

∇ **Selection process.** The employee also has a responsibility to interview the employer before accepting a job. If this is done well, there should be few, if any, organizational surprises for the employee after starting the job. Unfortunately, few potential employees know how to go about the process.

The employee who either bluffs or deliberately misinforms during the hiring process can also run into performance problems on the job. Unless such employees are very quick learners, they usually discover through the firing process that bluffing and misinformation don't carry them very far.

New employees who have idealistic or unrealistic perceptions that have persisted through the hiring process may also be in for rude awakenings once they are on the job. The letdown can have debilitating effects on performance, to the point of failure.

∇ **Motivation changes.** Many factors, both corporate and personal, can change an employee's *desire* to perform up to acceptable standards. This is the first area for a manager to explore with an employee who was once a satisfactory performer but whose performance has slid below the acceptable level. When performance changes for the worse, there is usually an underlying emotional cause.

∇ **Burnout.** For a variety of possible reasons, the employee chooses to continue the behaviors that inevitably lead to burnout. If the manager has reflected this behavior back to the employee, along with the consequences and a course of remediation, yet the employee persists, then it is apparent that the employee has chosen to fail. In such cases, professional counseling help is indicated.

∇ **Physical health.** With the flood of self-help books on the subjects of nutrition and exercise, good physical health is now much more a matter of choice than of ignorance. Most of us know what we need to do to maintain our health; it's just a question of our will to do it. The employees whose performance seriously suffers because of avoidable health problems have made choices that are in neither their best interests nor those of the organization. It is often up to the employees' manager to point out both the choices and the organizational consequences.

∇ **Habits and attitudes.** Employees may bring with them basic habits or attitudes that interfere with effective performance. For example, the employee who, for whatever reason, believes that being on time is only for other people is going to have problems. So will employees who have difficulty with authority figures, deadlines, interpersonal relations, attention to necessary details, flexibility in changing, or ambiguous situations. If taken to extremes, all of these can ultimately be a factor in dismissal.

Is Firing Necessary?

If all reasonable attempts at coaching, problem-solving, and remediation have failed, then termination may be the only remaining alternative. Because of the difficulties and general unpleasantness of the process, many managers will put it off as long as possible: "Well, one more chance, just one." Once termination is inevitable, however, such procrastination can cause several problems for the manager:

- The ineffectual worker drags down the performance and morale of other work unit members.
- The manager is seen by members of the work unit as being unwilling or unable to deal with difficult managerial issues.
- The ineffectual worker continues to require an unequal amount of the manager's time.
- The longer the situation drags on, the more difficult the firing process becomes—it is not a process that gets easier with the passage of time.
- Other workers get a mixed message about their own value and skills from the continued retention of an inferior worker.

Because the firing process is difficult, it needs to be done with a great deal of professional care. When a firing decision is made, it is helpful for a manager to keep three necessary attributes of the firing process in mind:

1. *Timely.* There is a time to take decisive action. If you haven't exhausted all reasonable attempts at correction and remediation of the problem area, it's too soon. If you realize that firing is the only remaining alternative, and you procrastinate or let the process drag on, it's late. Once termination has been decided on, waiting is not fair to yourself, the employee, or the organization—it is time to make a clean break.
2. *Considered.* The firing process needs to be a considered, deliberate process, not one conducted at the height of anger or defensiveness. By keeping hard feelings at a minimum, the employee is helped to realize that all possible steps short of firing were taken prior to termination. To avoid guilt feelings—"Maybe I should have given him just one more chance, maybe there was something else I could have done"—the manager also needs to be assured that all avenues to remediation were explored.
3. *Thorough.* Given the complexity of today's labor relations laws, managers who are careless with the firing process can find both themselves and their organization with a very expensive lawsuit. Fired employees' accusations of discrimination, sexual harassment, inadequate training, or safety violations, even if untrue, can necessitate a very expensive defense, plus negative public relations. Before proceeding with the final stages of the termination process, get legal advice. If you do not have a legal or personnel department, check with an attorney who is knowledgeable in this area.

   Even if you are in an "at will" state, requiring no just cause for firing, an impetuous firing may still cost you dearly. Like it or not, the "Begone! The King has spoken!" days are over.

The Termination Session

This is the toughest part of the dismissal process. Every manager has a private scenario, a wish list, of how he or she would want such a session to go:

1. *No emotions.* "Please, God, what will I do if they scream, yell, throw things, faint, or cry their heart out?"
2. *Agreement.* "J. D., you are absolutely right. I was terribly wrong, and I understand your actions completely. I would have done the same thing if I were in your position."
3. *Disappear.* "This couldn't have happened at a better time. I've been offered a job in Brazil, and I'll be leaving the country forever tomorrow on the first plane."

Unfortunately, it usually isn't that simple. In order to help the termination session go as smoothly as possible, here are several suggestions:

∇ If at all possible, help the employee realize that once the consequences had been explained, continuing the unsatisfactory behavior was a matter of the employee's choice and responsibility.

∇ Give clear, specific reasons for the termination. Many organizations put these in writing, signed by both parties. If the employee chooses not to sign, a note to that effect is included.

∇ The focus of the termination is on unacceptable behavior, not the person.

∇ Remind the employee that this is the last step in an orderly process, beginning with warnings of unacceptable behavior or performance, and that the employee was advised of consequences.

∇ If the situation seems to call for it, have a "friendly witness" present during the session. This can be a safety factor with an unruly employee, or prevent later complications should the issue end up in court.

∇ Do your legal homework. Be sure that you have touched all bases required by both your organization and the applicable laws.

∇ If it is applicable, advise the employee of the legal implications of removing files, equipment, or other organizational property, as well as revealing trade secrets to competitors. All of this should be in the employment contract, a legally binding document, so this is only a reminder of what they have already signed.

∇ Not all employees will take termination calmly, although it should come as no surprise. Should the employee become upset, these steps will help:

1. Listen—let the employee vent emotions.
2. Share—let the employee know you realize how difficult this is for him or her.
3. Continue—when emotions have subsided, continue with the session.

Above all, stay in control of your own emotions. There's no need for you to feel threatened by words—you still work there.

If you are physically threatened, and there is no one with you, call someone else in *immediately.* Heroism probably isn't in your job description.

∇ Know your company policies concerning referrals, severance pay, outplacement, insurance, grievance procedures, and terminations.

∇ Help the employee realize that termination is painful for everyone—you and the organization would like everyone to succeed—and that you wish him or her well.

∇ Let the employee know where he or she stands with you. Will you provide references? What will you tell potential employers should they call to check on the employee's background?

A final word: your anxiety about the termination session is both normal and healthy—it is a sign that you are a caring, feeling person, involved with a very difficult task.

Debriefing

An exit interview with the dismissed employee, usually conducted by someone in the personnel or human resource development department, can be a very worthwhile part of the termination process. It gives the organization feedback on its own processes from the employee's point of view.

Even if it isn't part of your organization's termination procedures, debriefing the termination from your point of view with someone can help give you a better perspective of the situation. Ask yourself:

- Did the problem which resulted in the dismissal occur after the employee was hired, or was it something that the employee brought to the job? Were we part of the problem?

- Should our employment screening process have detected the problem? Do we need to change anything in that process?
- Could we have detected the beginnings of the employee's problem earlier, either in the course of normal management interactions or in the performance appraisal process?
- In retrospect, is there anything else we could have done to rectify the situation and avoid termination?

In Conclusion

Firing an employee is never easy. Like divorce, it is a symptom of the failure of a relationship between two parties, both of whom had certain expectations of the other. With such a parting of the ways, it is normal to have grief, guilt, anger, sadness, remorse, resentment, and pain.

But in any dynamic organization, firings are almost inevitable. Keeping to a minimum such personally and financially costly events requires that organizations have an effective employment screening system, active performance appraisal and remediation procedures, and managers who are capable both of coaching substandard performance and of making the tough decisions necessary when termination is the only remaining alternative.

∇ ***For additional information, see:***

Chapter 10. Helping the Problem Employee
Chapter 16. P = SOME: The Performance Equation
Chapter 18. Poor Performance Comes In for Analysis
Chapter 22. Performance Appraisal—Who Needs It?

Date ______________ Employee ________________________ MANAGER

∇ Firing Is Never Easy Checklist

Directions: Use this checklist to be certain that your have included all important components of the termination process.

Actions: **Date(s)**

[ ] 1. Performance appraisal ______________

[ ] 2. Documented evidence of performance problem ______________

[ ] 3. Verbal warning ______________

[ ] 4. Written warning ______________

[ ] 5. Personal interview(s) ______________

[ ] 6. Remedial actions:

- Type: ________________________________ ______________

  ________________________________ ______________

- Attempted ________________________________ ______________
- Documented ________________________________ ______________

[ ] 7. Consequences Interview ______________

[ ] 8. Check with Personnel Department ______________

[ ] 9. Check with next upper management level ______________

[ ] 10. Check with Legal Department or other legal resource ______________

[ ] 11. Termination notification ______________

[ ] 12. Termination interview ______________

[ ] 13. Explain legal rights ______________

[ ] 14. Exit interview ______________

[ ] 15. De-briefing with staff ______________

∇ 12. Meetings—Power or Punishment?

One of the most common events in American organizational life is the meeting. According to In-Person Communications, a New York consulting firm, the average manager spends a thousand hours a year in meetings. If those hours are well-managed, they can be both an efficient way to disseminate information and a creative method of problem-solving. Misused, they can have a decidedly negative effect on participants' morale, high performance, and the cost-effective use of time.

Drop in on the kind of meeting that many of us are often forced to attend, and what do you find? Often the participants are unable to answer the question, "Why am I here?" You may also find a competitive, free-for-all situation, where the most verbally aggressive are doing most of the talking, while the rest of the participants are an often-reluctant audience.

You're also likely to find several different varieties of *Participants typicalus* in our hypothetical meeting: the consistent latecomer, the small clique (who talk mostly to each other—usually while someone else is speaking), the subject-changer, the lecture-giver, the putdowner, and the persistent devil's advocate (who disagrees with almost everything). You may also discover participants who brought their own agendas and are doing their best to carry them out, often to the great discomfort of the leader and the rest of the participants.

Why do nonproductive meetings featuring the above participants happen with such discouraging frequency? There are a number of reasons. Following are a few of the major ones, along with suggestions for possible improvements:

∇ **The nature of the meeting was not clearly established** either in the mind of the leader or in the information given to the participants.

There are two distinctly different types of meetings, informational and problem-solving, each with different intended outcomes:

- The informational meeting is intended to disseminate information efficiently to a group of people. A meeting format instead of written material, for example, gives participants the opportunity to ask questions, clarify, and offer suggestions and opinions. If another form of communication is more efficient, then *don't call the meeting.* Many meetings aren't effective because they also aren't necessary.
- The problem-solving meeting is intended to produce a solution to a problem when a collective approach is considered the most effective. If having these specific people gather together to attempt a solution isn't clearly the best way to handle the problem, *don't call the meeting.* Too many meetings are really an attempt on the part of the manager to spread responsibility for the problem, rather than a legitimate attempt to make the hard decisions necessary to solve it.

∇ **The purpose, process, and payoff for the meeting have not been clearly spelled out.** Participants in a meeting need to know why they are there, what they are going to do, how they are going to do it, and what benefits the meeting will have for them.

Because you are the manager, the meeting is going to be viewed as *your* meeting. If the participants can't see that they are also going to get something of value out of it, their meeting behavior may not be productive.

∇ **There is not a clear agenda.** One of the best methods to ensure that everyone is clear about the purpose, process, and payoff is to have a clearly defined agenda. This enables everyone to be aware of the content of the meeting, what is to be accomplished, and how much time is available for each topic to be covered.

Ideally, the agenda is given to each participant in advance. This helps both leader and participant to prepare adequately for the meeting. In short, one of the secrets for holding effective meetings is *planning.*

∇ **The person calling the meeting has not taken full responsibility for it.** There are two primary functions for which those who call the meeting must be responsible, for no one else should be expected to do them:

1. *Start and end the meeting on time.* Waiting for latecomers punishes those who are on time and rewards those who are late. The probable result? Next time, more people are late! Ending the meeting on time is part of the bargain with participants for which they exchange their attention, input, and cooperation.
2. *Moderate the meeting* in such a way that all the announced objectives are met and that all the participants leave with a feeling that their attendance was worthwhile. Even if the manager who called the meeting doesn't moderate personally, he or she is still responsible for seeing that it is done effectively.

Getting Air Time

One of the problems for the leader of even the best-organized meeting is how to give participants the air time necessary to express their thoughts and ideas. Individuals who can't get a word in edgewise soon give up, depriving the group of the potential benefits of their presence.

There are several reasons why people may not actively participate in a meeting, no matter how valuable their contributions could be:

∇ **The meeting is too large.** A rule of thumb for group dynamics is that when a meeting size reaches fifteen, at least three people will drop out and not actively participate. They are uncomfortable speaking in front of that many other people. Conversely, some people don't open up until the audience is large enough to warrant getting on their personal soap box. "Monster meetings" are generally useful only for disseminating information to a large number of people at the same time.

∇ **Some participants need to dominate the meeting.** There are those who feel threatened unless they can be in control—even if they aren't leading the meeting. Others have a need to be the focus of attention as often as possible, and a meeting gives them a captive audience.

∇ **The meeting lacks a clear structure.** The meeting leader has not established a clear agenda, a specific time frame, or the intended meeting outcomes.

This lack of focus allows some participants to move the meeting in directions that meet their personal needs. When this happens, other participants drop out. The leader needs to be aware that not everyone who leaves a meeting actually leaves the room.

∇ **The meeting leader shifts roles.** A cardinal rule of meeting leadership is "You can either run the meeting, or participate in the discussion—but not both."

The meeting leader has all the power. Participants often won't risk sharing what might be considered controversial ideas when the meeting leader is also involved in the discussion. This is especially true when the leader is also the participants' manager. Who wants to play poker with dealers who can change the rules at any time—in their favor?

The exception to this can be small groups that function well as a team and have established a high trust level. Even then if the meeting leader has power and authority that extends beyond the meeting itself, the dynamics can get complicated and the communication less than open. For that reason, peer-led meetings are often the most frank and productive.

Methods

No matter what type of meeting you're conducting, there are several methods for allowing meeting participants air time, the meeting time necessary for them to say what they want to say:

∇ **Free-for-all or competitive.** The floor is left open, and those who are most verbally assertive get and maintain the floor. If there is any recognition by the meeting leader at all, it goes to the participant who speaks first or loudest. This can be the least effective form of meeting leadership, as less-assertive participants are more likely to drop out than with any other method.

∇ **Rotation.** Each participant is recognized in a predetermined order, unless they prefer to pass.

∇ **By request.** Participants make a signal to the leader—usually a raised hand—that they would like the floor. A special example of this is the English system, in which meeting participants have a card with a different color on each side. When participants wish to speak, they signal the meeting leader by turning over the card, and are recognized in turn.

∇ **Time limit.** Each speaker is given an allocated amount of time, after which the floor is given to the next speaker, usually in a predetermined order.

∇ **By rank.** Those with higher authority positions are recognized first, on down the line to those with the least authority. In the free-for-all system, those with the greatest rank take precedence whenever they wish the floor.

- **By agenda.** Participants speak to predetermined agenda items, preferably announced in advance of the meeting.

- **Moderator's prerogative.** The meeting leader, because of the position as chair, takes precedence over requests for air time by other participants. To avoid abuse of this method, it is best to select a moderator, even temporarily, who does not have a strong personal agenda or need to speak to agenda items.

- **Disruptive behaviors.** Cross-talk (talking to others while someone else has the floor), nonverbal signals to other participants, coming late, or other disruptive behaviors force the meeting leader to give the offender air time in an attempt to rectify the situation and get the meeting back on track.

  It is generally best for the meeting leader to deal with these behaviors directly, either at the time they occur or following the meeting, whichever is most appropriate. To allow them to continue is not only a waste of other participants' valuable time, but also encourages others to engage in the same disruptive behaviors.

In Conclusion

Good managers learn to design the size and format of meetings to fit both the personalities of the participants and the intended outcomes. If in doubt, stick to the basics: be sure that your participants are fully aware of the purpose for the meeting, the process you're going to use, and the payoffs for their attendance and productive participation.

If you do, you should find a significant improvement in the quality and effectiveness of the valuable time spent on what may have been your most dreaded event—the meeting.

- ***For additional information, see:***

Chapter 3. If I'm Talking, Who's Listening?
Chapter 13. Creative Problem-Solving for Fun and Profit

Date ______________

∇ Meetings Assessment

Directions: Place a square around a number to indicate how important you think that item is to holding productive meetings.
Place a circle around a number to indicate the normal situation with regard to meetings in your organization or work unit. [If there is a significant difference between the two, use separate assessment forms.]

Scale: **5-Always 4-Usually 3-Occasionally 2-Seldom 1-Never**

Purpose

1. The purpose of the meeting is clear to everyone. 5 4 3 2 1
2. The purpose is available in written form prior to the meeting. 5 4 3 2 1
3. The purpose of the meeting is made clear by the leader at the start. 5 4 3 2 1
4. Questions about meeting purpose are clarified before other business is conducted. 5 4 3 2 1
5. There is a clear distinction in the planning process between an information meeting and a problem-solving meeting. 5 4 3 2 1

Process

6. Meetings are announced far enough in advance to allow for adequate preparations. 5 4 3 2 1
7. Meetings are long enough to get results, but short enough to maintain interest. 5 4 3 2 1
8. Each meeting has a specific agenda, with subjects and time-frames. 5 4 3 2 1
9. Written agendas are given to participants prior to the meeting. 5 4 3 2 1
10. Presentations are planned, appropriate, and time-conscious. 5 4 3 2 1
11. Participants keep their contributions short enough that everyone gets a fair share of time. 5 4 3 2 1
12. The leader keeps the meeting on track, drawing participants back to the purpose/agenda whenever necessary. 5 4 3 2 1
13. The meeting has an overall time-frame and a time allotment for each agenda item. 5 4 3 2 1

continued

Meetings Assessment, continued.

14. Specified time-frames are adhered to, including beginning and ending. 5 4 3 2 1

15. Audiovisual materials are used whenever necessary to help explain points and concepts. 5 4 3 2 1

<u>Outcomes</u>

16. People leave the meeting with a clear sense of what was accomplished. 5 4 3 2 1

17. There is a commitment by those involved to implement decisions reached during the meeting. 5 4 3 2 1

18. There is a method for checking that information was understood. 5 4 3 2 1

19. There is a clear indication that meeting results will be supported by appropriate levels of management. 5 4 3 2 1

20. The meeting outcome includes a suitable plan of follow-up and action. 5 4 3 2 1

Overall rating of the quality of the meetings in your organization or work unit:

Very high - 10 9 8 7 6 5 4 3 2 1 - Very low (circle one)

Note: Circled items in the 1-2 area may require immediate attention to improve the quality and efficiency of your meetings. Also give close attention to items in which the circle is two or more numbers to the right of the square as this indicates a gap between importance and the situation.

∇ Meeting Skills Assessment

Directions: Place a square around a number to indicate how important you think that skill is for conducting good meetings.
Place a circle around a number to indicate your estimation of your present skill level in conducting meetings.

Suggestion: Have your employees fill out the "Employee" version. Place their averaged scores in the appropriate places and compare their perceptions with yours.

Scale: **High/Excellent - 5 4 3 2 1 - Low/Poor**

Skills		Employees ☐ O
1. Organizing meeting material.	5 4 3 2 1	___ ___
2. Planning a meeting agenda.	5 4 3 2 1	___ ___
3. Structuring meeting time for agenda items.	5 4 3 2 1	___ ___
4. Keeping the group on-task.	5 4 3 2 1	___ ___
5. Mediating disagreement among participants.	5 4 3 2 1	___ ___
6. Generating participation.	5 4 3 2 1	___ ___
7. Maintaining a positive meeting climate.	5 4 3 2 1	___ ___
8. Conducting group problem-solving activities.	5 4 3 2 1	___ ___
9. Using audiovisuals to improve presentations.	5 4 3 2 1	___ ___
10. Getting participants' commitment to action.	5 4 3 2 1	___ ___
11. Handling disruptive behaviors.	5 4 3 2 1	___ ___
12. Reinforcing on-task behaviors by group members.	5 4 3 2 1	___ ___
13. Communicating meeting purpose, process, and payoff.	5 4 3 2 1	___ ___
14. Anticipating meeting problem areas and planning for them.	5 4 3 2 1	___ ___

Overall rating of the quality of your meeting leadership skills:

Very high - 10 9 8 7 6 5 4 3 2 1 - Very low (circle one)

Note: Circled items in the 1-2 area may require immediate attention to improve your meeting leadership skills. Also give close attention to items in which the circle is two or more numbers to the right of the square as this indicates a gap between importance and skill level.

Date ____________

EMPLOYEE

∇ Meeting Skills Assessment

Directions: Place a square around a number to indicate how important you think that skill is for conducting good meetings.
Place a circle around a number to indicate your estimation of your manager's present skill level in conducting meetings.

Scale: **High/Excellent - 5 4 3 2 1 - Low/Poor**

Skills

1. Organizing meeting material.	5 4 3 2 1
2. Planning a meeting agenda.	5 4 3 2 1
3. Structuring meeting time for agenda items.	5 4 3 2 1
4. Keeping the group on-task.	5 4 3 2 1
5. Mediating disagreement among participants.	5 4 3 2 1
6. Generating participation.	5 4 3 2 1
7. Maintaining a positive meeting climate.	5 4 3 2 1
8. Conducting group problem-solving activities.	5 4 3 2 1
9. Using audiovisuals to improve presentations.	5 4 3 2 1
10. Getting participants' commitment to action.	5 4 3 2 1
11. Handling disruptive behaviors.	5 4 3 2 1
12. Reinforcing on-task behaviors by group members.	5 4 3 2 1
13. Communicating meeting purpose, process, and payoff.	5 4 3 2 1
14. Anticipating meeting problem areas and planning for them.	5 4 3 2 1

Overall rating of the quality of your manager's meeting leadership skills:

Very high - **10 9 8 7 6 5 4 3 2 1** - Very low (circle one)

∇ 13. Creative Problem-Solving for Fun and Profit

A hen is only an egg's way of making another egg.
—*Samuel Butler*

Albert Einstein once said, "A problem can't be solved at the same level it was created." This speaks directly to the contemporary manager's need for creative problem-solving skills that are more sophisticated than the factors that created the problem.

Barriers to Creative Problem-Solving

In almost any organization there are barriers that can get in the way of creative thinking and problem-solving. The following are some that may be a problem in your organization or work unit:

- **Managerial support.** No seed is any better than the soil in which it is planted, and no creative problem-solving method is any better than the work culture in which it is used. The work culture is created in large measure by both the decisions and the example presented by the manager's behavior. Without managerial understanding and support, creative thinking lasts about as long as ground fog in the noonday sun.

- **Feedback.** Any individual or group that does not get adequate managerial feedback on the results of the problem-solving process soon loses motivation, and the process becomes an activity grounded in futility.

- **Responsibility without authority.** An employee or group that is given the responsibility to solve a problem without the authority to carry out the solution may also soon lose motivation. Having the apparent solution to a problem but needing to rely on someone else's authority to carry it out can be another exercise in futility. It's like fishing without barbs on the hook—you're engaged in the right activity, but it's not likely to result in anything for the frying pan.

  In short, if you're a manager who has delegated a problem, place the authority to solve it in the same hands to which you delivered the problem.

- **Loss of control over the implementation.** Related to the problem of responsibility without authority is the frustration and demotivation of the creative problem-solver that can result from loss of control over implementation of the solution. This is especially true if the implementer has no real understanding of all elements of the proposed solution.

  This loss of control is more likely to occur if people higher up on a hierarchical management scale attempt to carry out the solution, as they may feel no obligation or responsibility to check back with the creators of the original solution.

  An added hazard to the continued motivation of the problem-solver is the upper manager's almost irresistible urge to change the solution, even if only slightly, so that the solution carries the manager's personal stamp.

  Unfortunately, if the manager wasn't in on the creative process that developed the solution, such "This is mine" changes can be detrimental to the solution's effectiveness. To avoid this employee demotivating situation, managers need to be in touch with their own motivations before making arbitrary or unilateral changes in their employees' proposed solutions.

- **Manager takes the credit.** The manager's reluctance to give full credit or recognition to the creators of the original solution can compound the employee motivation problem even further. The net result can be an understandable attitude on the part of the creators, "If they're so anxious to change the solution and then take credit for it, next time let them solve their own damn problem!" And another valuable organizational resource goes down the drain.

Managers who unwisely attempt to take credit for employees' creative solutions quickly lose credibility and respect in the eyes of both their employees and anyone else who knows where the idea really came from. Such misappropriation of credit is one of the quickest and surest ways to demotivate conscientious employees. The truly innovative thinkers among them will soon find other outlets for their creativity.

∇ **"Mistakes" are punished.** Creative mistakes need to be examined, not punished, as they provide an excellent opportunity to learn. New growth seldom results from doing things "right," since that obviously indicates that those skills have already been acquired. New learning occurs from the stretch required when things don't turn out the way they were intended.

If the work unit culture punishes creative mistakes, the manager can kiss creative risk-taking goodbye. The trust level for employees to put their creative ideas out for public scrutiny is often very fragile. Being thoughtlessly shot down in flames by a manager can keep creative employee problem-solving grounded for the duration.

Nor does the crash have to occur to the individual employee to have a negative impact. Let the manager or peers turn their missiles on anyone's creative suggestion, and all but the bravest will prudently decide to keep their ideas safely on the ground.

Here are a few of these creativity-killing missiles that frequently traverse organizational skies:

"Management would never buy it."
"That's much too radical."
"Be practical."
"Probably costs too much."
"You've got to be kidding!"
"Come on, be *realistic*."
"Have you really thought that through?"
"We need to follow the rules."
"That's just *your* opinion."
"It's too obvious."
"Why stick our necks out?"
"It's too much trouble."
"That's contrary to policy."
"We don't do that around here."
"That isn't my area."
"We tried it once, and it didn't work."
"Where's the research to back it up?"

Any of these—and many more that you can probably add from your own experience—can serve to shoot down employees' creative problem-solving ideas in a way that will deter them from launching new ideas in the foreseeable future. Only the diehard masochist enjoys being shot at.

∇ **Risks vs. rewards.** Employees will take risks, the very heart and soul of creative problem-solving, if the reward is compensatory with the risk. You only bet the farm if the potential reward is an even bigger farm.

As a manager, if you are expecting or requesting innovative solutions from your employees, be sure that you've clearly spelled out the rewards for the risks involved. Otherwise, "safe, known, and normal" looks much more appealing to anyone without an inordinate taste for adventure.

∇ **Recognition.** Most, although not all, creative problem-solvers want and need recognition for their contribution. Even if you can't tie financial rewards to creative problem-solving, at the very least be sure that public recognition accompanies innovative solutions.

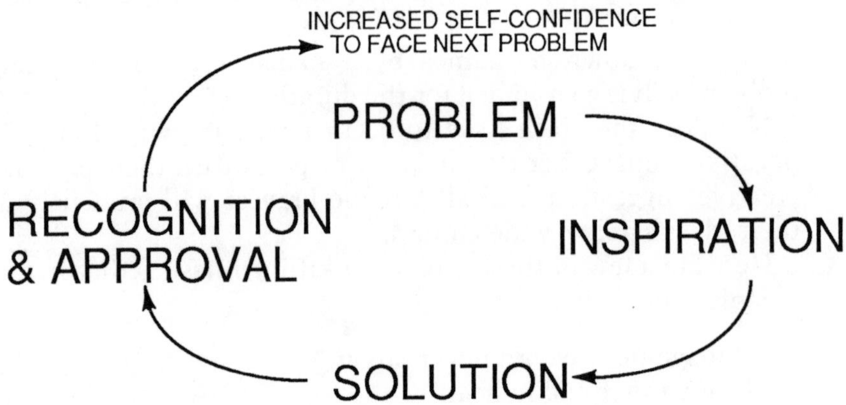

Figure 3. ***The creative problem-solving cycle***

Figure 3 illustrates the creative problem-solving cycle. Once a problem has been solved, the problem-solvers generally require at least some approval and recognition to reinforce the creative process. Without that vital step, employees are much less likely to expand their self-confidence and ability to take on the next problem.

Some people can give themselves sufficient approval for a job well done to improve their self-confidence, but most of us need at least some recognition and approval from other people.

∇ **Lack of freedom.** If too many committees, reviews, signoffs, evaluations, and implementation feasibility studies stand between the generation of a creative solution and its implementation, there is little incentive for employees to start the creative process—it is simply too frustrating.

This is especially true when employees don't perceive the people on committees and conducting the reviews as being as knowledgeable or creative as the problem-solver. In many cases if they were, employees reason, they would have solved the problem themselves.

∇ **Beliefs and attitudes.** Group norms—ideas or beliefs held by a majority of employees—can also be a work-culture factor limiting the freedom to come up with creative solutions. These are a few examples of work-culture norms that can act as barriers to creative thought:

"It doesn't pay to make waves in this department."
"You're safer around here running with the pack."
"In this place, a truly creative idea stands out like a crow in a snowstorm."
"We don't rock the boat with something really new."
"New ideas just end up causing everyone a lot of work."
"You put yourself in jeopardy around here if your idea isn't along party lines."
"In this office you're better safe than sorry."

If such group norms are believed by employees and exemplified by managers, they can be difficult to change. Each one has to be brought into the open by the manager or employees and confronted, and an example of new behavior has to be demonstrated by the manager before employees are convinced that anything has really changed. As long as the negative norms continue to operate, creative thought may be mostly underground and even counterproductive.

∇ **Restricted communication.** For the creative problem-solving processes to really hum, communication needs to be open and flexible. This is an area which the manager needs to monitor continually.

∇ **Staffing.** While almost everyone has creative talents if the work culture allows them to be expressed, to quote George Orwell, "Some are more equal than others." If a work unit faces new or unique problems, one of the major criteria for adding new staff needs to be the potential member's track record for creative problem-solving. Straight technical skills or a scintillating personality may be of little value if they can only be applied at the same level on which the problems exist.

∇ **Follow-through.** The most ingenious solution in the history of creative thought is of little value in the workplace unless there is sufficient follow-through to ensure its complete and successful implementation. Conceptual art, in which art activities or works are described in great detail by the artist but not carried out, may have had its day in the art world, but creative ideas without follow-through have very little positive effect on an organization's bottom line.

Individual vs. Group Problem-solving

I'm often asked by managers in creative problem-solving seminars which is most effective, individual or group methods? The answer is *both.*

Group problem-solving methods work best when:

- Many ideas need to be generated in a short period of time, as in a brainstorming session.
- A number of experts or interests from different areas need to be gathered together at the same time.
- The problem to be solved is one that affects an entire group.
- The potential solution needs to be agreed to by the group that either is affected by it or will need to implement it.
- Good politics dictates that specific people need to be present when the problem is tackled to make implementing the eventual solution more efficient or palatable.

Individual problem-solving works best when:

- A unique and personal answer is called for.
- The potential problem-solver does not work well in a group because of shyness, language differences, personality traits, and so forth.
- Individual skills—such as music, dance, the arts, scripts, graphics, highly specific technical knowledge—will be part of the proposed solution.
- An individual, meditative activity is a component of the problem-solving process.

Not everyone is equally effective problem-solving in a group, for a variety of reasons. Some people are visual thinkers, and get left behind in highly verbal sessions. Others are shy in groups and prefer to work one-on-one or by themselves. All of this needs to be taken into account when a manager delegates problem-solving responsibilities or decides on problem-solving processes.

Creative Problem-solving Methods

Many effective problem-solving methods have been developed in recent years, all of which can help the manager approach problems from new directions. Following are brief outlines of several time-tested methods:

∇ **Brainstorming.** Perhaps the oldest and best-known of all the creative idea-generating methods is brainstorming. It is done by having a group contribute ideas in a free-flowing, "stream of consciousness" session, without any initial evaluation of the ideas.

Brainstorming was originally developed by Alex Osborn, who introduced it in his 1952 book, *Applied Imagination.* Since then it has been successfully used to generate innovative ideas by everyone from rock musicians to church sewing circles.

The function of brainstorming is to generate a wide variety and number of ideas quickly, without censorship, judgment, or premature evaluation. Remember these ground rules:

- No comments or judgments on the ideas until it is time for discussion and voting.
- Record all ideas, using a flipchart or blackboard. (I highly recommend the flipchart, as it provides a permanent record. The paper size should be large enough to allow writing that can be easily seen by all participants. Use different color markers for greatest visual impact.)
- Share all ideas that come to mind, without prejudging before they're put out for the group.
- The idea-generating time period can be either specific or open-ended. In my experience, specific time periods work best, as it helps to keep the group on task. Brainstorming can generate an amazing number of ideas in a very short time.

Idea generation. Here are various methods you can use in brainstorming sessions:

- In a free-for-all, the group produces ideas as quickly as possible, and the ideas are recorded as they are generated. This method works best for a group that is not hesitant to generate ideas, and that has a strong enough leader to keep it under control.
- The rotation method involves participants in the session contributing ideas in sequence, with those who don't have an idea when their turn arrives passing until the next round. The rotation continues until all ideas are exhausted. This system works best with groups in which participants may be more hesitant to express their ideas than in a free-for-all session.
- Index cards can be used when it is advantageous to keep the ideas anonymous. Ideas are written anonymously on index cards, or other pieces of paper, and collected. They are then read aloud and recorded on a flipchart or blackboard. Quite often a second or third round follows the recording of the ideas from the first round, allowing the participants to build on the previous results.
- "Stacking" promotes the semianonymous building of one idea upon another. Each participant puts an idea on a sheet of paper and passes it to the next person. That person adds an idea to the sheet, folds it once so that only the last idea shows, and then passes it on.

  When the sheets have been around the group once or twice, they are collected and read aloud, and the ideas recorded. Depending on the nature of the problem under consideration and the number of responses desired, the process can be repeated as many times as necessary.

Evaluating the ideas. Depending on the nature of the problem and the uses for the ideas, they must be evaluated by the group before being put to use. There are two basic ways in which brainstorming ideas are usually evaluated:

1. *Voting.* With or without discussion, participants vote on the idea or ideas they prefer. This can be by secret or public ballot.
2. *Task forces.* The participants divide up into task force groups, each taking one or more of the ideas to discuss or convert into action plans. This can occur before or after voting on the ideas.

Action plan. Once the most promising ideas are selected, participants prepare action plans and discuss the necessary implementation strategies.

∇ **Analogies.** One of the major difficulties with creative problem-solving is our natural tendency to get tunnel vision in the face of problems, taking in even less information than we normally might. The use of analogies—a comparison between things that are similar in some respects but quite different in others—helps to open up our perceptions to other useful models in the world around us.

Idea generation. Participants in the problem-solving group are encouraged to think of parallel situations in other areas, especially nature. Essentials of that situation are then transferred to the problem situation as possible solutions.

For example, a group attempting to solve the problem of packaging delicate potato chips tried to think of other fragile and brittle items. The most obvious analogy was dried leaves. The solution for packaging potato chips came when they asked themselves, "Is there a time when leaves are *not* fragile?" The answer, of course, was when they are wet. The solution was to pack them when they are wet, and then dry them. The ultimate product: Pringle's potato chips.

The use of analogies—models found in other places with similar characteristics—can be a powerful tool for generating creative solutions to problems that don't yield to normal cause-and-effect reasoning.

∇ **"Magic wand."** One of the limitations we tend to place on ourselves when solving problems is to consider only some things as possible, and then automatically rule out all the rest. The "magic wand" method gets around that.

Idea generation. Once the problem has been carefully defined, participants are encouraged to "wave a magic wand over it"—to say, "Assuming that *anything* is possible, how would you solve this problem?" The resulting ideas are then examined for components or concepts that could be used or modified to solve the problem. Ideas generated in this way often have elements that would not have come up if only the "possible" had been considered.

∇ **"Like most . . . least."** One way to find out where the problem area is in a situation is to ask and list, "What do we like *most* about this situation?" This indicates the things that the new solution will need to retain. Next, asking and listing, "What do we like *least*?" indicates what needs to change. The size of the gap between what is liked most and what is liked least gives an idea of the scope of the problem.

∇ **Other media.** The structure or process for solving a problem in one area can often be found by looking carefully at the process of solving an entirely different kind of problem. For example, the process and structure that Mozart used to solve the problem of creating a symphonic work may give insights into arranging the layout for a new office complex. The way Indianapolis race drivers solve the problem of taking in sufficient information to drive a race car successfully at over two hundred miles per hour in traffic may give insights into ways for control tower operators to safely take in more flight control information.

Idea generation. Bring in someone who is expert in an entirely different field for an interview. This expert doesn't need to be an expensive outside consultant, but can be someone in your organization who once worked in another profession or is active in an unusual hobby or avocation.

The steps in this interview process are:

1. Carefully describe your problem to the expert, including the decision points and the desired outcome.
2. Have the expert do the same for problems in his or her own field.
3. Look for and list the parallels or commonalities between the two problem areas.
4. Have the expert describe how the problem is solved in his or her field.
5. Mutually examine the expert's solution for insights, suggestions, or methods as to how your problem could be solved along similar lines.

Once you and your work unit develop the skill of looking outside your immediate area for ideas, a whole new world of potential solutions opens up to you. Looking at how nature or experts in other fields solve problems is a good place to start.

∇ **Focus-relax-refocus.** Often some of our best and most original ideas come to us when we are relaxing—drifting off to sleep, singing in the shower, or staring into a camp fire. For our subconscious mind to do its essential part in the creative process, we sometimes need to let go of our conscious focus on the problem.

The focus-relax-refocus method is especially useful when you or your group becomes stuck and can't seem to go any further. The old problem-solving adage of "sleep on it" recognized the relaxed mind's ability to come up with new solutions when the conscious mind has run out of ideas.

Idea generation. Whether working alone or with a group, the method is to take a relaxing break at the point where you or your work team becomes stuck. Take a walk, sit quietly and let your mind wander, listen to relaxing music, or just look out the window. It should be a break in which your conscious mind is not active, so that creative subconscious thoughts can come through into conscious awareness.

The temptation on your break is to catch up on your phone calls or discuss another problem with a co-worker. This is not the kind of break that helps the creative problem-solving process! Let your conscious mind meander. Give it a little time to daydream.

When you've taken a 15 to 30 minute break, again focus on the problem. You may be surprised at what occurred to you on your break, or what new ideas may come to you or the group when you refocus on the problem. The most creative solutions are often a result of getting the conscious mind out of the way, after it has spelled out the problem, and letting the unconscious mind go to work on it and report back to you.

∇ **"If I were . . ."** We often feel powerless in the face of difficult problems. Once that happens, we start to focus on our feelings of helplessness, frustration, and inadequacy—and an innovative solution to our problem becomes even more unlikely.

One way to break that self-defeating cycle is to use the "If I were . . ." method, taking advantage of your mind's ability to imagine itself in other forms, times, places, and people. It can be used individually or in a group.

Idea generation. If you or your group begins to feel helpless or powerless, switch to "If I were . . . I would solve this problem by . . ." and imagine how this alter-ego would solve it. This often provides useful insights or strategies for a new approach.

You'll want to generate your own list of "If I were . . ." that is appropriate to your problem, but to get you started here are a few that others have found useful:

King Henry VIII
An eagle
Teddy Roosevelt
Helen Keller
Thomas Edison
Superwoman
Mickey Mouse
Albert Einstein
A porpoise
E. T.

The primary purpose of "If I were . . ." is for participants to really let themselves go and examine all the ways the problem could be approached from these new points of view and with these unique capabilities.

For example, a group of tool design engineers was stuck on a problem of how to distance a delicate cutting tool from the surface of the work. In using the "If I were . . ." method, one engineer elected to be a porpoise. As he thought about unique qualities of a porpoise, besides their having a brain potentially more powerful than that of humans, he remembered that they use their own "sonar" to determine how far away things are underwater. The net result of that line of thought was a laser "sonar" generated by the machine tool to determine precisely its distance from the work and position the cutting tool accordingly.

∇ **"What if . . .?"** This is another method that allows you or your group to break out of the "possible/practical" barrier to creative ideas. "What if . . .?" has been the creative artist's question for centuries: "What if I have the theme played only by the trumpets?" "What if I do an entire canvas in muted shades of blue?" "What if the audience sees only the shadows of the dancers?"

In an organization, it might be "What if we had outside contractors handle the entire project?" or "What if we put the whole operation under a single manager?"

The "What if . . .?" approach allows your imagination to simulate other situations without worrying about the possibility or practicality of the initial idea. The personal computer can help with this method, by using spreadsheet programs such as VisiCalc as an aid to doing quick "What if . . .?" computations and calculations.

Idea generation. The group or individual brainstorms as many "What if . . .?" situations as possible. The ones with the most potential are then selected for further examination by the voting process, with or without discussion. The examination focuses on what the imagined situations have in common with the problem situation and how the "What if . . .?" situation might be carried out, totally or in part.

In Conclusion

Research indicates that we are at our most creative up to the age of about five, when the school system starts to tell us what is "possible/practical." By the time we are forty, we are only about 5 percent as creative as we were thirty-five years earlier. By using creative problem-solving methods, you and your work unit can begin to recapture some of the creativity lost over the years.

All of the above problem-solving situations can be used by groups or individuals. What makes them work is not so much the techniques themselves, but the uninhibited spirit in which they are used. As you use these methods, preserve this almost playful approach to creative problem-solving. Not only is it fun, it seems to have the most profitable payoff in bottom-line results.

Date ______________

∇ Idea Systems Assessment

Directions: Place a square around a number to indicate how important you think that characteristic is for ideas and problem solutions.
Place a circle around a number to indicate your estimation of the present characteristics of ideas generated by your group problem-solving process.

Scale: **5- Always 4-Usually 3-Occasionally 2-Seldom 1-Never**

Our group problem-solving and planning system generates ideas that are:

1. Unique	5 4 3 2 1
2. Effective	5 4 3 2 1
3. Ahead of our competition	5 4 3 2 1
4. Innovative	5 4 3 2 1
5. Practical	5 4 3 2 1
6. Trend-setting	5 4 3 2 1
7. Profitable	5 4 3 2 1
8. Open-ended: can be expanded and built upon	5 4 3 2 1
9. Cost-efficient	5 4 3 2 1
10. "Leading edge"	5 4 3 2 1

Overall rating of the quality of our creative idea process:

Very high - 10 9 8 7 6 5 4 3 2 1 - Very low (circle one)

Manager's overall rating: ___________

Employees' averaged overall rating: ___________

Note: Questions 1, 3, 4, 6, 8, and 10 refer to the imaginative aspects of problem-solving, while questions 2, 5, 7, and 9 refer to the practical side of problem-solving. Examine the pattern of your circles to see which area may be favored. Effective and creative problem- solving requires a balanced mix of both practical and imaginative ideas.

Also note where there are gaps of two or more numbers between the squares and circles, the importance and the performance. Wherever the importance is greater than the performance is a place to start improving your creative problem-solving system.

Date ______________

∇ Creativity Barriers Assessment

Directions: Place a square around a number to indicate how important you think that item is as a barrier to creative ideas or problem-solving.
Place a circle around a number to indicate your estimation of the current situation in your organization or your work unit. (If there is a significant difference between your work unit and organization, use an additional assessment form.)

Scale: **5-Never 4-Seldom 3-Occasionally 2-Usually 1-Always**

The following factors are detrimental to our production of creative ideas:

1. Rigid or strict hierarchical authority structures.	5 4 3 2 1
2. Inappropriate people involved with review process.	5 4 3 2 1
3. Internal competition for leadership or credibility.	5 4 3 2 1
4. Lack of overall mission or purpose.	5 4 3 2 1
5. Requirements that proposals be overly detailed.	5 4 3 2 1
6. Segmented planning or research responsibilities.	5 4 3 2 1
7. Nonsupportive or harsh idea review process.	5 4 3 2 1
8. Inadequate rewards for creative ideas.	5 4 3 2 1
9. Excessive stress or burnout.	5 4 3 2 1
10. Resistance to change in key positions.	5 4 3 2 1

Note: Circled items in the 1-2 area may require attention and change if you are to improve your creative idea and problem-solving situation. Also give close attention to items which have gaps of two or more numbers between the squares and circles, the importance and the performance. Wherever the importance is greater than the performance is a place to start working on barriers to creative problem-solving.

∇ 14. Conflict and Resolution

You and me, we've made a separate peace.
—*Ernest Hemingway,* In Our Time

No matter how smooth-running an organization may be, there inevitably comes a time when an internal conflict becomes a problem, and a manager must step in to handle it. The manager who backs away from resolving a conflict, hoping that it will go away of its own accord, also backs away from one of the effective manager's most important functions and responsibilities.

Conflict in and of itself is not necessarily bad. In fact, a lack of overt conflict may indicate that important issues are being swept under the rug, rather than being dealt with openly. Organizational issues that lie hidden under the corporate rug have a way of tripping up even the most progressive organization.

Lack of conflict in an organization may also indicate that no new ideas are being tried, no new approaches investigated, no one daring to make waves. Such a static organization may fall victim to the first major change that comes along. The price of creativity and innovation is often conflict. Managing conflict therefore becomes a valuable and necessary managerial tool in the creative solution of difficult problems.

The Four Basic Steps

Although specific situations may vary considerably, conflict resolution usually consists of these four basic steps:

1. Clearly *identifying* the conflict or problem.
2. Openly *communicating.*
3. *Negotiating* a potential solution.
4. *Implementing* the negotiated solution or plan.

In actual conflict situations these steps may not be as easily or neatly defined, but they provide a practical model to follow. This allows the manager to divide into manageable units what at first may seem to be insurmountable problems or conflicts.

Let's look at each step of the process in more detail:

∇ **Identifying the conflict.** While some conflicts at first glance may seem obvious, they are often only the symptoms of deeper and more basic problems. Since curing the symptoms seldom cures the disease, the wise manager keeps digging until all parties concerned are certain that the *real* conflict or problem has been identified and brought up on the table.

For example, "Martha, you say that George here, and the rest of production, are dragging their feet on this new unit, while your customers are threatening to go somewhere else. George, you feel that Martha and her people in marketing jumped the gun on this one, promised it before it was fully tested. You know, George, compared to the 626, this one does seem to be slow getting out the door. What seems to be holding it up?"

"Ed, no one knows better than you that these things take time. Besides, with the hiring freeze, we just don't have the people. Of course, Martha here seems to be able to get new people whenever she smiles. And then put 'em in those fancy new offices, while we're lucky to have enough string and paper clips to hold our place together. Of course, when you get your department's picture on the cover of the newsletter, I suppose you can get whatever you want. Meanwhile, my guys are back there bustin' their butts in the heat so they'll have something to sell out of those fancy new offices. What happened to *their* picture?"

"Now I think we're getting somewhere."

- **Open communication.** The second step is to be certain that communication is open between all parties, and that the conflict identification is clearly understood by everyone. This may be difficult, for the conflict has probably already generated a certain amount of fire, heat, and smoke. If at any time during the first step the manager realizes that communication is snarled, the communication process itself must be the next order of business. Without open communication, any further progress is highly unlikely.

"So what I'm hearing, George, is that production is a little out of shape by what appears to your people to be the favored treatment marketing has gotten the last couple of months. Am I right? Martha, what's it sound like to you?"

- **Negotiating a solution.** Once communication is open, the next step is to negotiate a resolution that is the best solution possible for all parties under the circumstances. The parties involved must not be allowed to engage in wishful thinking or might-have-beens. They must negotiate on the basis of the realities inherent in the initial conflict identification.

Also, unless the negotiated solution is seen as fair by all parties, then some sabotage of the solution by one or both parties is almost inevitable; if it is to be a lasting solution, it must be seen as win/win by both sides.

"O. K., that sounds good to me. Martha, you say that you're willing to go back to your customers and plead, promise, whatever is necessary, to get two more weeks for testing before production starts delivery.

"George, you say that if we can get you two more people, at least on a temporary basis, you can start shipping the new units to Martha's field people in two weeks.

"And I promise, if you can keep that schedule, George, your guys will be on the cover of the next newsletter—in color!

"Does that sound fair?"

- **Implementing the negotiated solution.** The final step is to implement the solution arrived at during the negotiating stage, for no agreed-upon solution will resolve a conflict unless it is effectively carried out.

As obvious as this may seem, carrying out the solution is often more difficult than facilitating the negotiations, for up to this point the proposed solution hasn't cost anybody anything, either actually or psychologically. Even negotiations in the best of faith often run into snags when the parties attempt to carry out the solutions—witness many international agreements. If the solution is not fully implemented, however, the negotiations are seen as having been in bad faith. This sows the seeds for further conflict, and an even more difficult restart at square one.

"George, I'll speak to Wilma about authorizing two more people for production. I'm sure she can juggle things somehow. Meanwhile I'll authorize any necessary overtime until your people are on board.

"Martha, you hit the telephones to your field people about the two-week extension. Get back to me by tomorrow noon as to how it's going.

"Good job, both of you. Now I think we're on top of it. Thanks for your time."

In Conclusion

This model, although simple, will help you put conflict into a manageable perspective, whether it be between your two best supervisors, or two growing children. Don't be surprised, however, if at some stage in this process you run into some new barriers, conflicts, or problems. In that case, you may need to return to step one and repeat the process. In fact, you may need to do this several times before you identify the real conflict and can begin to deal with the real issues involved.

In terms of creating a high-performance organization, where open disagreements over new ideas and methods are not discouraged but welcomed, conflict resolution is a necessary skill for the contemporary manager.

∇ ***For additional information, see:***

Chapter 2. When Manager and Employees Communicate
Chapter 3. If I'm Talking, Who's Listening?
Chapter 5. Growing the Corporate Culture
Chapter 12. Meetings—Power or Punishment?

Date______________

∇ Conflict Resolution Worksheet

1. Identifying the problem.

a. As "A" ________________ sees it, the situation is: ______________________________

____

____

b. As "B" ________________ sees it, the situation is: ______________________________

____

____

c. The problem really seems to belong to (A, B, or both): __________________________.

2. Communicating.

a. The major barriers to open communications among all parties seem to be: ___________

____

____

b. Communications would be improved if: ___________________________________

____

____

continued

Conflict Resolution Worksheet, continued.

3. Negotiating a solution

a. Possible solutions seem to be (list as many as possible): ______________________

____

____

____

b. The most feasible solution seems to be: ______________________

____

c. This solution has these benefits for each party involved: ______________________

____

____

4. Implementing the solution.

a. The biggest barrier(s) to implementation could be: ______________________

____

____

b. The solution will be successful if: ______________________

____

____

c. The following implementation steps need to be taken:

Sequence	Steps	Date
____	______________________	____
____	______________________	____
____	______________________	____
____	______________________	____

∇ 15. The Manager-as-Coach

If you were manager of an oceanarium, such as Florida's Sea World, how would you go about getting a large whale that could jump over a rope suspended fifteen feet above the water? Ken Blanchard, co-author of *The One-Minute Manager*, contends that your only managerial options would be either to spend a lot of time searching the world's oceans for a jumping whale, or to train the one you have.

Sounds logical—but how does that apply to employees? How can a manager help employees improve performance, clear higher and higher hurdles? As Blanchard also points out, the manager who wants better performance has three basic options:

1. Hire better people (costs money).
2. Train your people to be better (costs time and money).
3. Pray (requires good connections Upstairs).

Left with those alternatives to obtaining higher performing employees, many managers seem to be relying on number 3—often, it seems, without the necessary connections.

There are more reliable ways, however, and one of the most cost-efficient is to train your present employees. In many organizations this may put you, the manager, in the role of coach. Not that you have to don baseball cap, stopwatch, and whistle, but several things distinguish coaches from managers or teachers.

∇ **Performance orientation.** While managing and teaching have many common components and functions, the primary focus in coaching is better performance. So when do you put on your coaching hat? When the purpose of a session is showing an employee how to achieve higher performance.

∇ **One-on-one.** Coaching may include one-to-group sessions if there are higher performance issues more than one employee needs to know about at the same time, but most coaching is done one-to-one.

∇ **"How to" emphasis.** The main reason for coaching is that the employees being coached will come away from a coaching session with both the knowledge and the experience necessary to do a task or job better than they did before the session. Basically the coach is saying, "Here's how you do this. Now you do it and I'll tell you how you're doing until you get it right."

∇ **Feedback, feedback, feedback.** The good coach is constantly giving feedback on how the student is doing, realizing it is the only way to improve performance, other than by sheer accident. And without feedback, even that wouldn't help much.

∇ **Knowledge of the subject.** The coach must have a thorough knowledge of the subject being coached if the student's performance is to improve significantly. There is no other way.

You may be able to fake it and sell it, but you can't fake it and coach it.

Does that mean the only way to learn a subject is to be a star performer? Would we expect the venerable Pop Warner, coach of Olympic track champion Jim Thorpe, to be able to run faster than Thorpe? Hardly. The main prerequisite of being a good coach is to be an astute student of the area being coached, no matter how the information is acquired. For example, the leading high school football coach in the state of Minnesota a few years ago had never played an organized game of football in his life!

∇ **Communication skills.** No matter how well the potential coach knows the performance area to be coached, that knowledge must be accompanied by good communication skills. Knowledge and good intentions alone don't carry you very far as a coach. An effective coach must be able to explain the subject clearly in the first place and follow it up with easily understood feedback. And, of course, if your coaching communication skills are good enough, you can go on to a lucrative career in television!

∇ **Vested interest in and responsibility for performance.** Unlike teaching, which has many of these same knowledge and communication requirements, in coaching the coach usually has a direct responsibility and accountability for improving the student's performance. "No wins, no contract" holds true whether you're a major league sales manager or baseball manager.

∇ **Patience, patience, patience!** Despite the coaching fireworks and forensics seen on television, every good coach is patient in his or her own way. They realize that, motivation being equal, each student being coached learns and performs at his or her own speed. If there's one thing you learn about coaching before your first heart attack, it is that "you can't push the river." Once you've mastered that, you can begin to learn about coaching.

Coaching Suggestions

If you haven't had the opportunity for much managerial coaching experience, and you don't consider yourself the next Earl Weaver or Tom Landry, here are a few coaching suggestions that might help:

∇ In coaching employees, or anyone else, **start from where they are**. No amount of wishful thinking or browbeating will give employees a background other than what they already have. Don't make assumptions about what employees know or don't know—check it out before you start.

If necessary, begin with the basics. Vince Lombardi, legendary coach of the Green Bay Packers, used to start the training season each fall by holding up a familiar object and stating, "Gentlemen, this is a football."

∇ **Put the learning experience in perspective.** Right up front, the employee needs to know at least these four things:

1. Goals—what is the purpose of the training?
2. Rewards—what is the employee going to get out of it?
3. Support—what will be there when the training is over?
4. Context—what is the overall picture into which this training will fit? This gives the training much more meaning.

∇ **Coach in the employee's strongest learning modes.** How many times have you heard a manager or parent complain, "If I said it once, I said it a thousand times . . . and they still don't get it!"

True—and they may not get it if you *say* it a thousand more times. Research indicates that people learn in three basic modes—verbal, visual, and kinesthetic—and most people are stronger in one mode than in another. That is, some people learn better by being told or reading how to do it, others by seeing how to do it, and still others by going through the process themselves.

Sometimes, if a manager who is strong at telling tries to coach an employee who is visually oriented, they may as well be on separate planets. The employee isn't dumb, the manager is just speaking the wrong coaching language for that particular employee.

If you don't know which is the employee's strongest learning mode, just ask how he or she likes to receive new information. If that's not possible or adequate, present material in all three media—visual, verbal, and kinesthetic—just to be sure that you cover all three learning modes.

For example, if you are coaching someone on a new production process, tell how to do it, give reading materials about it, show visuals of the process, and have the employee physically go through it while you give feedback.

∇ **Create an image of what you want to happen.** To see what I mean, try this experiment:

> Follow my instructions explicitly. I do not—repeat, do NOT—want you to imagine that you see a purple elephant.

Despite those explicit instructions, and probably the best of intentions to follow them, you still are likely to have seen a purple elephant in your mind's eye. And how many times does the child who has just been told by a coaching parent, "Now don't knock over your milk!" or "Don't run in the street!" do just the opposite? Was the child disobedient, lacking intelligence, revolting against parental authority—or was the problem the way the coaching instructions were given?

In many cases the problem is that the strongest mental image created in the student's mind by the coach's instruction is the very thing the coach *doesn't* want him or her to do! In these examples, the mental images created were of spilled milk and a very fascinating street.

We generally act on images, not words—the most powerful words are those that conjure up strong images. As a coach, be sure that you give training instructions that create a strong mental image of what you want to happen. There is no mental image for *not* or *don't*, so it doesn't have much instructional impact—just ask any parent!

∇ Finally, **reinforce your coaching.** Some things are easy to understand, but hard to do. Be sure that you follow up with adequate support until the new skill is fully integrated into the employee's performance. Since mastering a skill is a series of closer and closer approximations to the desired level of performance, praise the employee each time he or she gets closer to the coached behavior.

In Conclusion

Teaching a whale to jump rope may be simple compared to the complexities of modern business, but one fact remains the same: in both arenas, good managers also need to be good coaches.

∇ ***For additional information, see:***

Chapter 2. When Manager and Employees Communicate
Chapter 4. Feedback Is Free

Date ______________

∇ Coaching Skills Assessment

Directions: Place a square around a number to indicate how important you think that skill is for coaching your employees.
Place a circle around a number to indicate your estimation of your present skill level in coaching your employees.

Suggestion: Have your employees fill out the "Employee" version. Place their averaged scores in the appropriate places and compare their perceptions with yours.

Scale: **High/Excellent - 5 4 3 2 1 - Low/Poor**

Skills		**Employees** □	○
1. Using language level appropriate to skill level and employee being coached.	5 4 3 2 1	___	___
2. Giving clear instructions.	5 4 3 2 1	___	___
3. Having patience.	5 4 3 2 1	___	___
4. Setting example by consistently using skills.	5 4 3 2 1	___	___
5. Providing follow-up to the coaching.	5 4 3 2 1	___	___
6. Giving good examples or analogies.	5 4 3 2 1	___	___
7. Providing resources/materials.	5 4 3 2 1	___	___
8. Efficient use of coaching time.	5 4 3 2 1	___	___
9. Willing to answer questions.	5 4 3 2 1	___	___
10. Explaining why as well as how.	5 4 3 2 1	___	___
11. Available if problems arise.	5 4 3 2 1	___	___
12. Knowledge of subject being coached.	5 4 3 2 1	___	___

Overall rating of the quality of your coaching skills:

Very high - 10 9 8 7 6 5 4 3 2 1 - Very low (circle one)

Your employees' averaged rating: ___________

Note: Circled items in the 1-2 area may require immediate attention to improve your coaching skills. Also give close attention to items in which the circle is two or more numbers to the right of the square, as this indicates a gap between importance and skill level.

Date ______________

EMPLOYEE

∇ Coaching Skills Assessment

Directions: Place a square around a number to indicate how important you think that skill is for coaching.
Place a circle around a number to indicate your estimation of your manager's present skill level in coaching employees.

Scale: **High/Excellent - 5 4 3 2 1 - Low/Poor**

Skills

1. Using language level appropriate to skill level and employee being coached.	5 4 3 2 1
2. Giving clear instructions.	5 4 3 2 1
3. Having patience.	5 4 3 2 1
4. Setting example by consistently using skills.	5 4 3 2 1
5. Providing follow-up to the coaching.	5 4 3 2 1
6. Giving good examples or analogies.	5 4 3 2 1
7. Providing resources/materials.	5 4 3 2 1
8. Efficient use of coaching time.	5 4 3 2 1
9. Willing to answer questions.	5 4 3 2 1
10. Explaining why as well as how.	5 4 3 2 1
11. Available if problems arise.	5 4 3 2 1
12. Knowledge of subject being coached.	5 4 3 2 1

Overall rating of the quality of your manager's coaching skills:

Very high - 10 9 8 7 6 5 4 3 2 1 - Very low (circle one)

∇ 16. P = SOME: The Performance Equation

Managers frequently ask management and training consultants, "Can you come in and do a program for my employees that will improve their performance?" Sound familiar? If you haven't actually asked that yourself, chances are you've at least thought about it.

If so, you're certainly not alone, because there are good reasons for wanting that kind of quick fix: it seems inexpensive, it doesn't involve much of the manager's time or energy, and it gets directly to the heart of the performance problem—the employee. Right?

Wrong. Unfortunately for all concerned, the quick fix approach is often less than satisfactory, for the simple reason that it is seldom a cost-effective solution to the employee performance problem—because it doesn't solve the problem.

Why doesn't employee-only training solve troublesome employee performance problems? Essentially because it is usually based on the erroneous assumption that the problem lies only with the employee. This is often not the case. A look at what I call The Performance Equation may explain why:

P = SOME
PERFORMANCE = SKILLS—*what* I can do
OPPORTUNITY—my *chances* to do it
MOTIVATION—my *willingness* to do it
ENVIRONMENT—the *support* when I do it (resources and work culture)

All of these factors are closely interwoven. For example, no matter how high your skill level, if you are not given the opportunity to use what you know, you are likely to be frustrated in your job situation. That frustration, in turn, may have a detrimental effect on your motivation, impeding your job performance. It may also have a negative impact on the work culture environment in your organization, adversely affecting everyone's performance level.

As another example of the interrelation of the SOME components, imagine that you are consistently reprimanded, criticized, or belittled by your manager whenever you make a mistake. That will likely have a detrimental effect on your motivation. Once that happens, you probably won't accept an opportunity to use your skills, even if it is offered to you. Why should you set yourself up for more trouble and grief? The result is that you will probably follow the old military axiom, "Don't volunteer for *anything*!"

Performance Responsibility

With the four SOME performance factors in mind, who is ultimately responsible for employee performance? Skills are certainly the responsibility of the employee, for knowledge, ability, and experience are unique to each person. However, the remaining three factors—opportunity, motivation, and environment—are largely the responsibility of the manager.

It is the manager who gives employees the opportunity to demonstrate their skills. It is also the manager who has the greatest impact on the environment, or work culture, which is a major factor influencing employees' motivation. We've all seen examples of a manager's sarcastic remark or unwarranted criticism taking the steam out of what had been a highly motivated employee. We may even have had that experience ourselves. Unfortunately, it is an experience too easily forgotten when we become managers.

Skills

What we call *skills* really consist of several distinct, yet interrelated, components:

1. *Knowledge* (training, education, book learning)
2. *Experience* (practice, on or off the job)
3. *Self-management* (work habits, use of time, self-talk, stress management, diet, interpersonal skills)

Managers can use these components to analyze problem areas of either their own skill situation, or that of their employees. An example would be taking a ride with me in an airplane: from reading and talking with pilot friends, I have a good idea about how to take off and land a small plane (knowledge). What might be unnerving to you as a passenger is that no matter how well I can talk about takeoffs and landings, I've never done it!

What's more, the self-management of my anxiety might be so poor that I would forget what little I did know.

For managers wanting to improve the skills of their employees, it becomes a matter of analyzing which of the three skill components need work: knowledge, experience, or self-management. Here are some suggestions for each of the three areas:

∇ **Knowledge.** At first glance, you might think that knowledge would have to precede experience, but that's not necessarily so. Like the football player who, in the heat of the game, carries the ball across the wrong goal line, employees may think they're doing the right thing, but be going about it all wrong—lots of practice, but in the wrong direction.

This is especially true in the area of quality. For example, American automakers had been building cars for years, but when foreign competition arrived on these shores in force, the difference in quality was obvious. American workers didn't know how to build cars to a quality standard that was up to the level of their foreign competition. It has taken a massive education program aimed at both skills and motivation to change that.

If your analysis of your employees' skill situation indicates that they don't know how to do their jobs at the required level—if they don't know what "quality" looks like in your organization's product or service, for instance—then additional training or education is called for.

∇ **Experience.** As any manager who has ever hired anyone right out of school can attest, knowledge isn't everything. In some cases it takes years of experience before reaching truly high performance. This is one of the factors that makes employee turnover in some organizations so expensive—it may take months or even years before the new employee is performing at the level of the person being replaced. Some unfortunate organizations have such high turnover rates that they may never realize the levels of performance that can come with extended experience.

Other organizations, for a variety of reasons, rotate people through positions so quickly that they never really get a chance to reach a high performance level. This can be expensive for the organization—either things have to be redone or quality isn't what it needs to be—and demoralizing for the employees; they know they're not doing as good a job as they could if they had a chance to get more experience.

∇ **Self-management.** If employees are poor at self-management, all their practice and training may be virtually useless.

For example, employees who lose their temper at the slightest provocation can cause more public relations havoc in a customer-contact situation than they're worth. Without good time management skills, the best education and greatest experience can be frittered away in meaningless activity. Salespeople whose self-talk when they don't close a sale consists of "You're such a wimp, such a failure!" will probably never make full use of the best sales training and experience available.

Self-management is harder to analyze than experience or knowledge. One way is to measure performance against established goals. If the employee seems to have the necessary experience and knowledge, the problem may be inadequate self-management.

Opportunity

The opportunity for employees to use their skills is largely under the control of the manager. The exception is the self-starting employee who does everything possible to create the necessary opportunity. The judicious use of new opportunities for employees to use and test their skills provides the necessary challenge, variety, and sense of accomplishment to keep employees motivated to perform.

What can get in the way of employees getting the opportunities to prove themselves?

- Some employees are not assertive enough either to make their wants known for more opportunities or to get their needs met for a greater variety of work. The manager has to be especially aware of these needs with shy or reserved employees, as many of them will not come to you first.
- Some opportunities have stereotypes attached to them that have to be broken before everyone has an equal opportunity. For example, "I'm sorry, but we've always had somebody from production handle that. I'm not sure you know enough about it."
- Organizational politics can also get in the way of providing appropriate opportunities, unless you have the ability to cut through them: "Look, let's not kid ourselves. The boss's niece is slotted for that project, and your chances of getting it are about as good as a snowball on a July day in Death Valley."

Motivation

This is perhaps the most critical factor in the P = SOME equation. If motivation is high enough, all things are possible—mountains are brought to Muhammad. It is difficult to measure in and of itself, as it is most evident by its impact on results and is almost impossible to separate from the other components of the equation. It is made up of numerous elements, of which these are some of the most important:

- Self-concept, the value I place on myself, will have a great deal to do with how motivated I am to perform well. If "high performer" doesn't match my image of myself ("I'm such a loser"), chances are high performance will occur only by accident, if at all. We will go to great lengths to remain true to the image we have of ourselves.

- The balance of rewards/punishments in any given situation will greatly influence my performance in that situation. (See Chapter 18 for a complete discussion of the rewards/punishment balance and how to analyze it.)
- Self-confidence has a great deal to do with how much I'm willing to risk in situations calling for high performance. If I don't think I can do it, or am worried about looking like a fool for trying, I probably won't risk it.
- My past experience in similar situations may also determine how motivated I am to perform in this situation. If my manager has put me down every time I made a mistake with this kind of job in the past, I won't be very motivated to tackle it again.
- My personal goals are powerful motivators for performance. If I want it bad enough, I'll do everything possible to make it happen. If my personal goals are at cross-purposes with the organization's, however, my job performance is likely to be low.
- My personality is such that I'm self-motivated, not requiring much push from outside to get me going. My office partner, on the other hand, is more externally motivated, needing more guidance, direction, and approval to be motivated. The manager must be sensitive to these needs to help maintain motivation—which employees need a little push in the right direction, and with which employees to just get out of their way.

Environment

The environment in which employee performance takes place can have a major effect on the level of that performance. Like opportunity, it is largely under the manager's control. Here are some of the major components:

- It is difficult to perform if you don't have the physical resources—the equipment, all the parts, enough supplies, the ancillary services, and so forth. There are organizations that can be temporarily brought to their knees by running out of toner for the copy machine. The accidental cutting of a telephone cable can be a disaster to a telemarketing firm. The most skilled lathe operator is not at his or her best if the lathe is outmoded or inadequately maintained.
- High performance usually requires support: manager, co-workers, family, social contacts. Nearly every employee needs consolation in defeat and cheers in victory, whether the employee admits it or not. It is often up to the manager to grease the skids a little to make sure it happens. And the best grease is a good example.
- An unpleasant physical environment—factors of light, heat, color, noise, odor, aesthetic design, ergonomics of equipment—can have very debilitating effects on employee performance, and we're still learning more about

it. Sufficient to say that if these physical elements aren't part of the performance solution, they're probably part of the problem. They are seldom a neutral influence.

- Corporate culture, the invisible working environment of beliefs, values, attitudes, stereotypes, and behavior norms, has a profound effect on the psychological environment in which each employee performs. It, too, is greatly influenced by the behavior of managers, and managers must take the lead in producing positive change if this is an area that is impeding employee performance.

A Case History

At a midwestern manufacturing firm, a vice-president was taking a shortcut through the machine shop. He noticed that none of the lathe operators was wearing safety goggles, a flagrant violation of company safety regulations.

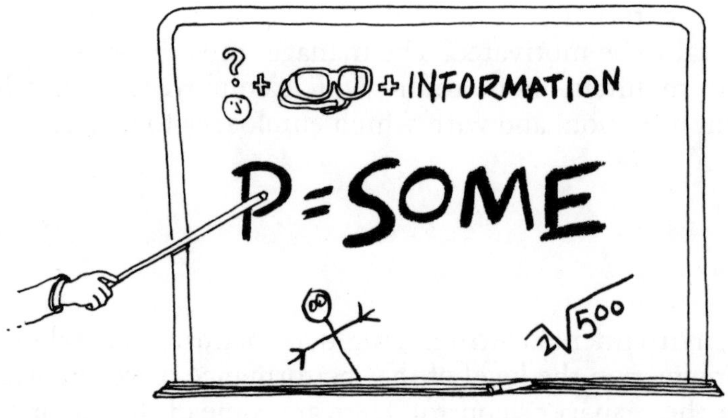

A few short minutes later the incensed vice-president strode angrily into the corporate trainer's office, reporting his experience and demanding an immediate safety training program for the company's lathe operators. Between the lines was the implication that if the training department had been doing its job, all the lathe operators would be safely goggled.

The training director was puzzled, and being more performance-analysis oriented, went down to investigate personally. A few P = SOME questions in the machine shop revealed that all the operators *knew* they should wear goggles and had previously done so (skill), they all *wanted* to wear goggles (motivation), and they had eight hours of opportunity to wear them. That line of questioning ruled out lack of training as the problem.

One more question solved the problem: What about resources (environment)? "Well, Henry—he's the foreman—sometimes forgets and puts the key to the goggles cabinet in his pocket. Henry's home sick today, so we can't get in the cabinet."

Making a second key and hiding it in the first aid kit solved the "training" problem. Using the P = SOME performance equation up-front made the difference between a seventy-nine-cent key and $2350 worth of training time and materials.

The Performance Development Plan

Included with this section is a performance development plan based on one first used by the farm team organization of the Milwaukee Brewers baseball team, named Organization of the Year in 1985 by *Baseball America.* I designed it as part of an ongoing effort by the Brewer organization to encourage and assist young ballplayers in taking a more active role in their own professional development.

The performance development plan is easy to use, fosters cooperation between employee and manager, and begins to train employees to take charge of their own careers. It provides an excellent system for anyone interested in fine-tuning job performance and can be used as an integral component of a performance appraisal system.

In Conclusion

Using the P = SOME performance equation helps managers realize that in order to improve employee performance with additional training, they first need to determine the nature of the problem. Is it a *skills* problem, in which employees don't have the necessary knowledge, experience, or self-management? Is it an *opportunity* problem, in which the people with the skills are not being given a chance to use them?

Is it a *motivation* problem, in which employees' attitudes or beliefs are causing them to be unwilling to perform at their highest possible level? Or is it an *environment* problem, in which either the physical environment or the psychological environment—the work culture—is not sufficiently supportive to allow a high level of performance?

Try the P = SOME analysis yourself the next time you're faced with a performance problem. It can save you both time *and* money.

∇ ***For additional information, see:***

Chapter 5. Growing the Corporate Culture
Chapter 15. The Manager-as-Coach
Chapter 17. Team-Building for All Seasons
Chapter 18. Poor Performance Comes In for Analysis
Chapter 24. To Train, or Not to Train?

Date ______________

∇ P=SOME Checklist

May be used individually or in groups

1. Description of the performance problem--be as specific as possible:

____

____

____

2. Once you have the performance problem completely described, go through each of the **P=SOME** components below until you locate the cause of the problem. Then use your creative problem-solving skills (Chapter 13) to generate a solution.

What do you know about each of these components, relative to the performance problem you described in Section 1?

Skills [S=K+E+SM]

- **Knowledge** ______________________________

____

- **Experience** ______________________________

____

- **Self-management** ______________________________

____

Opportunity ______________________________

____

____

Motivation (attitudes, beliefs, past experience, rewards) ______________

____

____

Environment (resources, support, logistics) ______________

____

____

∇ Performance Development Plan

Directions:

1. Under Performance list the most important skills or activities of the job. (Example: "Produce the annual budget.")
2. Under Goals list what you want to do to improve each Performance item. Goals should be specific and measurable. (Example: "Finish this year's budget in 3 days.")
3. Under Time Frame put in the date when you plan to have reached the goal.
4. Under Priority rank order the importance of reaching each Goal or improving each Performance item. This tells you where to begin and in what order to start work.

Priority		Performance	Goals	Time Frame
______	1.	______	______	______
______	2.	______	______	______
______	3.	______	______	______
______	4.	______	______	______
______	5.	______	______	______
______	6.	______	______	______
______	7.	______	______	______
______	8.	______	______	______
______	9.	______	______	______
______	10.	______	______	______

continued

Performance Development Plan, continued.

Directions: 5. Under Goal # transfer your highest priority goals from page 1.

6. Under Plans indicate--as specifically as possible--how you intend to reach your goal. (Example: "(a) delegate budget data-gathering; (b) sub-contract computer work; (c) block out staff time for final approvals")

7. Under Time Frame put target dates for each plan item.

Goal #	Plans (as specific as possible)	Time Frame

∇ 17. Team-Building for All Seasons

The [Chicago] Bears all hate each other, but they hate us a lot more.
—Hawg Hanner, Green Bay Packer tackle, 1963

For those of you who watch team sports, can you remember a game when you thought to yourself, "That's no team, that's a *group*!" In your own organization or work unit, the difference between a team and a group can make a crucial difference in overall performance.

What is that difference? Basically, a group is a number of people in the same place, sometimes for the same general purpose. A team is a number of people who not only have the same purpose and goals, but who also have the coordinated skills necessary to carry out that purpose successfully. The group down at the Fireside Tap after work on Friday evening is certainly gathered for the same purpose—socializing and liquid refreshment—but no one would ever mistake them for a team.

By the same token, it is not unusual for the top collegiate basketball team to beat a professional all-star team. Although the professionals are better and more experienced individually, they have played on different teams and haven't practiced much together. The college players, on the other hand, while less experienced, have perfected their coordinated game throughout a whole season of playing together.

Team Ingredients

Whether it is a work team or a rugby team, the formula for a *team* looks like this:

TEAM = Efficiency + Mission + Leadership

Let's look more closely at the three components:

- **Efficiency.** Good teams get things done with an efficiency that exceeds that of any one team member alone. Not that they necessarily do it faster—it takes time to coordinate team members—but they will do a better job with combined skills and support than any team member could do solo. Otherwise, there's no need for a team.

  The level of efficiency is determined by a combination of skill and the ability to work with others. Neither one of those will do it alone. The all-too-familiar example is collegiate sports stars who don't make it in professional sports, not because of a lack of talent, but because they couldn't blend that talent with other players of equal ability. That is the real secret of an efficient, high performance team: *blending* high levels of individual skills.

- **Mission.** The major factor that blends the skills is purpose, or mission. The greater the sense of purpose on the part of all team members, the greater the motivation of that team to perform. The degree to which each individual member's purpose is aligned with the overall team mission is a large measure of how efficient that team will be.

- **Leadership.** Without a sense of direction and strategy, even the most motivated and skilled groups will probably remain just that—a group. Strong leadership is often what provides the needed direction. Ever watch six people try to decide where to eat lunch? Plenty of skill and motivation, but no direction.

Team Commonalities

If you've ever played team sports, think back to the best team you ever played on, even if it was only a pickup volleyball game at the company picnic. What were the characteristics that made it a better team than some of the others you played on?

The majority of people who are asked that question will mention *commonalities*—"We had a lot of things in common." Commonalities are the things that help bind a team together. Here are several of the commonalities most frequently mentioned:

∇ **Purpose, goals, mission.** These are the most important areas of commonality. It is what keeps the team moving in the same direction. If the goals of individual members differ significantly from those of the team, the team either is not very productive, it falls apart, or the member with different goals leaves the team. This difference in goals and purpose has led to the demise of everything from rock bands to revolutions.

∇ **Activities.** Even when members have different job skills and roles within the team, generally there are activities that team members do together. The less often team members get together for a common activity, the more "special" the occasion needs to be in order to maintain the feeling of unity and commonality.

∇ **Rituals, symbols, and uniforms.** Most teams have some special indications that set them apart from non-team members. It may be a ritual that they do before or during their mutual activities, such as the team cheer before an athletic event.

It may be symbols or emblems, everything from special coffee cups to warm-up jackets, or it may be the same or similar clothing—a uniform. In some organizations, the three-piece business suit is the uniform, right down to the suggested color, pattern, shirt, and tie. "Dress for success" also often means "Dress for conformity . . . for the team."

Of course, symbols and rituals are not effective for everyone. Some people are natural team players and love team jackets, caps, or T-shirts, while others are individualists who rebel against it. Everyone has to be treated individually for the most effective overall results.

∇ **Adversaries.** The adversary can be the Green Bay Packers, salespeople from a competing firm, natural disasters, or reported aliens from another planet, but the effect of an outside force whose potential threat or impact is greater than individual differences is another element that can bind a team together and motivate its performance.

Nearly every winter we ask, "Why can't people work together and help each other without needing a sixteen-inch blizzard to motivate them?" The answer, of course, is that during most other weather conditions, individual purposes are stronger motivators than the weather. It isn't until weather becomes life-threatening that it gets our team-building attention for mutual support.

∇ **Trust level.** An old army saying is, "If you can't trust a man with your watch, you can't trust him with your life." A normal characteristic of successful and smoothly functioning teams is a high level of mutual trust. There is not only a trust in each members' skills and intent, but also a trust in each member's regard of teammates as people. As William Ouchi writes in *Theory Z*, "Productivity and trust go hand in hand."

What this means in practice is that team members can trust one another:

- To be frank and open with communication.
- Not to put personal interests in front of team interests.
- To be mutually supportive when the going gets tough.
- Not to resort to blaming if things go wrong.
- To share resources and knowledge with other team members.
- To keep personal issues confidential within the team.
- To air complaints openly and objectively.

Teams that do not have mutual trust in these areas are teams that may never reach their full performance potential. It requires energy to protect oneself, either physically or psychologically, and if team members' efforts have to be expended to ensure that their personal flanks are protected, that energy is not available for team performance. The effort to protect oneself also diverts concentration and attention from accomplishing team goals.

∇ **Communication.** Another factor that the members of strong teams usually have in common is a desire for, and a willingness to engage in, honest and open communication. There is a chicken-and-egg relationship between communication and trust: without honest communication, it is difficult to establish an atmosphere of trust, yet without trust it is also difficult to have honest communication.

Generally, it is best to start with improving communication, and let the trust follow. If the intent to communicate is there, communication is a trainable skill. On the other hand, since trust is an emotion, it is almost beyond the reach of training. You can build it, but, like love, it's hard to train for it.

∇ **Home base.** Most teams have some place they can call their own, where victories are celebrated and memorialized, and where the wounds of defeat can be tended. This can be a conference room, someone's office, or a corner of the lab. The home base becomes headquarters for the team and, like a home, may be decorated with their personal items—posters, mementos, paperwork, photos, and so forth. Other company personnel are not encouraged to use this area.

Unfortunately, this need for a team to have its own home base is often overlooked in the modern organization's quest for efficiency and conformity. A successful team usually has character, and that is often indicated by the character of its home environment.

∇ **Enjoyment of working together.** Finally, members of a good team enjoy working with each other. They are comfortable with each other and, win or lose, they feel rewarded by the opportunity to work together. This adds motivation, trust, and pride in the team and its performance. As the memorable collegiate coach A. J. Shortenwyde once said, "Truly great teams might lose a game, but they won't lose their pride."

Team Cautions and Concerns

Despite the many values of having a closely knit, high-performance team, there are also some cautions and concerns that a manager or team leader needs to be aware of:

- **Turnover.** Once you have a smoothly functioning team, the loss of a team member can be more serious than the loss of an employee from a group. Therefore the manager must often work harder to make the tasks and work environment such that valued team members will be retained.

- **Employee personalities.** Not all employees have the personality traits or the necessary interpersonal skills that allow them to be good team members. For example, those who place a high value on independent action may have difficulty accepting the compromises that teams often require for smooth functioning.

  Employees who have trouble with authority figures may engage in fight or flight behavior—either power struggles or avoidance of the team leader. Insecure employees who require a large amount of supervisory attention may not make good team members, nor may employees with inadequate abilities to make the necessary interpersonal adjustments.

  In short, not everyone is suited for team activities. Pick your team members with as much care as possible under the circumstances. If you need to make a team out of your entire work unit, transfer or retraining may be the answer for those who don't fit into the team concept.

- **External relations.** A closely knit team is often perceived by outsiders as snobbish or cliquish. They may also be viewed with envy or even jealousy by less cohesive co-workers.

  I call this the "Damn Yankees" syndrome—everyone hated the perpetual winners. It can seriously interfere with successfully meshing the operations of the team with those of other departments and work units. It is especially detrimental to cooperation if it develops into an us vs. them attitude on the part of either the team or other groups within the organization.

- **Team-other relationships balance.** The team usually expects, and often demands, total allegiance to its goals and activities—team members are expected to give first priority to team requirements. The team becomes a very demanding mistress, not only naming the game, but also inventing the rules.

  Relationships outside the team are often suspect, since they divide the member's allegiance, and have the potential to dilute the leader's power. Other team members may develop feelings of betrayal or disloyalty if a fellow team member expands beyond the team. Threatened team members can be hard on such relationships, to the extent of attempting to belittle or sabotage them.

Outside the team, those with close relationships to a team member often feel frustration and jealousy in attempting to compete for time, attention, and loyalty with the team. Peer pressure is very strong and, combined with a job role, puts most of the leverage on the side of the team.

Caught in the middle of this rivalry between team and relationship, the team member often becomes unduly stressed and guilty that one or the other is being neglected. The result is that the team member, feeling entrapped, often ends up leaving either the relationship or the team, and sometimes both.

∇ **The team vs. dissent.** A team can be equally hard on dissent for the same reasons: it threatens the homogeneity of the team and the power of the team leader. Dissenting views or opinions may therefore be squashed "for the good of the team."

A team burdened with this totalitarian view may find itself unable to mature and grow. It develops tunnel vision, a "not invented here" attitude, that severely limits the amount of new information and ideas it can accept. Internal creativity and uniqueness of vision not only become limited, but may even be actively discouraged.

More seriously, the team afflicted with such internal provincialism also begins to lose the nerve to question itself, to examine the validity of sincere yet opposing viewpoints. This self-isolation weakens the team's ability to adapt to changing situations, leaving it as vulnerable to change as an aging dinosaur.

∇ **Competition.** Internal competition between work units can sometimes stimulate higher performance, as Tracy Kidder reports in his *Soul of a New Machine.* On the other hand, work teams occasionally lose sight of the purpose of a team: performance that exceeds the capacity of any one team member alone. They begin to think the team's purpose is competition with other teams or units.

A work team that falls into this self-laid trap may end up setting goals that are far short of its potential—just high enough to "win"—or expending valuable energy on the competitive element of its performance. It becomes reactive to other teams' actions, rather than pro-active in setting its own course toward its common goals.

The manager who cannot help the team balance external competition and internal cooperation may find that the team's energies become misdirected into the competitive effort, while neglecting the cooperation essential to high performance. The experienced manager and team leader has learned that there is nothing that can trip up a team faster than its own overly competitive feet.

Team Leadership

Managing a team requires additional skills to those required for managing units where teamwork is not a major consideration. In *Leaders,* Warren Bennis contends, "The problem with many organizations, and especially the ones that are failing, is that they tend to be overmanaged and underled."

The increasing complexity of organizational functioning requires that work units be molded into work teams, which also requires new managerial skills. It has become the era of the leader-manager.

What distinguishes the new breed of leader-managers from their more traditional manager counterparts? Bennis again, expanding on an idea of Peter Drucker's, says, "A *manager* does things right; a *leader* does the right things."

More specifically, there are several significant differences between traditional managers and leader-managers, the understanding of which is important to developing effective teams in today's organizations:

∇ **Diffusion of power.** The greatest consistent source of power over the ages has been knowledge. Even if large armies could temporarily hold power, smart armies with more recent technology soon prevailed. For example, a comparative handful of Spanish conquistadors defeated Indian tribes throughout Mexico and the southwestern United States. The difference? Gunpowder. A little later, when the Indians acquired firepower of their own, General Custer was unpleasantly surprised at Little Bighorn.

In the same way, the person at the top of an organization was usually there because he or she knew more about how to do things than anyone else. In any kind of organization from ancient Egypt to Industrial Revolution steel mills, there was a "priesthood" that held authority because of their special knowledge. Power and authority were then delegated vertically downward to those with less knowledge and therefore less power.

This worked fine as long as an organization's chief assets were things. People were needed primarily to carry out the systems necessary to produce and move the things. But Gutenberg and his simple little printing press had started an information revolution of enormous proportions. The personal computer, electronic libraries, and a giant publishing industry have now accelerated that revolution to the point where everyone can know as much about anything as the boss.

Moreover, in specialty areas it is now necessary that some employees know *more* than the boss; the power of knowledge is now diffused throughout the entire organization. The manager who fails to realize this also fails to recognize one of the major differences between successfully managing people in the latter half of the twentieth century and managing in the Middle Ages.

Rosabeth Moss Kanter, in her book *The Change Masters,* states, "Today 25% of all people who work are college graduates who have learned attitudes about dignity, entitlement, and using their skills. This educated work force cannot be managed in the same way that seemed acceptable for a low-skilled, largely immigrant labor force." An authoritative management style does not sit well with employees who have been educated to think for themselves.

∇ **The organization's resources.** Once employees begin to know more about some things than the boss, the organization's assets begin to shift from things to people, from tangible goods to the almost intangible qualities of the human brain. This also requires a parallel shift in management style, for people cannot successfully be managed in the same way as things.

For managing things, *push* will often be sufficient. For people, however, *pull* is a much more effective management approach, because it allows people to be drawn forward using the power of their own dreams, goals, and purposes. In automobiles, it is the difference between front-wheel drive pulling, or rear-wheel drive pushing. And when the going gets slippery or tough, there's no question that front-wheel drive is much more likely to get you to your destination.

Think of your own preference when you've been in tough situations: did you want someone leaning and pushing on your backside, or putting out a hand to help pull you out of the difficulties? Your employees are no different.

∇ **Authority delegated upward.** Voltaire once wrote, "I am a leader, therefore I must follow." When Voltaire wrote this it was considered heresy—kings don't often approve of that sort of thinking—and some contemporary managers still don't fully understand the implications: the power to lead really flows upward from those who are being led.

A classic example of where the authority to manage contemporary employees really lies is the case of the new plant manager, fresh M.B.A. degree in hand, who charged out onto the plant floor and announced to the veteran union steward that as the new plant manager, he was there to shape up the operation and would be totally in charge. In response, the wizened old man silently held up his right arm. All the plant's equipment suddenly stopped, and the workers stood motionless behind their expensive machines. "That's fine, lad," the old steward finally said, softly, "go ahead and run it."

Comparisons

There are some clear-cut differences between the traditional "push" authority-manager, and the more "pull"-oriented leader-manager. Here are a few of those differences:

Authority-Manager	Leader-Manager
Authority-based	Influence-based
Position power	Personal power
Tell-oriented	Ask-oriented

Authority-Manager	Leader-Manager
Retains authority	Shares authority
Defines limits	Expands limits
Enforces	Reinforces
Restricts creativity	Encourages creativity
One-way communication	Two-way communication
Personal distance	Personal interest
Mandates	Persuades
Dictates	Sells
Task orientation	Human resource orientation
Arbitrates	Negotiates
Requires loyalty	Obtains commitments

For the team, these managerial traits may result in:

Dependency	Interdependency
Reluctant production	Voluntary performance
Compliance	Commitment
"Crisis" problem-solving	"Prevention" problem-solving
Stress	Challenge
Malicious obedience	Creative performance
Discouragement	Empowerment

The authority-based manager may have been appropriate in the days of the Sun Kings, self-anointed with the power to rule from on high, but the "Do as I say because I said it" approach is increasingly less viable with modern employees. Today's managers who put themselves at the head of an employee parade using an authority-based management style may find that their employees have zigged when the managers have zagged and, looking back, discover that no one is behind them.

The Manager's Role as Team Leader

In addition to the usual managerial skills, here are several that the leader-manager of a team must develop or possess:

∇ **One-to-group skills.** Most traditional managerial training focused on one-to-one skills, but the leader-manager must also possess a full complement of one-to-group skills. These skills include:

- Conducting effective meetings.
- Leading group problem-solving sessions.
- Developing and maintaining communication networks.

- Setting team goals and priorities.
- Implementing plans and strategies.
- Assessing team strengths, weaknesses, and opportunities.

∇ **How to build a supportive work culture.** For a team to live up to its performance potential, it must focus its available energy on the task, not on individual or mutual self-defense. To allow this to happen, the leader-manager needs to build a culture that is:

- Nonthreatening—no fear of managerial retribution for honest mistakes or sharing of sincere ideas, thoughts, opinions, or feelings.
- Mutually supportive—team members unselfishly help each other.
- Reinforcing and rewarding of team performance—rewards reflect the fact that when the team performs well, everyone wins.
- Maintaining a high level of trust—excessive individual ego needs are checked at the door, reputations are safe, backup support is available when needed, and sexual harassment is something that only happens somewhere else.
- Expanding—help is available to learn new skills and take on new responsibilities.

∇ **Sustain positive beliefs and values.** Finally, the leader-manager needs to sustain the positive employee beliefs and values that result in high team performance, pride, and self-satisfaction. To do this the manager needs to:

- Be an example of the desired team behaviors.
- Keep the organization's mission out front and visible.
- Confront, discuss, and change negative beliefs and values whenever they surface in the work unit.

The team leader-manager who can implement these functions in the managerial role will be well on the way to building a high performance team.

Leaderless Teams

Despite our emphasis on the qualities of leadership necessary for the contemporary leader-manager, there are also good examples of effective leaderless teams. For example, have you ever watched a group of women put together a church supper? Hardly a wasted motion, but no apparent leader. In this case, everyone on the team knew how to do every activity, what needed to be done, and in what order. When all of the team functions are interchangeable and the goals are clear, very little overt management is necessary to get the job done.

What about a team of highly specialized teachers, with no leader? Here the goals, mission, and purpose are also very clear, and the awareness of each other's strengths is understood and appreciated by all team members. Typically, on this kind of team if there is leadership at all, either it moves through the team by rotation, or it is determined by the nature of the project.

Is Building a Team Always Necessary?

Probably not, for there are some organizational functions that are often best done individually. For example:

- Individuals in staff positions who report directly to upper-level managers.
- Some field personnel who operate independently most of the time.
- Some problem-solving activities which are best done on an individual basis rather than in a group environment.
- "Art"—such as film, video, theater, dance, music, fashion, or industrial design—which is often conceived or designed by an individual and then produced by a team.

  For example, in automotive design, an Italian Ferrari has traditionally been designed or approved by one individual, Señor Ferrari, while a German Mercedes-Benz is designed by a team of specialists. You can appreciate the engineering and technical qualities of the Mercedes—but you can fall in love with the Ferrari.

In Conclusion

The essence of building a strong team comes down to a conscious move by the leader-manager to reduce individual differences below the level of team commonalities, and to develop and maintain a work culture sufficiently supportive to allow the team to focus its energies on performance. The contemporary team leader-manager realizes that people are the organization's single greatest asset, and as such need to be led, not pushed.

Retired general Sheldon J. Harmony, responding to a reporter's question about the teamwork necessary to carry out the Normandy invasion in World War II, replied, "As long as team members consider the mission more important than individual differences, you have a team. If individual differences become greater than the mission, you *don't* have a team. We had a team."

∇ ***For additional information, see:***

Chapter 2. When Manager and Employees Communicate
Chapter 4. Feedback Is Free
Chapter 5. Growing the Corporate Culture
Chapter 12. Meetings—Power or Punishment?
Chapter 24. To Train, or Not to Train?

Date______________

∇ Team Leadership Assessment

Directions: Place a square around a number to indicate how important you think that skill is for good team leadership.
Place a circle around a number to indicate your estimation of your present skill level in these aspects of leading your employee team.

Suggestion: Have your employees fill out the "Employee" version. Place their averaged scores in the appropriate places and compare their perception of your team leadership skills with yours.

Scale: **High/Excellent - 5 4 3 2 1 - Low/Poor**

Skills		**Employees** ☐ ○
1. Supporting a high level of effective communication within the team.	5 4 3 2 1	___ ___
2. Conducting team meetings that produce results worth the time and energy involved.	5 4 3 2 1	___ ___
3. Getting the team going again if it is stuck.	5 4 3 2 1	___ ___
4. Helping to maintain a high level of team morale.	5 4 3 2 1	___ ___
5. Using group problem-solving methods with the team to address and solve work-related problems.	5 4 3 2 1	___ ___
6. Bringing out and using the talents and creativity of team members.	5 4 3 2 1	___ ___
7. Establishing a clear sense of purpose within the team.	5 4 3 2 1	___ ___
8. Maintaining a team "climate" in which members freely contribute suggestions and solutions to work-related problems.	5 4 3 2 1	___ ___
9. Helping the team recognize and overcome barriers that limit a creative approach to problem-solving.	5 4 3 2 1	___ ___
10. Analyzing and changing the team climate if it is having a negative effect on performance.	5 4 3 2 1	___ ___
11. Assisting the team in identifying areas of greatest opportunity for improving performance.	5 4 3 2 1	___ ___

Overall rating of the quality of your team leadership skills:

Very high - 10 9 8 7 6 5 4 3 2 1 - Very low (circle one)

Your employees' averaged rating: ___________

Date______________

EMPLOYEE

∇ Team Leadership Assessment

Directions: Place a square around a number to indicate how important you think that skill is for good team leadership.
Place a circle around a number to indicate your estimation of your manager's present skill level in these aspects of leading your team.

Scale: **High/Excellent - 5 4 3 2 1 - Low/Poor**

Skills

1. Supporting a high level of effective communication within the team.	5 4 3 2 1
2. Conducting team meetings that produce results worth the time and energy involved.	5 4 3 2 1
3. Getting the team going again if it is stuck.	5 4 3 2 1
4. Helping to maintain a high level of team morale.	5 4 3 2 1
5. Using group problem-solving methods with the team to address and solve work-related problems.	5 4 3 2 1
6. Bringing out and using the talents and creativity of team members.	5 4 3 2 1
7. Establishing a clear sense of purpose within the team.	5 4 3 2 1
8. Maintaining a team "climate" in which members freely contribute suggestions and solutions to work-related problems.	5 4 3 2 1
9. Helping the team recognize and overcome barriers that limit a creative approach to problem-solving.	5 4 3 2 1
10. Analyzing and changing the team climate if it is having a negative effect on performance.	5 4 3 2 1
11. Assisting the team in identifying areas of greatest opportunity for improving performance.	5 4 3 2 1

Overall rating of the quality of your manager's team leadership skills:

Very high - 10 9 8 7 6 5 4 3 2 1 - Very low (circle one)

Date______________

∇ Team Management Assessment

1. How would you rate your overall performance as an effective team? (circle one)

   Very high - 10 9 8 7 6 5 4 3 2 1 - Very low

2. No matter how dedicated we are, in almost any work situation not all of our personal energies are directed toward the job. On your work team, what percentage of the group's energies would you estimate are consistently directed toward work? (circle one)

   100% 90 80 70 60 50 40 30 20 10 0%

3. Realizing that there are many different and successful management styles, where would you place yourself on these management style scales? Neither are right or wrong, just different. (circle one)

A. "ASK": Two-way communication with team	**• 5 4 3 2 1 •**	"TELL": One-way communication with team
B. Group solves problems	**• 5 4 3 2 1 •**	Manager solves problems
C. Higher performance achieved by one-to-group interactions with the team	**• 5 4 3 2 1 •**	Higher performance achieved by one-to-one interactions with the team

4. On almost every team there are three levels of performers: high, acceptable, and low. On your work team, what would you estimate to be the number and percentages of each category of performer?

   ______ **High** = ______%

   ______ **Acceptable** = ______%

   ______ **Low** = ______%

   Total = ______ = **100%**

5. **Overall rating of your team management skill level:**

   Very high - 10 9 8 7 6 5 4 3 2 1 - Very low (circle one)

Your employees' averaged rating: ___________

Suggestion: Have your work team do the "Employees" version and compare your results with theirs.

Date____________

EMPLOYEE

∇ Team Management Assessment

1. How would you rate your overall performance as an effective team? (circle one)

   Very high - 10 9 8 7 6 5 4 3 2 1 - Very low

2. No matter how dedicated we are, in almost any work situation not all of our personal energies are directed toward the job. On your work team, what percentage of the group's energies would you estimate are consistently directed toward work? (circle one)

   100% 90 80 70 60 50 40 30 20 10 0%

3. Realizing that there are many different and successful management styles, where would you place your manager on these management style scales? Neither are right or wrong, just different. (circle one)

A. "ASK": Two-way communication with team	**• 5 4 3 2 1 •**	"TELL": One-way communication with team
B. Group solves problems	**• 5 4 3 2 1 •**	Manager solves problems
C. Higher performance achieved by one-to-group interactions with the team	**• 5 4 3 2 1 •**	Higher performance achieved by one-to-one interactions with the team

4. On almost every team there are three levels of performers: high, acceptable, and low. On your work team, what would you estimate to be the number and percentages of each category of performer?

   ______ **High** = ______%

   ______ **Acceptable** = ______%

   ______ **Low** = ______%

   Total = ______ **= 100%**

5. **Overall rating of your manager's team management skill level:**

   Very high - 10 9 8 7 6 5 4 3 2 1 - Very low (circle one)

∇ 18. Poor Performance Comes In for Analysis

The trouble with the term *poor performance* is that it doesn't mean anything useful to a manager. It is about as helpful as telling your mechanic "The car isn't running right." In all gears? In cold weather? Only in the mountains? A mechanic needs much more specific information if your car is to be restored to full performance. Likewise, if a manager is going to do anything concrete about an employee's "poor performance," there needs to be an analysis that provides equally concrete information about the nature of the problem.

On the other hand, the analysis process must not be so complex or cumbersome that it can't be done rather easily, quickly, and inexpensively. If the initial assessment points in directions where an in-depth analysis is called for, that is the time to get complex.

Included in this section are three such relatively simple analysis systems. However, don't let their simplicity fool you about their effectiveness, for they have been used successfully with everything from upper management teams to baseball teams.

These systems look at three aspects of "poor performance":

1. *Internal/external causes.* The first thing a manager needs to know is if the employee's subpar performance is being caused by internal or external factors. In other words, is the cause something over which the employee can develop control (internal), or will external changes have to be made or taken into account?
2. *Skills/motivation dilemma.* If the cause of the poor performance is indeed internal, is it a problem with skill or motivation, the interwoven twins of all performance? And once you have some clues about the balance, what do you need to do next?
3. *Rewards/punishment balance.* Once you've analyzed the causes and applied the appropriate remedial actions, why does the employee still persist in the poor performance? Where have you failed?

   Chances are you haven't. You just need to carry the analysis process a little further to determine the rewards and punishments balance between the employee's taking up the new and desired behavior, or staying with the old undesirable variety. Once you know and understand that, helping the employee improve performance is much easier.

Uses for the Assessments

These three systems have proved useful to managers for a wide variety of situations, including:

- Performance appraisal interviews.
- Before and after changes or transitions.
- Career development and planning.
- Selecting employees for training.
- Coaching strategies.

As you work with them, you'll find other practical applications. (They have been known to find their way home to help with school performance problems.)

Internal/External Causes Assessment

∇ **Directions.** Place a mark on each scale according to whether the answer to each question indicates an external or internal cause for the employee's performance problem.

Internal Causes | **External Causes**

A. Performs other tasks poorly:

ALWAYS • USUALLY • OCCASIONALLY • SELDOM • NEVER

B. Performs this task poorly at other times:

ALWAYS • • • • NEVER BEFORE

C. Extent to which others perform this task poorly:

NO ONE ELSE • • • • EVERYONE

Figure 4. ***The Internal/External Causes Assessment***

∇ **The questions.** This assessment looks at three primary areas of the employee's problem performance:

1. **Scale A.** *Does the employee perform* other *tasks poorly?* If other tasks are also performed poorly, then it is likely that the cause is internal. If this is the only task that is a performance problem, the cause is much more likely to be external. The exceptions can be lack of knowledge or experience.
2. **Scale B.** *Does the employee perform this task poorly at other times?* If the poor performance is an exception to the norm, then the cause is most likely external. If the task is always performed poorly, the cause is more apt to be internal.
3. **Scale C.** *What is the extent to which* others *perform this same job poorly?* If other people are having trouble with it too, it is probably an external problem, although here again lack of knowledge or practice can be a factor. If no one else seems to be having problems with the task, then the first place to look for causes is internal.

∇ **The causes.** Here is a list of internal and external causes which can be contributing to the employee performance problem. Add to this list from your own experience.

Internal causes	**External causes**
Lack of self-confidence	Distressing news/events
Change in attitude	Lack of opportunity
Excessive stress/tension	Confusing instructions

Internal causes	**External causes**
Insufficient challenge	Lack of managerial support
Lack of apparent rewards	Unclear organizational goals
Changed priorities	Excessive changes
Lack of task knowledge	Difficult work environment
Insufficient practice	Responsibility without authority
Performance anxiety	Personality clash
Fear of failure	Task overload
Procrastination	Inadequate resources
Lack of motivation	Lack of recognition
Other: ________	Other: ________

∇ **The patterns.** When you have positioned the employee on the A-B-C scales, connect the three points with lines. There are four major patterns that can emerge that will be helpful to your analysis of the employee's performance:

1. *Task/job problem.*

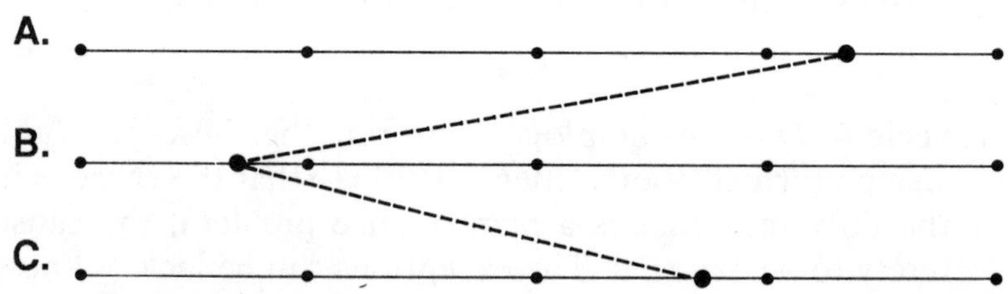

Figure 5. ***The task/job problem pattern***

Since the employee apparently performs other tasks satisfactorily, and everyone else seems to be having trouble with it as well, this pattern may indicate that the problem really lies within the job or task itself. Unless you think that no one has the necessary training or experience, the causes probably are in the "external" list.

2. *Employee internal problem.*

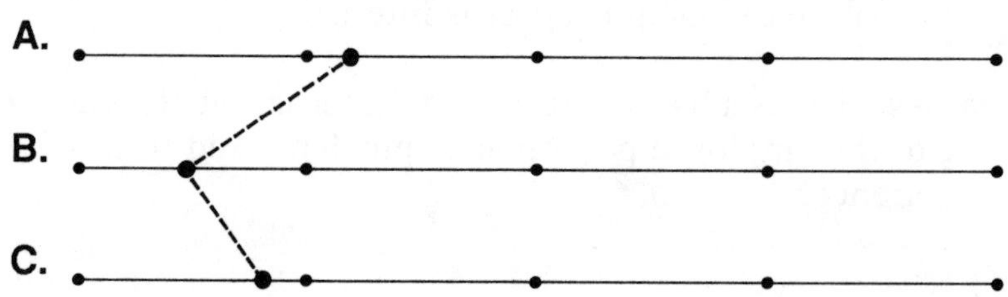

Figure 6. ***The employee internal problem pattern***

Since all tasks are performed poorly, and others are not having a problem with it, the problem would appear to be internal, and for only this individual employee.

3. *Individual skill problem.*

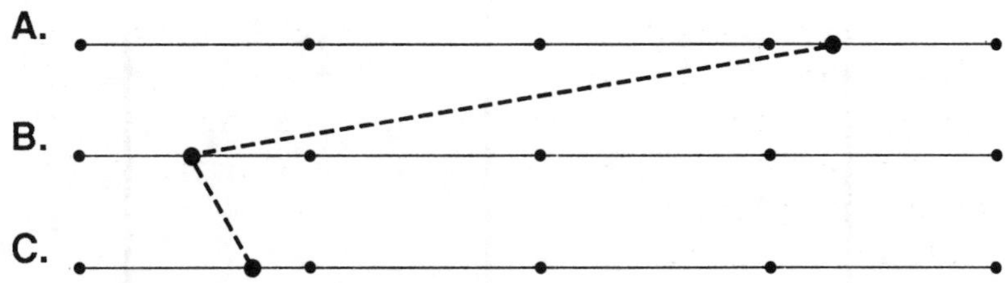

Figure 7. ***The individual skill problem pattern***

Since this seems to be the only area giving the employee a problem—and others aren't having a problem with it—then the first place to look would be the employee's skills for this particular task: knowledge, experience, or self-management.

4. *External impact on work environment.*

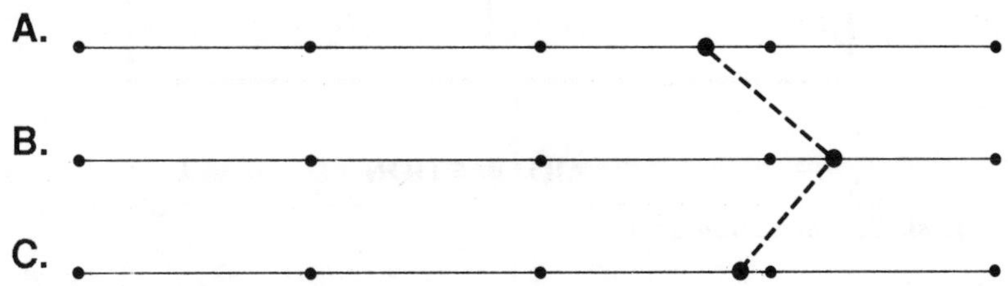

Figure 8. ***The external impact on the work environment pattern.***

Since other tasks are performed well, this task has never been a problem before, and everyone else is having problems with it as well, this pattern indicates that some sort of "shock wave"—an external event—may have gone through the work environment, affecting everyone's performance, and that the employee's poor performance is likely to improve when the environment improves.

∇ **Summary.** This assessment does not give you an ironclad analysis of the employee's performance problem, nor is it intended to. What it does provide is a quick, organized look at the problem's pattern, and start you in the right direction for pinning down the exact causes.

It is also a helpful document to work on together with the employee, for it serves as an excellent basis for discussion.

The Skills/Motivation Assessment

This assessment is useful in helping to separate a poor performance issue into its skills and motivation components, never an easy task. It can be used with either an individual or an entire work unit team.

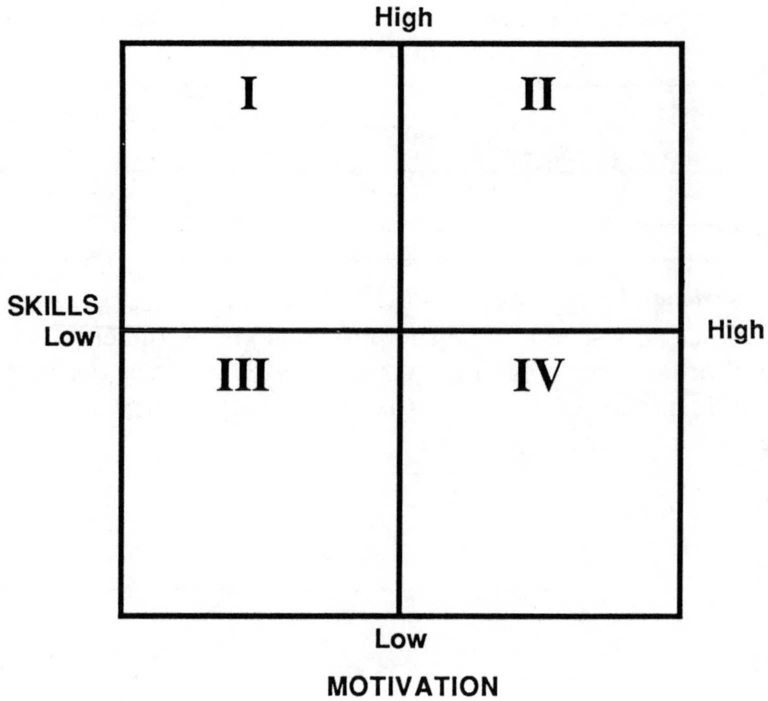

Figure 9. ***The skills/motivation grid***

∇ **Observing behavior.** One of the questions that sometimes arises in using the Skills/Motivation Assessment is "How do I distinguish skill from motivation just by observing? Motivation is an emotion, a feeling—how does it show up in behaviors?" A legitimate question. To help answer it, here are several observable behaviors that may help you when placing individuals on the skills/motivation grid:

Behaviors

Motivation	**Skills**
Energy level	Finished outcome
Enthusiasm	Efficiency
Concentration	Speed
Perseverance	Can explain to others
Positive attitude	Ease of execution
Conscientiousness	Quality of work
Other: ________________	Other: ________________
________________	________________

No single one of these terms is sufficient to rate an individual as to skills or motivation. For example, someone may be very skillful when judged by the finished outcome, but also be very slow and methodical in the way it is done. For that reason, try to use as many of these behaviors as possible, plus your own, when placing an individual on the grid.

∇ **Directions.** Place an individual's name or initials on the roster list beneath the grid. Use the roster number to position the individual on the grid according to your perception of his or her skill level and motivation. Figure 10 shows an example of a completed grid.

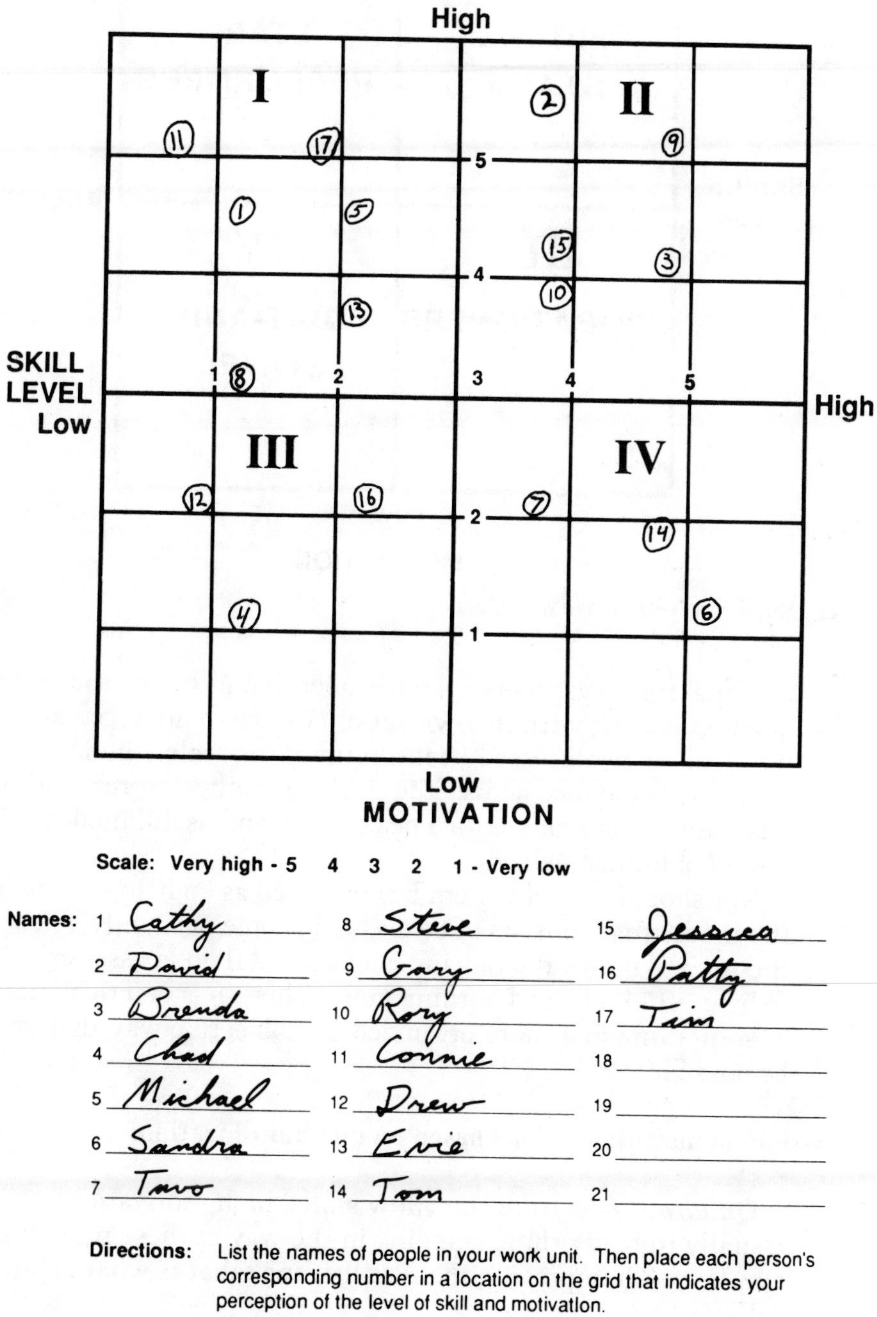

Figure 10. ***Example of a completed grid***

∇ **The quadrants.** Once you have placed an individual or work unit members on the grid, you can use the grid location to give yourself a basic idea of what actions you may want to carry out next.

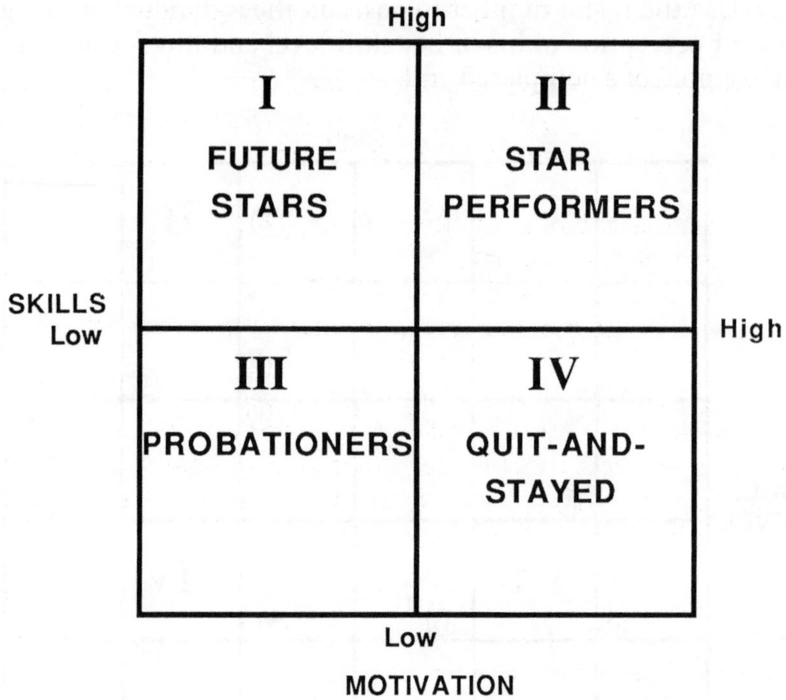

Figure 11. ***Skills/motivation grid quadrants***

In making an assessment, remember that although the grid is divided into quadrants, each with its own set of possible managerial actions, it is really made up of two crossed "continuums," or scales, indicating a continuous range of behaviors across the scale. In other words, although the grid/quadrant system makes for a neat, clean, and useful model, it is only that—a *model* of human behavior.

Nor should such a system be construed as "putting people in boxes." It is the model that consists of boxes, and people need only be compared against the model, not evaluated and packaged. All good assessments are designed to be useful tools, and nothing more. They are a practical method of looking at something in a more organized and objective way than might otherwise be possible.

∇ **Possible managerial actions based on quadrant location:**

Quadrant I—Future stars (low skills, high motivation).
Usually the only thing standing in the way of these more highly motivated employees is improving their skills, since that is what is low. More specifically:

- Offer training.
- Provide practice.
- Allow them to gain experience.
- Set realistic performance goals.
- Use performance development system (see Chapter 16).

Quadrant II—Star performers (high skills, high motivation). These are your high performers, but don't neglect them. Here are some specific suggestions for managing them:

- Reinforce their high performance.
- Let them teach others.
- Help them reset goals upward.
- Use their high performance as basis for new growth.

Quadrant III—Probationers (low skills and motivation). These probably verify the 80/20 rule, in that they're usually the 20 percent of your employees who need 80 percent of your time. They're probationers because if they're low enough in the corner of the quadrant, they're in danger of being fired. Here are some suggestions:

- Help them set specific performance goals (use the performance development system, Chapter 16).
- Provide coaching in subpar skills.
- Provide job or task training.
- Offer self-management training or counseling, for motivation.
- Allow time for practice, with coaching.
- If all else fails, "career re-adjustment" (firing) may be necessary.

Quadrant IV—Quit-and-stayed (high skills, low motivation). As a manager, this may be your most frustrating group, because you know they have the skills to do the job if they *want* to. They also offer you your greatest opportunity, because if you can remotivate them, they can also be star performers. In many cases they once were.

Give this group a very careful look with regard to burnout, especially if they have been there about three, seven, ten, or fourteen years. Burnout research, including my own, indicates that these are the points where job performance can be most seriously affected by burnout, often to the point that the employee leaves the organization.

Here are some suggestions for this group:

- Improve self-management skills (use assessments in Chapter 25).
- Evaluate reward/punishment balance.
- Help them reset personal and professional goals.
- Evaluate internal/external causes.
- If other strategies fail—and they have fallen low enough on the motiva-

tion scale—you may want to suggest counseling or other professional assistance.

Once you are able to determine the skills/motivation balance, you are in a position to help the employee move toward Quadrant II. If low skills are the problem, training, practice, and more experience are called for. If low motivation seems to be the principal issue, discuss the demotivating issues involved with the employee and take appropriate action.

In almost every case it is best to use the assessment in conjunction with the employee. It is your discussion and interaction with the employee that will bring about improved performance, not the assessment.

Rewards/Punishment Balance

One of the laws of inertia states that once something is headed in a given direction, it requires energy to change that direction. The law holds as true for poor employee performance as it does for subatomic particles. People are no more anxious to change directions than are particles. We often have much of our self-image and habit patterns at stake in any given set of behaviors.

The Rewards/Punishment Balance Assessment lets you get additional insight into why improved employee performance may not have occurred despite your best efforts. It can be used either before starting to work with an employee on subpar performance, to establish the context within which you'll want to work, or afterward, if there isn't sufficient improvement.

∇ **Directions.** Under Present Behavior, put the behavior that is causing the problem. Under Desired Behavior, put the behavior you would like from the employee. Under Rewards, put the apparent positive outcomes for the employee for each behavior. Under Punishment, put the apparent negative consequences for each behavior. (See Figure 13 for an example.)

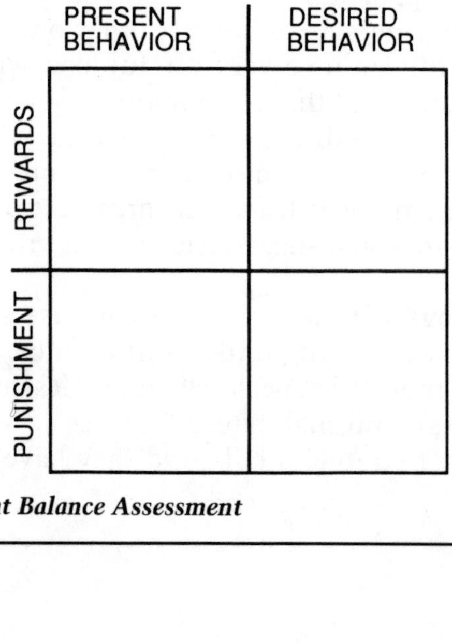

Figure 12. ***The Rewards/Punishment Balance Assessment***

∇ **Mickey.** The rewards/punishment balance worksheet itself may be found at the end of this chapter, but here is a case history that will give you an idea of how it works.

Mickey was frequently late for work. This can be enough of a problem under normal circumstances, but in this case it was even worse: Mickey had exceptionally good skills, and because of that was the set-up person in the work unit. Until Mickey got there, not much happened. Mickey's lateness therefore was not only a bad example to the newer employees, but was also very expensive in terms of production.

Mickey's immediate supervisor, Randy, finally decided to get help, because repeated warnings weren't accomplishing anything. Mickey continued to be late, each time with a more inventive excuse than the last. The work unit wasn't much help, either. They were amused at Mickey's inventiveness, and secretly admired Mickey's nerve at flaunting authority. In fact, Mickey had become something of an underground celebrity.

Randy's manager, after hearing the situation, thought that doing a rewards/punishment balance on Mickey would be helpful. This is what it looked like:

∇ Rewards/Punishment Balance

NAME Mickey DATE 10/23

	PRESENT BEHAVIOR	DESIRED BEHAVIOR
	frequently late	be on time to work
REWARDS	sleep later	supervisor + peer
	avoid rush hour traffic	approval
	gets attention	increase job security
	express independence	full pay
	feeling of power:	easier parking
	others must wait	
	"live dangerously"	
	test authority's limits	
PUNISHMENTS	supervisor's disapproval	less sleep
	danger of getting fired	more traffic
	docked pay	less attention
	harder to find parking	less feeling of
		independence
		less excitement
		less personal power
		"just like all the
		rest"

I NEED TO: increase docked pay to include # of people who must wait; tie work-unit # to production; see if M. can be promoted to greater authority/responsibility; set limits/"probation".

Figure 13. ***Mickey's rewards/punishment balance worksheet***

Notice that the rewards for Mickey continuing the late behavior exceeded both the current punishments and the rewards for changing to the desired behavior. Likewise, the punishments for changing behaviors exceeded the rewards. In short, with a balance like that, Mickey would have to be a little crazy to start reporting for work on time.

With Mickey's apparent rewards and punishments laid out before the two managers, it became a lot easier to work out a strategy to change Mickey's problem behavior. Because of Mickey's skills and experience—not to mention a very creative imagination—firing was to be the last possible option. Mickey could not be easily replaced, a fact of which Mickey was equally aware. To shift Mickey's balance of rewards and punishments, they decided to do the following:

- Increase the amount of Mickey's pay docked for lateness to include the wages of anyone who had to wait until Mickey got there. This raised Mickey's potential financial penalty by a factor of eleven!
- Tie the pay of Mickey's fellow workers more closely to work-unit production. This would greatly increase the peer pressure on Mickey and take away the hero status; while they were waiting for Mickey, they wouldn't be making any money. Mickey's lateness would hit them right in the pocketbook.
- Inquire in personnel as to whether Mickey would be promotable to a position of greater authority and responsibility, putting Mickey's skill and ingenuity to work for the organization, instead of against it.
- Put Mickey on probation, with finite limits, beyond which Mickey and the organization would part company.
- Discuss the rewards/punishment balance worksheet with Mickey, indicating the reason for the probation, and the clear consequences of breaking it.

Did it work? Within six months Mickey was promoted to a supervisory role, where the creativity could be channeled into more constructive directions. Is Mickey now a model of punctuality? No, but arrival is well within acceptable organizational limits, and is no longer accompanied by excuses such as, "Well, Aunt Hazel couldn't get the old tractor started, so I . . ."

∇ **Summary.** The rewards/punishment balance gives you additional insights into why employees don't improve performance even when it seems to be in their best interests. To get some experience with it, try it on one of your own behaviors that you know you should change or would like to change. That will give you a better idea of why improving poor employee performance has to go beyond just telling them what they need to do. "Shape up or ship out" only goes so far—especially with employees you don't want to ship out.

In Conclusion

There's an old question in customer service businesses that seems to get at the heart of analyzing employee performance problems: "If your people know how to smile, why don't they?"

When you can accurately answer that kind of performance question, separating the skills and motivation issues, you're well on the way to determining the real causes of employee performance problems. Then, and only then, can you apply cost-effective training, coaching, and performance improvement strategies.

∇ ***For additional information, see:***

Chapter 10. Helping the Problem Employee
Chapter 16. P = SOME: The Performance Equation
Chapter 22. Performance Appraisal—Who Needs It?
Chapter 24. To Train, or Not to Train?

Date ______________

∇ Analyzing Poor Performance

Directions:
1. Place a mark on each scale in response to the statement regarding the employee's performance.
2. Draw a line connecting the three marks. (See Chapter 18 for illustrated examples.)
3. Refer to examples in Chapter 18 to interpret the pattern.

A. Performs <u>other</u> tasks poorly:

ALWAYS USUALLY OCCASIONALLY SELDOM NEVER

•________•________•________•________•

B. Performs <u>this</u> task poorly at <u>other times:</u>

ALWAYS NEVER BEFORE

•________•________•________•________•

C. Extent to which <u>others</u> perform this task poorly:

NO ONE ELSE EVERYONE

•________•________•________•________•

<u>Internal causes</u>:

- Lack of self-confidence
- Change in attitude
- Excessive stress or tension
- Insufficient challenge
- Lack of apparent rewards
- Changed priorities
- Lack of task knowledge
- Insufficient practice
- Performance anxiety
- Procrastination
- Fear of failure
- Lack of motivation

<u>External causes</u>:

- Distressing news or events
- Lack of opportunity
- Confusing instructions
- Lack of managerial support
- Unclear organizational goals
- Excessive changes
- Difficult work environment
- Responsibility without authority
- Personality clash
- Task overload
- Inadequate resources
- Lack of recognition

∇ Skills/Motivation Grid: 1

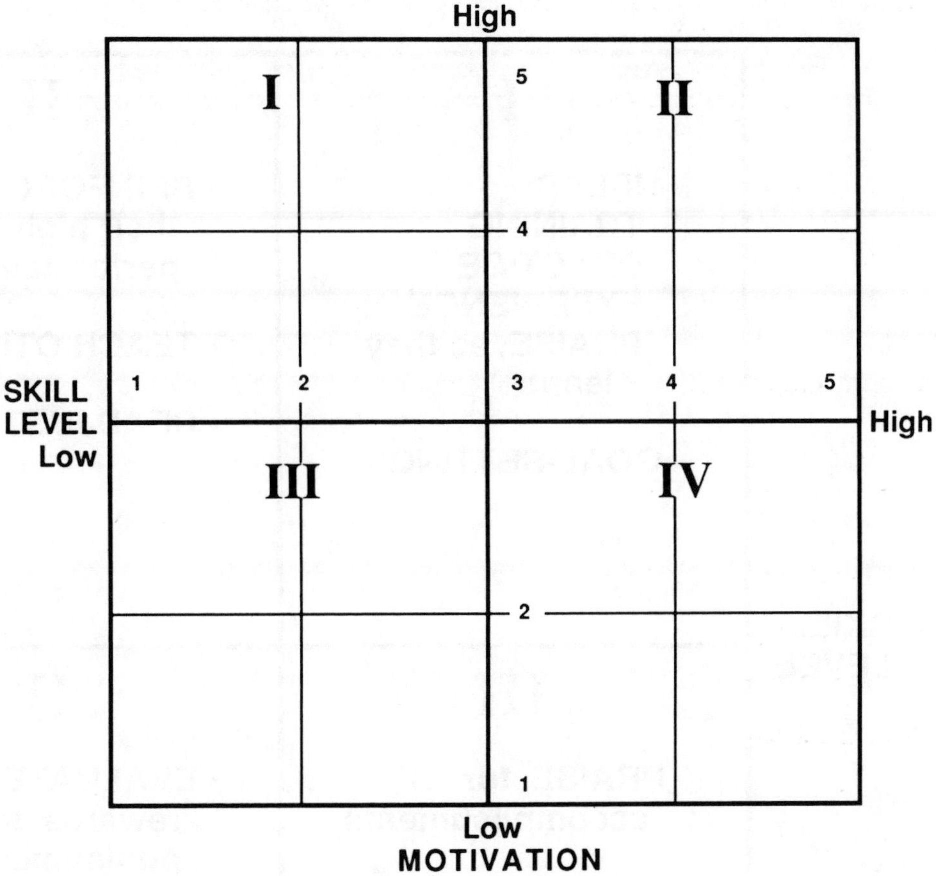

Scale: Very high - 5 4 3 2 1 - Very low

Names:

1 ______	8 ______	15 ______
2 ______	9 ______	16 ______
3 ______	10 ______	17 ______
4 ______	11 ______	18 ______
5 ______	12 ______	19 ______
6 ______	13 ______	20 ______
7 ______	14 ______	21 ______

Directions: List the names of people in your work unit. Then place each person's corresponding number in a location on the grid that indicates your perception of the level of skill and motivation.

∇ Skills/Motivation Grid: 2

SKILL LEVEL	**I** • NEEDS: TRAINING PRACTICE EXPERIENCE PRAISE, as they learn • GOAL-SETTING	**II** • REINFORCE their high performance • TEACH OTHERS • READJUST GOALS
	III • PRAISE, for accomplishments • GOAL-SETTING • COACHING and COUNSELING • TERMINATION, if all else fails	**IV** • EVALUATE rewards and punishment ratio • RESET GOALS and OBJECTIVES • STRESS MGMT. • NEW CHALLENGES

MOTIVATION

∇ Rewards/Punishment Balance

NAME ______________________________ DATE ____________

	PRESENT BEHAVIOR	DESIRED BEHAVIOR
REWARDS		
PUNISHMENTS		

I NEED TO: ______________________________

____

____

____

∇ 19. Mapping Career Development

I believe the most fortunate people on earth are those who have found an idea that's bigger than they are.

—*Richard Leider,* The Power of Purpose

At the turn of the century, there were only about 270 careers open to men, and even fewer open to women. Now, in the 1980s, almost any large corporation has more than that open to both men *and* women.

The enormous number of possible career choices provide a great deal of career freedom, but it also makes the task of career development that much more complex for both manager and employee. Contemporary workers' value systems have changed, and so have the things they want out of a career. As Steve Buchholz, a vice-president of Wilson Learning Corporation, one of the nation's leading training organizations, states, " 'Performance with Fulfillment' is the motto of today's employees. The role of today's successful managers is to help bring about both the performance *and* the fulfillment."

The Need for Career Development: Organization

Both organizations and individual employees need more effective career development programs, although not necessarily for the same reasons. Some of the organization's essential career development needs include:

- **Employee loyalty and retention.** As jobs become more complex, workers necessarily become more educated and sophisticated about both the quality of their training and the work they do. As a result, organizations without adequate career development and training programs are finding it increasingly difficult to retain the bright young employees they need to develop into the managers of tomorrow. Hiring the competition is no longer a reliable way to hedge against the future, if indeed it ever was.

- **Avoiding future shock.** As the rate of cultural and organizational change accelerates, more and more organizations will be caught unprepared, with inadequate human resources, when their particular "future" arrives. Alvin Toffler, originator of the term, says that to avoid future shock, individuals and organizations need to learn to learn, learn to choose, and learn to relate. All three of these can be integrated into a good career development program.

- **Performance motivation.** Research continues to indicate that money is not a reliable motivator of high performance, especially over the long term. Not that most of us don't need jobs to keep up with our credit cards, but unless we work on commission or piecework, there is often little direct connection between our performance and our compensation. Money is a great motivator to get and keep a job, but once on the job the performance motivators have to come from other sources.

  Most employees are more likely to be motivated to high performance over the long haul by knowing the context within which their particular job fits, both for the organization and for their own career aspirations. To establish that context requires a well-planned career development system. As an old Down East saying goes, "If you want that mail to get there, then you'd better give it to somebody who knows where they're goin'."

Individual Needs for Career Development

Someone once calculated that the average individual spends less time per year on career plans than watching television per week—a rather sobering thought, considering the investment of time and energy we place in the jobs that over a lifetime make up a career.

Despite the lack of planning, the individual employee has needs that are quite similar to those of the organization. In fact, one of the best ways for individual employees or managers to think of themselves is as personal corporations with the same concerns for the efficient use of time, energy, and resources as their parent organization has.

With regard to planning the individual's career development program, however, there is one important difference: whereas the organization can be considered to have a theoretically unlimited future, the individual employee does not. A lifetime is finite. How far the employee is along the road of that lifetime has a great deal of influence on how and which career decisions may need to be made. The bifocal generation has far different career decision needs than the Pepsi generation.

We can look at it this way: because of the time left to them, employees entering the work force typically have available a wide range of career opportunities and very few professional responsibilities. As employees progress along their career paths, however, the time remaining dictates that they will have fewer and fewer career alternatives remaining, while the level of their professional and personal responsibilities has probably gone up.

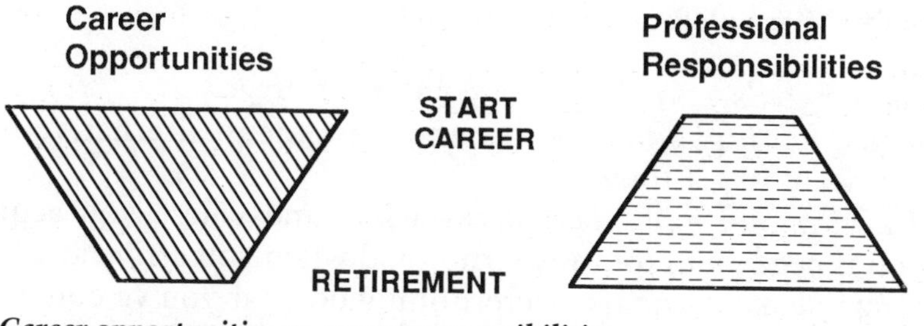

Figure 14. ***Career opportunities vs. career responsibilities***

With current information indicating that American workers now change careers three to five times during their working years, it is apparent that the more linear career paths of a generation or two ago—one basic set of skills used in a limited number of organizations—are no longer common. This combination of increased responsibilities and decisions, with decreasing career options, dictates the need for increasingly sophisticated methods of career planning and development. This is especially true as the employee grows older and the options grow smaller.

The Manager's Role

In addition to planning and implementing their own career development programs, managers also need to play a major role in helping their employees to establish satisfying career paths—where they want their career to go and the best route to take to get there. Here are two specific ways in which managers can do this:

1. *Include career development planning with performance appraisal sessions.* Performance reviews offer an excellent opportunity for the manager to act as a consultant and assist employees with their career path planning and implementation, as well as to determine an employee's career aspirations. The need for a good manager to be "growing people" requires that career paths, job descriptions, performance appraisals, and feedback be considered as a unified concept.
2. *Facilitate job experiences and training that fulfill the employee's career plan.* No matter what employees do on their own, often a manager must help them get the training and job experiences they need to reach their career goals. Employees who feel that their manager has their best career interests at heart are also much more likely to be both loyal employees and high performers.

Strategies

Most career development systems consist of four basic components, analogous to a road map:

1. *Career goals*—deciding where you want to go.
2. *Career path planning*—since there are many alternative routes, how do you want to get there?
3. *Training and job experiences*—when and where you acquire the skills you'll need, both for the journey and when you arrive at each destination.
4. *Ongoing assessments*—determining how far you've come, how far to go, and what else you'll need to get there.

Continuing the travel analogy, planning a good career path is much like traveling with a comprehensive guidebook: it allows you to read about the next destination before you get there. This not only saves you time and energy once you arrive, but lets you get the most experience possible out of the trip. The alternative is to look around once you get there and wonder where you are.

Unfortunately, career planning in many organizations tries to operate without the guidebook. For example, Leslie in accounting does such a good job at one level that at the earliest opportunity, without much advance preparation, Leslie is promoted to the next level on the organizational ladder. Not having been adequately prepared for the jump, Leslie now spends a good bit of nonproductive time trying to figure out how to do the job. And by the time Leslie really gets this job under control, it will be promotion time again.

In an organization with that kind of system, most employees and managers are constantly learning their job responsibilities through on-the-job training. Carried to an extreme in a fast-track organization, the cost in added employee stress and lowered productivity can be enormous.

The smoother alternative is to start preparing the employee for the next job as soon as he or she has been moved into the current one. The only catch is that both the organization and the employee need to have planned what that next job is going to be. This becomes one of the prime benefits of a good career development system to both organization and employee.

Assessments

Good assessment tools let you find out how far you've traveled along your career path, how far you have to go, and what additional supplies and skills you're going to need to reach your destination successfully. Not that your career destination need be carved in granite—you can change your destination any time you want to. It is just that when you do, you'll also want to change the routing on your map and assess your new requirements.

Planning a solid career path becomes a matter of developing two basic skills:

1. Designing a well-planned trip to your current career destination.
2. Redrawing your map if and when you decide to change either your route or your destination.

For the organization, good career planning requires that a comprehensive career development system be put in place for all employees. "Comprehensive" doesn't necessarily equate with "expensive" or "elaborate," but organizational thought should be given to the way career pathing interrelates with all other aspects of employees' jobs and responsibilities.

Good employee career development also means that the organization provides adequate management training to ensure that career development is most effectively used. Many managers don't have the opportunity for any training or experience in career development consulting, either for themselves or their employees.

In organizations large enough to support personnel departments, "career development" may be a departmental function, but not all organizations have that luxury. Even those that do have often found that in order effectively to link performance appraisal and career pathing, *all* managers need some background with at least the rudiments of employee career development consulting.

For the individual employee, career development assessments can provide the data necessary to manage one's own career, if that is the option the employee selects from the three basic career development patterns.

Three Basic Career Development Patterns

Short of marrying the boss's favorite offspring or inheriting a business, these are the three basic strategies people use to select jobs within their career paths:

- **Serendipity.** The employee relies on pure chance and Lady Luck to provide the right job. This system also requires that the user be in the right place at the right time. Despite the element of chance involved—and the high disappointment rate—it is amazing how many employees continue to use it.

  The best advice for the employee using the serendipity system is to keep moving. Give yourself every opportunity to be in the right place at the right time. No good hunting dog ever found game by sitting in one spot.

- **"The organization knows best."** This adult variation of "My parents know best" has the individual moved from job to job by the needs (or whims) of the organization. It was a perfectly appropriate strategy when we were younger and dependent on adults for protection and life's essential ingredients. For independent adults, however, this approach often leaves employees who use it feeling like puppets on a string, jerked about solely by organizational dictates.

  This system is at its best when used in a paternalistic organization that consistently has the employees' best interests at heart. Unfortunately, such organizations are often hard to find.

  The best strategy for users of this system is to sell yourself and do your homework. If you're going to wait for the organization to reach out and anoint you, at least know which way they're going to reach and remind them whom they should reach for. No need to make a big production of it, but like eager young singles at a wedding, be there when the garter and bouquet are thrown.

- **Self-designed.** This is the system most likely to produce performance with fulfillment. Employees themselves set their own career course, with organizational assistance, and are primarily responsible for its implementation, monitoring, and assessment. Employees who have their career destinies in their own hands are far more likely to be high performers.

  Assessment tools help the self-designing employee answer such basic career development questions as:

  - What are my goals, skills, and motivation? In other words, where do I want to go, what are my abilities to get there—and how badly do I want to make the trip?
  - Am I in my present job by design, or by accident? If by accident, can I count on such accidents happening again if I don't stay in this job, or with this organization, until retirement?
  - What am I doing to prepare myself for the next step up the ladder?

- In any way I choose to calculate it, how much is this career path costing me? Is it worth it?
- How much of the apparent stress in this job is produced because I don't know where the job leads? Where would I like it to lead?

Assessments don't provide all of the answers for midcourse corrections of a career path, of course, but they are far better than having no compass at all.

Organizational Career Development Systems

Each organization has its own specific career development needs that will determine the final design and implementation of its career development system. Here are several basic tenets of successful systems, however, which may be helpful:

∇ Integrate employees' career development planning with the organization's performance appraisal system. Of course, the organization first needs to *have* a performance appraisal system. This needs to be at least as formal as a regularly scheduled meeting between manager and employee to discuss performance and career issues.

∇ Create basic job descriptions that define the skills, training, job experiences, and other requirements needed to do any given job in the organization. This helps with both career development and hiring. Keep the descriptions flexible enough that they don't arbitrarily limit a given employee's talent, skills, or growth.

∇ Use career and performance assessment tools that enable employees to build profiles of themselves. These can then be compared against the job descriptions, giving managers and employees a much more accurate picture of what else may be needed to prepare employees for a given job. This profile/job description comparison becomes the basis for the employee's career path map.

For example, if I am a young salesperson in a department store and my current career destination is to be a department store general manager, knowing the job descriptions and requirements of each position along the path to general manager will allow me to plan my training and experience map accordingly.

∇ Provide the necessary career development consulting assistance by managers or the personnel department to enable employees both to plan their original maps and to redesign them if career goals or plans change. Books such as Richard Boles's *What Color Is My Parachute?* and *The Three Boxes of Life* can also be very helpful in mapping career plans.

∇ At every possible step, encourage employees to manage their own careers. This not only develops responsible employees but also increases the investment in their own performance. In the truest sense, they are now fully self-employed.

Career Development Plans for Small Businesses

Small businesses face a special set of problems when it comes to career development programs for their employees:

- Most of the jobs in a small business (five to fifty employees) are essentially dead-end; i.e., there's no place much to go within the organization, either laterally or vertically, except out. The top job, that of owner, is already taken.
- The personnel department resources for career planning that are available in larger organizations are lacking. The average manager has not had much training in career planning, so the employee basically has to learn to swim on his or her own.
- Many small business managers and owners feel like farm teams for the big leagues, knowing that some of their best people will ultimately leave for organizations with greater opportunities.

Can these factors be overcome for the small business? Here are some suggestions:

- To keep good people, make the business as comfortable and challenging a place to work as possible, with high-quality management and working environment, and as much opportunity to grow as possible.
- Take advantage of your small size to have as informal an atmosphere as people feel comfortable with, remembering that informal is not to be confused with disorganized.
- Encourage employees to take even greater charge of their own job descriptions and development than they might be able to do in a larger organization. Regular performance appraisals and job-enrichment sessions can occur in any size organization.
- Cross-train your employees to the greatest extent possible. This gives everyone greater flexibility and variety. Even if a job is dead-end, it does not have to be boring.
- Pay competitively. Small does not have to mean cheap—at least it didn't in Tiffany's marketing plan. Tie employee performance to some type of profit-sharing if at all possible.
- Be up-front about the possibility of employees moving on. It may not be ideal, but at least everyone is honest about the situation. Not everyone likes big organizations—help make your organization an attractive alternative.

In Conclusion

The values of today's more highly educated workers are changing the traditional parental relationship between employer and employee. To be effective, career development programs need to reflect that change and provide stronger links between planned employee career paths and performance.

Someone once described middle age crisis as "that time when you ask yourself once again, 'What do I want to be when I grow up?' " Good career development programs are an ongoing attempt to answer that question.

∇ ***For additional information, see:***

Chapter 22. Performance Appraisal—Who Needs It?
Chapter 24. To Train, or Not to Train?

∇ Career Self-Assessment

Directions: Place a square around a number to indicate how important you feel that item is to your career situation.
Place a circle around a number to indicate what you perceive your present situation to be.

Scale: **High/Excellent - 5 4 3 2 1 - Low/Poor**

Items

1. Making as much money as is normal for your job in other organizations.	5 4 3 2 1
2. Making as much money as you need.	5 4 3 2 1
3. Making as much money as you want.	5 4 3 2 1
4. Having the opportunity to significantly increase your income while in this organization.	5 4 3 2 1
5. Having vertical growth opportunities in this organization (upward in management).	5 4 3 2 1
6. Having lateral growth opportunities in this organization (other jobs or career paths).	5 4 3 2 1
7. Living in the part of the country where you want to live.	5 4 3 2 1
8. Living locally where you want to live.	5 4 3 2 1
9. Having a satisfactory time/energy balance between job and personal life.	5 4 3 2 1
10. Having job security.	5 4 3 2 1
11. Having your family/Significant Others satisfied with your career path choice.	5 4 3 2 1
12. Having your family/Significant Others satisfied with your present job.	5 4 3 2 1
13. Being generally satisfied with this organization.	5 4 3 2 1
14. Having the opportunity to be creative in this organization.	5 4 3 2 1
15. Having a reasonable work schedule.	5 4 3 2 1
16. Having a satisfactory physical work environment.	5 4 3 2 1
17. Having opportunities to update/learn new skills.	5 4 3 2 1

continued

Career Self-Assessment, continued.

18. Taking pride in your job.	5 4 3 2 1
19. Having opportunities for career path counseling.	5 4 3 2 1
20. Taking pride in the organization.	5 4 3 2 1
21. Being satisfied with your co-workers.	5 4 3 2 1
22. Being satisfied with your supervisor/manager.	5 4 3 2 1
23. Being satisfied with upper management.	5 4 3 2 1
24. Avoiding excessive job stress and burnout.	5 4 3 2 1
25. Making a positive contribution to the organization.	5 4 3 2 1

Your present overall career satisfaction:

Very high - 10 9 8 7 6 5 4 3 2 1 - Very low (circle one)

• Taking into account your present career situation--age, experience,skills, talents, contacts, and so forth--what do you think your job satisfaction could be?

Very high -10 9 8 7 6 5 4 3 2 1 - Very low (circle one)

• If there is a significant difference between your present career satisfaction and what you think it could be, what might you need to do to narrow the gap?

____

____

____

• What might you need to do to lessen any significant differences between the squares and the circles--the importance and the current situation--in your self-assessment?

____

____

____

Date ________________ **MANAGER**

∇ Career Development Checklist

Directions: Place a square around a number to indicate how important you think that item is in a good career development system.
Place a circle around a number to indicate your estimation of the present career development situation in your organization.

Suggestion: Have your employees fill out the "Employee" version. Place their averaged scores in the appropriate places and compare their perceptions with yours.

Scale: **5-Always 4-Usually 3-Occasionally 2-Seldom 1-Never**

Items		**Employees** □ ○
1. You are actively interested in your employees' career development.	5 4 3 2 1	___ ___
2. Career development is an integral part of the performance appraisal system.	5 4 3 2 1	___ ___
3. The organization has an overall concern with employees' career aspirations.	5 4 3 2 1	___ ___
4. Time and resources are made available to employees to plan and implement career development.	5 4 3 2 1	___ ___
5. Other job opportunities within the organization are announced publicly before being filled.	5 4 3 2 1	___ ___
6. Professional assistance is available to employees for career counseling.	5 4 3 2 1	___ ___
7. There are opportunities to learn about other employees' jobs and career paths within the organization.	5 4 3 2 1	___ ___
8. It is possible for employees to design/develop their own job descriptions.	5 4 3 2 1	___ ___

Overall rating of your organization's career development system:

Very high - **10 9 8 7 6 5 4 3 2 1** - Very low (circle one)

Your employees' averaged rating of the career development system:___________

Note: Circled items in the 1-2 area may require attention to improve your organization's career development system. Also, give close attention to items in which the circle is two or more numbers to the right of the square, as this indicates a gap between importance and the present career development situation.

Date ________________

EMPLOYEE

∇ Career Development Checklist

Directions: Place a square around a number to indicate how important you think that item is in a good career development system.
Place a circle around a number to indicate your estimation of the present career development situation in your organization.

Scale: **5-Always** **4-Usually** **3-Occasionally** **2-Seldom** **1-Never**

Items

1. Your manager is actively interested in employees' career development.	5 4 3 2 1
2. Career development is an integral part of the performance appraisal system.	5 4 3 2 1
3. The organization has an overall concern with employees' career aspirations.	5 4 3 2 1
4. Time and resources are made available to employees to plan and implement career development.	5 4 3 2 1
5. Other job opportunities within the organization are announced before being filled.	5 4 3 2 1
6. Professional assistance is available to employees for career counseling.	5 4 3 2 1
7. There are opportunities to learn about other employees' jobs and career paths within the organization.	5 4 3 2 1
8. It is possible for employees to design/develop their own job descriptions.	5 4 3 2 1

Overall rating of your organization's career development system:

Very high - 10 9 8 7 6 5 4 3 2 1 - Very low (circle one)

∇ 20. About Time for Time Management?

Managers around the country seem to be in general agreement that the need for good time management skills gets more critical as business becomes more complex. Lack of these skills causes problems for customers, employees, family, and friends. It also increases the stress load on the manager.

When I ask groups of managers how many are frequently late for appointments or meetings because of time pressures, many hands go up. If I ask, "How many of you think that you could use better time management skills?" the show of hands is almost unanimous. However, if I ask, "How many of you who fly are frequently late enough to miss your plane?" almost no one raises a hand.

How does that relate to your own experience? Do you have trouble managing your time well at the office, yet consistently get to airports on time? If so, why? What motivates you to be so punctual?

One of the most obvious answers is that while people will usually wait for you, airlines won't. Work schedules can be changed, but takeoff schedules can't—at least not by you. You can take home a bulging briefcase or sink into workaholism, but it won't impress the friendly skies when the loading ramp doors close.

So how *do* you consistently get to the plane on time? It seems that you already have all of the basic time management skills you need. What you may need, however, is the necessary focus to apply them consistently.

A Time Management System

If you take a closer look at how you manage to catch Flight 392 for Denver at the end of a busy workday, you will probably find that you do three important things, in this order:

∇ **Set priorities.** You decide the order of importance of tasks that must be done before you leave. A necessary part of that process is determining your specific goals and purpose. The importance of getting on that plane will help put other activities into their proper perspective.

Managers with poor time management skills often don't have a clear sense of goals or purpose on which to base their priority decisions. They may also have difficulty distinguishing between levels of importance or estimating how long tasks will take.

Probably the best-known method for setting priorities is the A-B-C strategy, in which you make a list of your tasks in advance and then identifying them as A, B, or C:

A = the "drop deads" that must be done before you go.
B = the "important but not crucial" tasks you do if you have time before airport departure.
C = the world won't end if these aren't done before you get back.

If you find that you are not completing all of your A projects before you leave, you need to:

1. Reevaluate your priorities.
2. Delegate more tasks, making sure those to whom tasks have been delegated also know what your priorities are.
3. Sharpen your time estimating skills.
4. Get more help.

∇ **Plan.** Once you've decided on your priorities, plan how you'll carry them out:

1. The sequence.
2. The who, what, where, and when.
3. Resources needed.
4. Follow-up required.
5. Contingency plans.

I suggest putting your plans in writing—it is easier to remember, organize, and delegate to someone else at the last minute.

∇ **Protect.** Now that you have priorities and plans established, you must *protect* that time. This usually means improving your ability to say "no" appropriately and emphatically. A colleague has a reminder fastened above the office desk: "If it isn't good for me—say 'No'!"

What if the request comes from a higher authority? Explain your time schedule and priorities and that honoring the request will require a shift in priorities and plans. Then ask for assistance in setting new priorities.

For example: "I'd like to help you with this, Pat, but I have two rush reports for marketing already in the works. If this is a higher priority, how should we handle the marketing reports?"

Protecting also means building contingency time into your schedule to allow for the inevitable emergencies—and then safeguarding it for real emergencies. If you find that you consistently use up most of this emergency time, then look carefully at your planning process. You may be engaging in some magical thinking as to how long things really take to get done.

More Strategies

Although setting priorities, planning, and protecting are valuable time management strategies, there are others:

- If you haven't already done so, take a few minutes to figure out how much you're paid an hour: how much it costs your organization for an hour of your time. It's a good figure to have in mind when you're setting time priorities.
- Some of us are morning people, while others are sharper at the other end of the day. Try to schedule your most difficult tasks during your best time—don't waste it opening mail or writing routine reports.
- Whenever possible, go to someone else's office or an appropriate neutral ground for meetings and conferences—especially if you are not in charge of the meeting. You want to position yourself so that you're free to leave if things aren't productive, get boring, or otherwise turn into a waste of your time.
- Keep people on their feet for short meetings or conferences. It is amazing how quickly things get accomplished. This may be one of the world's oldest business time-savers, but it still works.
- If at all possible, have someone screen your phone calls. If people have easy access to you by phone at any time, you end up managing your day on their schedule, not yours.
- Try to handle a piece of paper only once. Paper handled twice should either be filed—preferably by someone else—sent out, or sent back to where it originated.

- Let the size of a purchase determine who needs to spend time making the purchasing decision. A committee spending four hundred dollars' worth of staff time to make a two-hundred-dollar purchase decision isn't practicing good time management—but it happens.
- Use contemporary electronic assistance whenever possible. You can dictate into a portable recorder when out of the office, use a portable computer or electronic typewriter while traveling, or use conference phone calls or teleconference to cut back on travel time and dollars. Many of these will easily save you enough time to justify the price.

  And don't necessarily wait for the company to buy it—it's your time, energy, and mental health.
- For more in-depth information on time management, the following are several popular books on the subject:

  Getting Organized, Stephanie Winston
  How to Get Control of Your Time and Your Life, Alan Lakein
  How to Put More Time in Your Life, Dru Scott
  The Organized Executive, Stephanie Winston
  The Time Trap, Alec Mackenzie

In Conclusion

If you can catch planes consistently, then you already have good time management skills. The next step is to bolster your intent to use those skills on a regular basis. No matter what time management skills you have, it is the motivation to put them into regular practice that will make the real difference in your stress and productivity levels.

Date ____________

MANAGER

∇ Time Management Self-Assessment

Directions: Place a square around a number to indicate how important you think that skill is for good time management.
Place a circle around a number to indicate your estimation of your present skill level in time management.

Suggestion: Have your employees fill out the "Employee" version. Place their averaged scores in the appropriate places and compare their perceptions with yours.

Scale: **High/Excellent - 5 4 3 2 1 - Low/Poor**

Skills		**Employees** ☐ ○
1. Scheduling difficult tasks for best times during the day.	5 4 3 2 1	___ ___
2. Setting priorities.	5 4 3 2 1	___ ___
3. Planning activities.	5 4 3 2 1	___ ___
4. Protecting scheduled times.	5 4 3 2 1	___ ___
5. Saying "No" appropriately.	5 4 3 2 1	___ ___
6. Estimating time needed to do tasks.	5 4 3 2 1	___ ___
7. Meeting deadlines.	5 4 3 2 1	___ ___
8. Efficient use of time available.	5 4 3 2 1	___ ___
9. Being on time for meetings and appointments.	5 4 3 2 1	___ ___
10. Staying on task when necessary.	5 4 3 2 1	___ ___
11. Avoiding procrastination.	5 4 3 2 1	___ ___
12. Delegating appropriate tasks.	5 4 3 2 1	___ ___

Overall rating of the quality of your time management skills:

Very high - 10 9 8 7 6 5 4 3 2 1 - Very low (circle one)

Your employees' averaged rating: ____________

Note: Circled items in the 1-2 area may require immediate attention to improve your time management skills. Also give close attention to items in which the circle is two or more numbers to the right of the square, as this indicates a gap between importance and skill level.

Date _____________ EMPLOYEE

∇ Time Management Assessment

Directions: Place a square around a number to indicate how important you think that skill is for good time management.
Place a circle around a number to indicate your estimation of your manager's present skill level in time management.

Scale: **High/Excellent - 5 4 3 2 1 - Low/Poor**

Skills

1. Scheduling difficult tasks for best times during the day.	5 4 3 2 1
2. Setting priorities.	5 4 3 2 1
3. Planning activities.	5 4 3 2 1
4. Protecting scheduled times.	5 4 3 2 1
5. Saying "No" appropriately.	5 4 3 2 1
6. Estimating time needed to do tasks.	5 4 3 2 1
7. Meeting deadlines.	5 4 3 2 1
8. Efficient use of time available.	5 4 3 2 1
9. Being on time for meetings and appointments.	5 4 3 2 1
10. Staying on task when necessary.	5 4 3 2 1
11. Avoiding procrastination.	5 4 3 2 1
12. Delegating appropriate tasks.	5 4 3 2 1

Overall rating of the quality of your manager's time management skills:

Very high - 10 9 8 7 6 5 4 3 2 1 - Very low (circle one)

∇ 21. Detoxifying the Workaholic

Work keeps us from three great evils: boredom, vice, and need.
—*Voltaire*

Recently there has been a great deal of discussion among managers regarding "work addiction"—the compulsive need to work. Since it often leads to managerial burnout, many organizations are now looking at the workaholic, the compulsive worker, as a serious problem.

Let me make a clear distinction, however, between the workaholic and the hard worker, the person who thoroughly enjoys his or her job, is good at it, and may prefer doing it to anything else on earth. There are some important differences.

Like other addicts, workaholics may exhibit three basic symptoms:

1. They crave the work activity, much as the alcoholic craves alcohol.
2. They develop a capacity to handle larger and larger quantities.
3. They suffer withdrawal symptoms if the addictive activity is taken away. Illness, vacations, retirement—even weekends—can be a problem for the seriously work-addicted.

Recent research indicates that there are also other symptoms of work addiction. Christopher Hegarty writes in *How to Manage Your Boss* that "workaholics have an anxious relationship with their job. They are obsessed with the need to be busy, fearing that if they slack off for a minute, failure will darken their door instantly . . . true workaholics can't tolerate free time."

Other experts point out that work-addicted managers and employees often feel guilty when not working, may have problems with low self-esteem or self-confidence, and can have a strong tendency toward perfectionism. Such a manager may also have an unbalanced life-style, to the extent that most rewards and feelings of satisfaction come from work, rather than a healthier balance of personal relationships, off-the-job activities, and leisure.

Hard workers, on the other hand, even though they may also put in long hours, usually have a high self-concept, are relaxed when not working, enjoy their leisure time, and are motivated by reaching results or goals, rather than the work activity itself.

Advantages

But is work addiction really a problem for managers and their organizations? Can there be some advantages to the long work hours associated with being a workaholic? If you are a compulsive worker, the following may seem to be benefits of a workaholic life-style:

∇ Long hours on the job can help you avoid areas of your life where your rewards are not as high as for working. Certain responsibilities and situations can also be avoided by the long hours: marriage, parenting, household chores, social engagements, or personal relationships.

∇ Working extra hours can also help you think that you are seen by others as a hard worker, conscientious, or devoted to the job. The fact is that a perceptive boss may actually see those extra hours as a sign of inefficiency, disorganization, or inadequate planning.

∇ Long hours may help you lower anxiety about job performance, thinking "They can't criticize me, just look how hard I'm working." This is especially true in industries in which working long hours are the norm, such as sales or advertising. The problems of workaholism remain the same, however, regardless of whether the workaholic is the exception or just one of an entire workaholic staff.

The truth is, most rewards come to managers who get the most done in the least time. It makes more sense to work smart, not long. (Although the Protestant work ethic might argue that one should work smart *and* long.)

Problems with Workaholism

On the other hand, there are very good reasons for managers to either avoid the work addiction syndrome, or cure themselves of it if they are already afflicted:

- Workaholic managers face the very real possibility of job burnout, along with all of the debilitating physical and psychological effects that go with it.
- Personal relationships may suffer, often tragically. Building and maintaining quality relationships requires a significant investment of time and energy.
- The work-addicted manager or employee may become less efficient if he or she falls into the "I can always do it at home tonight or on the weekend" syndrome. Workdays then become less productive than those of their co-workers, although the time spent working is longer.
- Studies show that there tends to be a relationship between work addiction and other addictions, often chemical: alcohol, nicotine, sugar, caffeine, or stronger drugs. Such chemicals are often used in an attempt to relieve tension, anxiety, or frustration, and work addiction can become part of the same self-defeating pattern.
- Work-addicted managers may also be less creative and innovative problem-solvers than their more relaxed co-workers. Since innovation requires some risk, the anxious workaholic manager may seek to avoid it.
- The workaholic manager can set a poor example for employees, either by implication or direction. Employees tend to believe what managers *do,* rather than what they *say,* so a manager modeling overwork can be a significant problem. Since the average employee will still feel managerial pressure likewise to overwork, this can result in employee resentment, burnout, absenteeism, high job turnover, or, worst of all, employees who quit and stay—they resign from high performance, but not from the organization.

Causes

The specific reasons for work addiction may vary with each manager, but there seem to be three major causes:

1. The manager's feelings of self-worth become connected primarily with work. Karl Albrecht, in his book *Stress and the Manager,* contends that "One reason a manager spends long hours at the job is that he gets psychic

rewards from it. Managing a group of people means having a chance to give orders to others, to judge the efforts of others, to make decisions, and, above all, to feel important."

2. The manager has a significant fear of failure. This is especially true when the Peter Principle has taken effect. This principle applies, according to Laurence J. Peter, when managers have been promoted to a level just beyond their abilities, through seniority, longevity, or just good salesmanship. This results in managers who are marginally competent and who feel perpetually on the brink of failure.
3. The manager has strong perfectionist tendencies. Research indicates a pronounced connection between the workaholic manager and perfectionism. Oddly enough, perfectionists often get less accomplished, with more stress, than do their more pragmatic counterparts. Things done perfectly are also often done carefully and slowly.

Enabling Behaviors

Workaholic behavior can't exist in a social vacuum. As with most addictions, other people usually have to act in a way that aids the workaholic, or the addiction can't continue. These conscious or unconscious acts are called enabling behaviors, for they enable the addict to carry on with the addiction. Enabling behaviors are often unconscious and may occur at the same time enablers are telling addicts that they must change their ways. Here are a few typical enabling behaviors that allow workaholism to continue:

- Close friends and family of the workaholic seldom confront the behavior and rarely make personal demands. Others in the workaholic's social network sacrifice their needs and wishes in the face of the addict's "necessity" to work extra hours.

  This often occurs because confronting either creates more interpersonal strife than it's worth, or threatens the relationship. For example, workaholics often are not confronted with demands to do their share of housework, parenting, or social entertaining. Often the spouse takes on the added burdens of these duties, despite the pressures of job or career, rather than confront the work addict with his or her selfish behavior.
- Others close to the workaholic may apologize, rationalize, or otherwise cover up the work addiction to those outside the family or social network in order to save face or maintain a facade of "Everything is still wonderful." This also results in workaholics not having to confront their own behavior.
- The enabler may have built a compensatory life outside the relationship—sports, volunteer work, school, part-time job—while enjoying the material rewards of the work addict's labor. Sometimes this outside life is complete enough that if the addiction was cured, that life would be

disrupted. In that case, attempts at a cure may be subconsciously sabotaged by the enabler.

- The enabler may take a certain amount of reflected pride in the work addict's activities, bragging to others about how hard the addict works, or what has been accomplished. This of course sends a reinforcement message to the addict.
- The enabler may have problems with the relationship, and may find it easier to maintain the distance the work addiction creates than to confront the relationship problems. This often becomes a tacit "You do your thing, and I'll do mine" arrangement.

Male-Female Issues

There are a number of sex-role issues in our culture that may also be a factor in the development of work addiction, especially among males.

∇ The culture has traditionally conditioned and trained males to feel more comfortable with work issues, and women to feel more comfortable with relationship issues. In fact, according to psychologist Ann Wilson-Schaef, men often base their self-concept on their work successes, while women are more likely to base it upon the quality of their relationships.

It is only human nature to do more of the things from which you get the most rewards, so men tend to work longer, while women become frustrated trying to relate to someone who isn't there. Since men often haven't developed relationship skills to the same level as their work skills, they're likely to retreat into work if the relationship becomes a problem. This, of course, only makes the situation worse and can cause a further deterioration of the relationship.

∇ For those men who haven't developed their relationship skills to the same level of sophistication as their professional skills, work often seems much more interesting and attractive than the relationship with wife, kids, relatives, and friends. After all, a man tells himself, he is making "significant contributions" to the world of art, advertising, science, or industry. It is more satisfying to work, where there is perhaps a greater sense of accomplishment.

∇ As more and more women take on demanding jobs, with increased professional responsibilities, relationship problems are beginning to arise with role reversals. The culture hasn't prepared the male to relate to a work-addicted partner! No amount of schooling or professional training has equipped him emotionally to deal with the same subsidiary role that women have found themselves in for generations.

As a result, the male doesn't pick up the loose ends of relationship, home, and family—or even the kids' dirty clothes. This often leaves the woman with two full-time jobs, one at work and one at home, causing further complications in the relationship.

Self-Assessing

How do managers know if they are truly work addicts? One of the greatest problems in the treatment of any addiction, whether chemical or psychological, is getting the addict to realize and admit that a problem exists. Many of the workaholics who read this probably consider themselves in the hard worker category, no matter what their families, friends, or fellow workers might say.

There are several questions you can ask yourself to begin a self-assessment process:

- Do I have feelings of guilt if I'm not working?
- How many hours a week do I actually work now?
- If more than forty-five hours a week, how long can I continue at this pace before burnout or other serious personal problems affect me?
- If I were to work only forty to forty-five hours per week, what would be the effect on these important areas of my life: job, home life, leisure time, personal relationships, social life, parenting?

Why forty-five hours a week as a demarcation point? The "normal" week for American workers is forty hours. Beyond that, hourly workers go on overtime, salaried workers may go on coffee and adrenalin. Adding commuting time to forty-five hours per week results in an eleven-hour or longer workday. Push the day beyond that, and there's not much time for family, social relationships, balanced diet, relaxation, outside interests, exercise, or the type of balanced life-style that research and clinical experience indicate resists burnout.

Long working hours per se are not a sure sign of a workaholic or a compulsive worker, but the *reason* for those long hours can be a signal that something is wrong. If important aspects of your life are suffering or being avoided with long hours on the job, then *these* are the areas of your life that need creative work, not your job!

Changing

If you want to make changes in a work-addicted life-style, there are several things you can do:

∇ **Develop a better balance** between working hours and other activities, including leisure. Leisure is a chance to unwind, shift gears, and recharge. The alternative? A recent bit of graffiti points out, "Death is nature's way of getting you to slow down."

- ∇ **Look carefully at your motives** for working long hours. Are you trying to impress someone—and if so, is this the way to do it? Realistically, is your job in danger?

- ∇ **Determine what other areas of your life you are avoiding or missing.** The time for extra work must come from someplace.

- ∇ **Calculate how much you really make per hour.** Determine how many hours you work in an average week. Better yet, let someone who is more objective do it! Then divide that into your weekly income.

  How does it look? Many workaholics claim they are working long hours just for the money. If that's true in your case, is there a better way you can earn that much per hour?

- ∇ **Learn to relax**—especially with other people. Research indicates that people who have good social networks live longer, happier lives than those who do not.

- ∇ **Take regular vacations.** If you can't get away for a big one, at least take long weekends on a regular basis.

Helping the Workaholic Employee

Too often, managers who find themselves with workaholic employees think they have died and gone to heaven. Dedication to the job, cheap source of labor (pay someone for forty hours and you get sixty), few outside distractions—what's the problem?

Your conscience aside, the problem is that at this pace these folks aren't going to be around very long. Burnout, divorce, chemicals, or competitors will usually get them, sooner or later. The human cost notwithstanding, the workaholic is generally only a short-term, nearsighted cost benefit for the organization.

If workaholism is a problem in your work unit, here are some things that you can do:

- ∇ Encourage your employees to keep regular hours, except in the time-crunch emergencies that every organization occasionally experiences. (If you find there are emergencies on a regular basis, see the section on stress junkies in Chapter 10.) If subtle hints are overlooked, a managerial "Get outta here!" seems to work fine.

- ∇ Make developing a balanced life-style part of your regular performance review sessions with your employees.

- Encourage outside interests by asking your employees about them and formally recognizing accomplishments outside the organization.

- Avoid setting impossible deadlines except in true emergencies. Consistently giving tight deadlines to a compulsive worker is like pouring drinks for an alcoholic—the results are inevitable.

- Be aware of how long your employees *really* work, and its impact on their lives outside the organization. What are they really being paid per hour?

- Let family responsibilities also be a priority when times are scheduled, or emergencies arise.

- If you feel, as I hope you do, that the contemporary manager's primary job is to shepherd your organization's best resource—people—then look for ways to cut costs other than letting your people overwork.

In Conclusion

If you can successfully make the distinction between hard work and compulsive work—and help your employees to do the same—both you and your organization are on the way to a healthier and more balanced life-style.

- ***For additional information, see:***

  Chapter 22. Performance Appraisal—Who Needs It?
  Chapter 25. Managerial Stress Management

∇ Workaholic Assessments

SELF-ASSESSMENT

Scale: **5-Never 4-Seldom 3-Occasionally 2-Usually 1-Always** (circle one)

1. I take work home evenings and/or weekends. 5 4 3 2 1
2. I feel uneasy or guilty if I'm not working. 5 4 3 2 1
3. I work late more frequently than my co-workers. 5 4 3 2 1
4. I play as hard as I work. 5 4 3 2 1
5. I avoid delegating work to others because no one else can do it quite right. 5 4 3 2 1
6. I become restless or uneasy on vacation. 5 4 3 2 1
7. Most of my reading is work-related. 5 4 3 2 1
8. I expect others to put in as many hours as I do. 5 4 3 2 1
9. I communicate better with my co-workers than with family or friends. 5 4 3 2 1
10. I find it difficult to relax. 5 4 3 2 1
11. I tend to schedule more and more activities into less and less time. 5 4 3 2 1
12. I work under a great deal of tension. 5 4 3 2 1
13. I equate success with hard work. 5 4 3 2 1
14. I have difficulty becoming involved with activities other than my job. 5 4 3 2 1
15. I would rather be at work than most other places. 5 4 3 2 1
16. My family and friends comment or complain about how much I work. 5 4 3 2 1
17. Those who know me well would say that I'm a perfectionist. 5 4 3 2 1
18. I work harder than most others in my organization or line of work. 5 4 3 2 1
19. I find myself working when I could be relaxing. 5 4 3 2 1
20. I take pleasure in telling others how hard or long I work. 5 4 3 2 1

continued

Workaholic Assessment, continued.

Note: Pay special attention to those items which you have circled in the 1-2 area, for these are most indicative of a tendency towards workaholism. If you wish to "kick the habit" of workaholism, these are the most likely areas in which to start.

SATISFACTION ASSESSMENT

Scale: **Totally satisfied - 100% ------- 0% - Totally dissatisfied**

Assess for satisfaction these areas of your life that you may be avoiding with work. The areas that score low may be the areas that need more of your time and energy, not your job.

_____ **Family life** _____ **Social life** _____ **Parenting** _____ **Friendships**

_____ **Leisure time** _____ **Close personal relationships**

JOB ASSESSMENT

Scale: **T (True) or F (False)**

Respond to this statement: **I work longer than normal hours because...**

___ 1. I'm slow or inefficient.

___ 2. I want to impress: __boss __co-workers __friends __family.

___ 3. I ___want ___need to make more money.

___ 4. I'm not well-organized.

___ 5. I have too many job-related responsibilities.

___ 6. We are short-staffed: ___temporarily ___permanently.

___ 7. I have inadequate assistance.

___ 8. We have insufficient budget to add more help.

___ 9. It is considered "normal" in this ___organization ___industry.

___ 10. Work gives me more satisfaction than almost anything else.

Note: Look carefully at those items you marked True. Although you may not be actually addicted to work for its own sake, these are the job areas that may require your immediate attention if you are to avoid excessive stress and potential burnout.

∇ 22. Performance Appraisal—Who Needs It?

Use every man after his desert, and who should 'scape whipping?
—*William Shakespeare*

Some managers contend that performance appraisals are like cleaning a teenager's room: everyone wants the results, but nobody wants to do it. Recent surveys indicate that 75 to 85 percent of American organizations now use one type of performance appraisal system or another. But why? Why would an organization burden itself when other studies show that most appraisal systems are considered less than 50 percent effective by their users? Is the performance appraisal just some recent organizational development fad, invented by human resource managers to enhance and perpetuate their jobs?

No, it's not. The first primitive performance appraisal system in industry was apparently used in the early 1800s by a canny Scotsman, Robert Owen, who hung a painted wooden cube over each work station in his cotton mills denoting the operator's "deportment." Performance appraisals were begun in the United States in the army in 1813 and introduced into the federal government in 1842. They came into use with industrial workers after World War I, but were not widely used with managers until after World War II.

But why use them? What function do they serve beyond keeping the personnel department and managers swamped with paperwork? Basically, performance appraisals serve several different functions:

- Provide input into administrative decisions, including salary adjustments, retention, job responsibilities, and promotions.
- Develop employees, especially in the areas of higher performance, motivation, and goal-setting.
- Identify training needs by locating employee skill deficiencies as early as possible.
- Help in planning future human resource development strategies based on

the level of talented and skilled people moving up the organizational ladder.

- Provide legal documentation of performance problems of marginal and poorly performing employees.

This is quite a load of functions for a system that has not been radically changed since World War II, when it was only expected to provide information to personnel departments for salary adjustments. How are performance appraisal systems holding up under the burden of modern demands?

Not very well, apparently. For example, a recent survey of 360 managers in 190 organizations found that 29 percent of those surveyed reported almost no rewards from their last performance appraisal, and most indicated that there had been no identification of ways to improve their performance, or any planned follow-up.

Other studies report similar findings. Why? What has gone wrong with a managerial activity that is used by the great majority of organizations? There seem to be several problems that stand in the way of performance appraisals being as effective in practice as they are in theory:

∇ They take time—not as long as it takes to maintain the performance of the company pickup truck, but some organizations are still having difficulty sorting out their priorities between maintaining the performance of equipment and maintaining the performance of people.

∇ Almost all performance appraisal systems are managed by the employee's immediate superior, yet a manager may not be in the best position to

evaluate the employee's performance. Studies indicate that managers often spend as little as 10 percent of their week in the working presence of any given employee. Appraisal systems that include input from the employee's co-workers, customers, or others that have contact on a day-to-day basis provide a more balanced source of appraisal information.

∇ Many managers have had little or no training in the skills necessary for conducting effective performance appraisals: data-gathering, performance record-keeping, coaching, setting developmental goals, or eliciting employee involvement in the process. In fact, one study found that eliciting employee involvement was one of the least likely skills possessed by the typical manager.

One of the first steps in setting up a performance appraisal system is to train the appropriate managers in the process, and then have them train their employees.

∇ Performance appraisals on an annual basis are very time-removed from the events and performance they are appraising. As a result, an undue amount of attention is often paid to the most recent aspects of the employee's performance.

Also, the infrequent nature of many appraisal systems, along with marginal follow-up, seriously diminishes the impact of the appraisal on an employee's performance. Many experienced managers feel that daily feedback and coaching have a much greater effect on employee performance than an annual review. Lee Iacocca, chairman of Chrysler Corporation, is a strong advocate of quarterly appraisals, from top to bottom of his staff.

∇ Many systems are outmoded, inadequate, or inaccurate. For example, many systems are still using the "trait rating" system in which employees are rated on such things as neatness, accuracy, or assertiveness. The fact that those traits may have no bearing on the employee's job description is ignored in some appraisal systems.

∇ Some characteristics of an employee—sex, race, performance level, age, position in the organization, job classification, and personality—can all influence the performance appraisal rating. A well-designed system will attempt to minimize these differences.

∇ Since most jobs can much more easily be rated than measured—how *well* you do, as opposed to how *much* you do—most appraisal rating systems are highly subjective, no matter how the numbering systems are structured. Of course, the more subjective the rating, the greater the chance for distortion.

Also, in a culture that is inclined to sue first and ask questions later, the more subjective a system is, the more likely it is eventually to end up in court.

∇ Current research also indicates that the characteristics of those who use the system—their training, appraisal and coaching skill, for example—may make much more difference in the effectiveness of a given system than the design of the system itself. It's like my getting on the tennis court with John McEnroe: the brand of racket I use isn't going to have a very significant effect on the outcome.

Improving the System and Process

Both experience and research seem to indicate that the most effective performance appraisal systems have five elements in common:

∇ **Informed participants at all levels.** This includes the use and support of performance appraisals by top management in the organization. This also means that all participants, top to bottom, know the hows and whys of the system, as well as having been trained in the necessary skills to make it work.

∇ **System looks at past, present, and future.** The appraisal takes into account how well the employee met previously set goals and targets, what the current state of his or her performance is, and sets new personal and professional goals for the next appraisal period.

∇ **System clearly defines what is expected.** The system itself contains clear indications of what is expected of the participants in regard to using the system and job performance criteria.

∇ **Process is separate from financial negotiations.** If the major intent of the system is to improve employee performance, it has been found to be more effective to separate that process from scheduled financial negotiations. A performance-oriented system works best if it is a coaching and mentoring relationship, whereas financial negotiations can be an adversarial relationship. Professional sports teams learned a long time ago not to have the coach or field manager handle player salary negotiations, just as the players learned to let an agent handle their end of salary issues. Money can motivate or reinforce high performance, but negotiating money issues can often get in the way.

∇ **System contains ongoing reinforcement.** A system that has no provisions for ongoing reinforcement of the goals and plans decided on during the appraisal session won't be much more effective in improving employee performance than New Year's resolutions. Reinforcement is the way that most significant behavior changes occur, and the effective appraisal system needs to have it as an integral component.

For example, even a very brief weekly or monthly update with the employee's manager can reinforce progress toward agreed-upon goals.

Manager's Role

How can we as managers make the best use of performance appraisals to ensure an experience that is productive for manager and employee alike? Following are several things that you can do:

- ∇ **Increase your performance appraisal skills.** If no training program is available, there are now a number of good books on the subject. Richard Olson's *Performance Appraisal,* David DeVries, Ann Morrison, Sandra Shullman, and Michael Gerlach's *Performance Appraisal on the Line,* and Howard Smith and Paul Brouwer's *Performance Appraisal and Human Development* can get you started.

- ∇ **Establish goals for the performance appraisal system itself.** Be sure that the system itself is performing the functions that you and your employees want it to achieve. If you're not sure that it is meeting everyone's needs, ask them. (See the assessment at the end of this chapter.) In your session with each employee, include mutual diagnosis and planning for any areas of weakness in the system. Organizational and employee needs change, and the system must be flexible enough to change along with them.

- ∇ **Relate ratings to employee's job description.** Be sure that any rating system you use relates directly to skills and attributes the employee needs to perform the job. The best appraisal systems rate job-related traits, behaviors, and performance outcomes.

- ∇ **Simplify any rating forms.** Experience indicates that in practice an overly complex system usually is ignored or treated superficially.

- ∇ **Establish specific employee performance criteria.** No measurement or rating system can in any way compensate for inadequate or vague performance criteria. Good performance criteria should allow anyone to answer the question, "How would I know one if I saw one?" In other words, if a stranger walked into your office, what would he or she see an employee doing that would identify that employee with a given job description?

  Another way to determine job descriptions is to imagine that you have a room full of people, half of whom have a given job description. What are they doing that would allow someone to distinguish one group from the other?

- ∇ **Use multiple rating sources,** especially if you do not have ample opportunity to observe an employee's job performance. Other sources of information may include co-workers, clients or customers, other managers, subordinates, or the employee's self-assessment. U.S. Army studies show that averaged ratings done by the employee's co-workers are generally more accurate than those done by the direct supervisor. Accuracy is further improved when the co-workers' ratings are done anonymously.

In Conclusion

Employee performance appraisals can range from an effective enhancement of job performance to a demoralizing disaster. Today's more highly educated, sophisticated employee wants to know more about his or her performance, and if the formal system is not adequate, the employee may be forced to jury-rig an informal system to provide it. A manager's attention to the appraisal basics of good performance information gathering and honest employee feedback can help make the formal system pay large dividends in improved employee performance and morale.

∇ ***For additional information, see:***

Chapter 16. P = SOME: The Performance Equation
Chapter 18. Poor Performance Comes In for Analysis
Chapter 24. To Train, or Not to Train?

∇ Quarterly Performance Appraisal

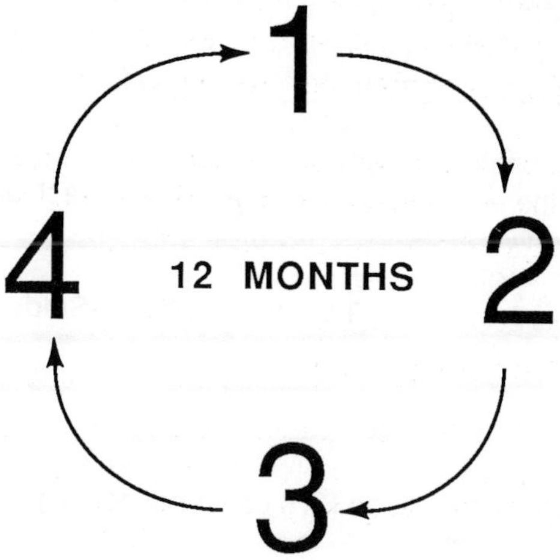

Following are suggested agendas for quarterly performance appraisal sessions. These may be on any yearly cycle that is appropriate for the individuals involved and the organization. When both manager and employee are properly prepared, the sessions need last no more than an hour, and often less.

SESSION	TASKS
1.	**Professional development**--plans for next six months. **Job feedback**--level of performance over past three months. **Job planning** --goals and specific plans for next three months. **Manager feedback**--feedback from employee on managerial performance.
2.	**Salary negotiations**--salary for the next 12 months. **Personal development**--plans for next six months. **Job feedback**--level of performance over past three months. **Job planning**--goals and specific plans for next three months.
3.	**Professional development**--plans for next six months. **Job feedback**--level of performance over past three months. **Job planning**--goals and specific plans for next three months. **Manager feedback**--feedback from employee on managerial performance.
4.	**Personal development**--plans for next six months **Job feedback**--level of performance over past three months. **Job planning**--goals and specific plans for next three months. **Career development**--progress report and plans for next 12 months.

Date ______________

MANAGER

∇ Performance Appraisal Assessment

Directions: Place a square around a number to indicate how important you think that function is for an effective appraisal system.
Place a circle around a number to indicate your estimation of how frequently your present appraisal system performs each function.

Suggestion: Have your employees fill out the "Employee" version. Place their averaged scores in the appropriate places and compare their perceptions of the appraisal system with yours.

Scale: **5-Always 4-Usually 3-Occasionally 2-Seldom 1-Never**

Functions		**Employees** □ ○
1. Administrative personnel information ("It's company policy").	5 4 3 2 1	___ ___
2. Increase employee's understanding of job role and employer's expectations.	5 4 3 2 1	___ ___
3. Improve employee morale.	5 4 3 2 1	___ ___
4. Uphold professional standards.	5 4 3 2 1	___ ___
5. Increase employee's self-awareness of job performance.	5 4 3 2 1	___ ___
6. Maintain discipline.	5 4 3 2 1	___ ___
7. Reward superior performance.	5 4 3 2 1	___ ___
8. Produce competition among employees.	5 4 3 2 1	___ ___
9. Reinforce boss-employee relationship.	5 4 3 2 1	___ ___
10. Improve employee performance skills.	5 4 3 2 1	___ ___
11. Weed out inferior employees.	5 4 3 2 1	___ ___
12. Increase employee's self-confidence and self-esteem.	5 4 3 2 1	___ ___
13. Inform supervisors/upper management of employee's performance.	5 4 3 2 1	___ ___
14. Basis for awards and/or promotions.	5 4 3 2 1	___ ___
15. Improve supervisor-employee relationship.	5 4 3 2 1	___ ___
16. Basis for changing financial compensation.	5 4 3 2 1	___ ___
Other: ______________________________	5 4 3 2 1	___ ___

Date _______________

EMPLOYEE

∇ Performance Appraisal Assessment

Directions: Place a square around a number to indicate how important you think that function is for an effective appraisal system.
Place a circle around a number to indicate your estimation of how frequently your present appraisal system performs each function.

Scale: **5-Always 4-Usually 3-Occasionally 2-Seldom 1-Never**

Functions

1. Administrative personnel information ("It's company policy").	5 4 3 2 1
2. Increase employee's understanding of job role and employer's expectations.	5 4 3 2 1
3. Improve employee morale.	5 4 3 2 1
4. Uphold professional standards.	5 4 3 2 1
5. Increase employee's self-awareness of job performance.	5 4 3 2 1
6. Maintain discipline.	5 4 3 2 1
7. Reward superior performance.	5 4 3 2 1
8. Produce competition among employees.	5 4 3 2 1
9. Reinforce "boss-employee" relationship.	5 4 3 2 1
10. Improve employee performance skills.	5 4 3 2 1
11. Weed out inferior employees.	5 4 3 2 1
12. Increase employee's self-confidence and self-esteem.	5 4 3 2 1
13. Inform supervisors/upper management of employee's performance.	5 4 3 2 1
14. Basis for awards and/or promotions.	5 4 3 2 1
15. Improve supervisor-employee relationship.	5 4 3 2 1
16. Basis for changing financial compensation.	5 4 3 2 1
Other: ____	5 4 3 2 1

What changes would you like to see in the present appraisal system? ____________________

____

Date ______________

∇ Performance Appraisals Checklist

1. What methods are currently used to evaluate employee performance?

___ Supervisor ratings
___ Self-ratings
___ Co-worker ratings
___ Outside consultant ratings
___ Other: ______________________________

2. What feedback does the employee get from the appraisal process?

___ None
___ Rating grade/letter/number
___ Written critique by rater
___ Verbal critique by rater
___ Conference with supervisor
___ Other: ______________________________

3. How frequently does a scheduled performance appraisal occur?

___ Annually ___ Semi-annually ___ Quarterly ___ Monthly ___ Weekly

4. At what point in the appraisal process are the evaluation criteria to be used communicated to the employee?______________________________

5. Who determines these evaluation criteria?

___ Top management
___ Immediate supervisors
___ Co-workers
___ Personnel department
___ Industry standards
___ The employee
___ Outside consultants
___ Other: ______________________________

6. Who do you think benefits <u>most</u> from the current appraisal process? (mark an '**X**') Who do you think benefits <u>least</u> ? (mark a ✔)

___ Top management
___ Immediate supervisors
___ The employee
___ Co-workers
___ Other: ______________________________

∇ 23. Contrlling Qualitey Conttrol

If the above title caused you to squirm, quiver, and reach for the correction fluid, read on. You're in the right place.

This past spring, after careful research and sale-watching, I bought a propane-fired barbecue from a local hardware store. The carton said it was built by one of America's foremost barbecue manufacturers, but I suspect that it was in fact built by saboteurs. After an assembly operation suitable for a Grand Prix race car, I found that the igniter that starts the whole thing didn't work, and the grill was miswelded and wouldn't let the top close.

I returned the offending parts, and the store manager graciously gave me another grill and ordered an igniter. On the way to my car the replacement grill's welds came apart in my hands. Back to the store and the manager. Graciously replaced grill number three was also miswelded, but at least allowed the top to close. I took it. With this firm, quality control was obviously *not* "job one."

But what to do for our dinner guests, arriving shortly to enjoy charbroiled Milwaukee bratwursts from the new (nonstarting) barbecue? Fortunately, I remembered a portable charcoal grill on sale at another store. I bought it, along with the necessary hand-blackening supplies, which I had hoped to be done with forever. Back to a tried-and-true technology, I reasoned.

Wrong. When I took the new charcoal grill out of the box, I found the top held down with a rubber band—the latch was about to part company from the firebox. It probably didn't leave the factory that way (well, maybe), so I can only assume that some other hapless consumer had discovered it first and returned it, and the store had put it back in stock. We used it anyway.

Quality control had come in last again.

In marked contrast, a few days later, I received a call from the service manager of the local auto dealer where my car had been serviced the week before. "Problem?" I asked, fearing a recall notification that my expensive new parts were about to fall off the car. "No", the manager replied, "just calling to be sure our service was O.K." Now, *that's* quality control. And that dealer had earned my business for as long as they keep it up. I can't say the same for the other two stores.

Quality in the Marketplace

As competition becomes tougher, quality control becomes an increasingly important issue for managers, whether their business is product- or service-oriented. Skill training is getting increasingly sophisticated in service industries, while computers are doing the same for products. The real competitive edge is now becoming the quality with which the people in the organization carry out what they and the new technologies know how to do. With other buying variables more equalized, quality—how well the design of the product or service is implemented—is the new primary buying criterion.

Improving Quality

As a manager, what can you do to help quality be "job one" in your organization? Here are some suggestions:

∇ **Recognize that most employees want to do a good job.** Using the P = SOME performance equation (Performance = Skills + Opportunity + Motivation + Environment) as a model, it is up to you as manager to ensure that employees have the skills, opportunity, resources, and supportive environment to do quality work.

∇ **Make quality tangible.** Be certain that your employees realize that quality is a tangible attribute of your product or service. Be clear in your own mind about whether, in a crunch, you will opt for quality or quantity—and then be equally clear with your employees. A mixed message from management regarding quality or quantity usually marks the death of quality control.

∇ **Educate employees as to what you mean by quality.** Too many managers assume that their employees already know what quality is in their product or service. As a quality-oriented manager, you cannot afford to make that assumption.

Ask yourself and your employees such questions as:

- What does quality in our product or service look like?
- How do our customers recognize quality?
- How might our customers feel when they receive it?
- What stands between us and achieving the highest possible quality? What can we do to get the barriers out of the way?
- How much would getting it right the first time be worth to us? What gets in the way of that, and what can we do about it?

Once you and your employees are very clear about the answers to such questions, you can develop specific standards from which to work and manage, and formulate the plans with which to implement those standards.

∇ **Get feedback from your customers.** Even if your customer is the department on the other side of the office partition, find out their perception of the quality of work you deliver to them. Don't assume that just because "They haven't complained lately" there aren't things you and your work unit can do to improve the quality of your output to them. Even small improvements in quality all along a linear process can make an enormous improvement in the final product.

∇ **Give feedback to your suppliers.** Tell anyone who supplies materials or services for your work unit where they stand with regard to their quality. If their quality is good, your unit's feedback will help to reinforce and maintain it. If their quality is not good, your supplier needs to know about it, for it also adversely affects *your* unit's performance and quality of output.

∇ **Make quality a part of your work culture.** Since quality involves every facet of an organization's operations, it becomes almost unmanageable unless it also becomes an integral part of the organization's culture—a part of everyone's belief system, from the top down and the bottom up.

Accomplishing this in an organization may involve everything from posters on the walls to the performance appraisal system. Building a quality-oriented organization requires more than just a Quality Awareness Week once a year. It requires reminders and reinforcements—visual, verbal, and written. A class operation is much more than skin deep.

∇ **Test, test, test!** Designing, building, and selling new products and services can be very exciting—it's where the action is. On the other hand, making sure they work—and keep on working—is often an unsung, laborious task. It requires patience, determination, commitment, and the ability to stick to one's guns in the face of pressures to "get it out the door."

∇ **Monitor quality on a regular basis.** Whether your work unit produces a product or a service, for internal or external customers, set measurable or observable quality standards and check them regularly.

The frequency with which you need to monitor your quality is a direct function of how frequently your product can change. For example, the quality of output from a high-speed printing press needs to be monitored constantly, but the quality of an engineering design process may need to be monitored only on a project-by-project basis.

∇ **Get agreement on quality standards from all departments.** Regarding quality control, there is usually a never-ending struggle between marketing and production over the standards met before a product or service goes on the market, with other departments sometimes caught in the crossfire.

Both positions are understandable. Marketing has already sold the new product almost before it's off the drawing board, with delivery promised for yesterday—at the latest. "Never mind all that testing," marketing demands. "If something's really wrong, we'll fix it in the field!" And why not push to have it yesterday? For those in marketing, the house payments and kids' shoes are riding on those sales. Promising customers the moon—and then delivering it ASAP—is what made them successful. From marketing we hear, "Production would do the same if they were working on commission."

On the other hand, production—which is usually not on commission—is successful by turning out a product or service with at least enough quality that it did not generate bushels of irate letters dumped on the CEO's desk. That quality is usually achieved by taking the time to do adequate and thorough testing before releasing it to the market.

And so we have the classic standoff: marketing wants it yesterday, while production wants to take time to refine it, to the point where marketing is sure it will be obsolete before it ever hits the market.

The first step in getting agreement from such opposing viewpoints is to help both sides realize that everyone involved has a common goal: to bring to market a product or service with the highest possible quality, at a competitive price and with competitive timing.

To do that, marketing has to realize that there are no magical shortcuts to high quality. Production has to realize that there are tides and currents in the marketplace that must be taken advantage of if the product or service is to be sold. Cooperation is improved to the extent that both needs are acknowledged and fully understood by all concerned.

In practice, there are several ways of improving the situation:

- Some firms have found that placing production in a bonus pool generated by sales is added incentive to get the product or service to market as quickly as possible.
- Training the organization's sales force to sell the product or service based on quality and value, rather than on low price, helps marketing to perceive quality as a saleable component of the product. If quality wasn't a tangible asset to a product, Mercedes-Benz would have been out of the automobile business years ago, followed by Porsche, Ferrari, and a number of others for which a major sales feature is quality, not price.
- It also helps if production and marketing are aware of each other's

problems firsthand. Getting production people out into the field with marketing, and marketing people spending time working in production, can prove to be time well spent in improving cooperation and communications.

∇ **Reward quality work.** It is amazing how many employees do not know how well they are doing their jobs. A manager cannot expect quality as an outcome when employees have no specific feedback on their performance. It's like trying to play golf at night—you only know that you hit the ball *somewhere.* That approach does not develop championship-quality golfers or employees.

∇ **Practice what you preach.** If high quality is to be achieved with your products or services, it needs to be a consistent concern throughout your organization. If you want to set an example for employees of quality awareness and performance, you'll need to monitor internal quality just as closely as you do products or services being delivered to your customers. Quality is seldom generated in an environment of "Do as we say, not as we do."

In Conclusion

Presenting your customers with a quality product or service is a multilevel process. You need employees who fully realize what quality is and how to deliver it, and who then get quality feedback from the manager about how well they're accomplishing it.

Especially when they're doing it *right.*

∇ ***For additional information, see:***

Chapter 5. Growing the Corporate Culture

Date__________

∇ Quality Control Assessment

Directions: Place a square around a number to indicate how important you think that item is for effective quality control.
Place a circle around a number to indicate your estimation of the current situation with regard to quality control.

Scale: **High/Excellent - 5 4 3 2 1 - Low/Poor**

Items		**Employees** ☐ ○
1. The organization's overall attitude toward quality control.	5 4 3 2 1	____
2. Measurable and/or observable quality criteria or standards.	5 4 3 2 1	____
3. The organization's attitude toward correcting products or services which are not up to par.	5 4 3 2 1	____
4. The attitude of upper management toward quality.	5 4 3 2 1	____
5. Direct supervisor's and manager's concern with quality.	5 4 3 2 1	____
6. A formal quality control system.	5 4 3 2 1	____

Scale: **5-Always 4-Usually 3-Occasionally 2-Seldom 1-Never**

7. Product/service comes before marketing expediency.	5 4 3 2 1	____
8. The quality of supplier input is monitored.	5 4 3 2 1	____
9. Feedback is given to suppliers regarding input quality.	5 4 3 2 1	____
10. The quality of output to customers is monitored.	5 4 3 2 1	____
11. Feedback is requested from customers about output quality.	5 4 3 2 1	____
12. Specific plans and strategies in operation to improve present quality of product/service.	5 4 3 2 1	____

The quality of products/service in the past 12 months:

Very high - 10 9 8 7 6 5 4 3 2 1 - Very low (circle one)

Compared to the previous 12 months, this is: (check one)

Great improvement__ Some improvement__ Same__ Less__

Note: Circled items in the 1-2 area may require attention to improve your quality control situation. Also give close attention to items in which the circle is two or more numbers to the right of the square as this indicates a gap between importance and the present situation.

Date___________ EMPLOYEE

∇ Quality Control Assessment

Directions: Place a square around a number to indicate how important you think that item is for effective quality control.
Place a circle around a number to indicate your estimation of the current situation with regard to quality control.

Scale: **High/Excellent - 5 4 3 2 1 - Low/Poor**

Items

1. The organization's overall attitude toward quality control.	5 4 3 2 1
2. Measurable and/or observable quality criteria or standards.	5 4 3 2 1
3. The organization's attitude toward correcting products or services which are not up to par.	5 4 3 2 1
4. The attitude of upper management toward quality.	5 4 3 2 1
5. Direct supervisor's and manager's concern with quality.	5 4 3 2 1
6. A formal quality control system.	5 4 3 2 1

Scale: **5-Always 4-Usually 3-Occasionally 2-Seldom 1-Nevcr**

7. Product/service comes before marketing expediency.	5 4 3 2 1
8. The quality of supplier input is monitored.	5 4 3 2 1
9. Feedback is given to suppliers regarding input quality.	5 4 3 2 1
10. The quality of output to customers is monitored.	5 4 3 2 1
11. Feedback is requested from customers about output quality.	5 4 3 2 1
12. Specific plans and strategies in operation to improve present quality of product/service.	5 4 3 2 1

The quality of products/service in the past 12 months:

Very high - 10 9 8 7 6 5 4 3 2 1 - Very low (circle one)

Compared to the previous 12 months, this is: (check one)

Great improvement__ Some improvement__ Same__ Less__

Date ______

Quality Control Assessment

Directions: Place a circle around a number to indicate how [illegible] you [illegible] the following quality control [illegible].

Place a [illegible] around a number to indicate your [illegible] with the [illegible] related to quality control.

Scale: [illegible] High/Excellent 5 4 3 2 1 Low/Poor

Items

1. The organization's overall attitude toward quality control [illegible] 5 4 3 2 1
2. [illegible] and [illegible] quality control [illegible]
3. The organization's [illegible] to correct [illegible] problems [illegible]
4. The [illegible]
5. [illegible] with quality [illegible]

Scale: [illegible] Always [illegible] Frequently [illegible] Occasionally 2 Seldom [illegible] Never

7. Product/service quality [illegible] expectations [illegible]
8. The quality of [illegible]
9. Feedback [illegible] quality [illegible]
10. The quality of output to customers is monitored.
11. [illegible] quality
12. [illegible] procedures [illegible] to improve [illegible] quality [illegible]

[illegible]

Very High 10 [illegible] Very Low

Compared to [illegible] months [illegible]

Great Improvement [illegible] Some Improvement [illegible] Same [illegible] Decline

∇ 24. To Train, or Not to Train?

This season, in a moment of athletic nostalgia perhaps only the middle-aged can fully understand, I agreed to pitch for our company softball team. (The last time I pitched in organized softball was before a couple of my teammates were born.) Being in the middle of the diamond, I could watch everyone's performance, much as a manager might observe employees.

Most of the time, however, I watched well-hit softballs headed toward the outfield, untouched by human hands (including, in all fairness, mine). This was usually followed by a steady parade of opposing baserunners that closely resembled the start of the Boston Marathon. One tactless spectator observed that our defensive efforts seemed more like middle-aged jazz-ercise without the music.

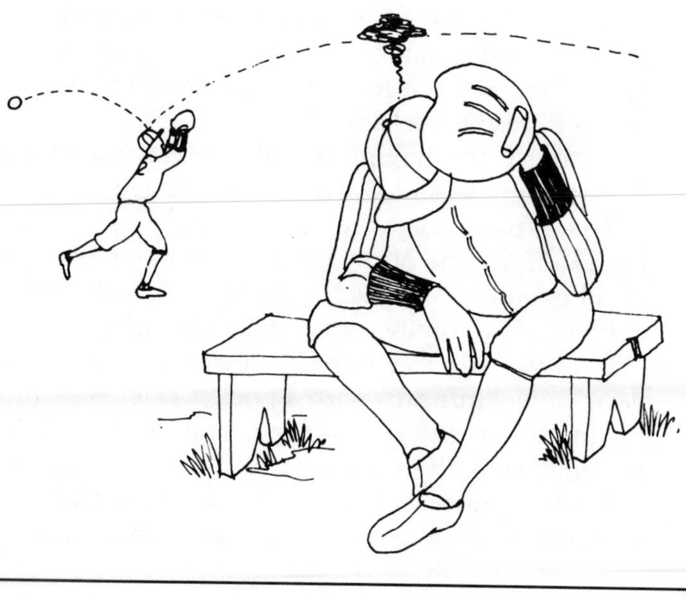

What was our performance problem? To put it simply, we seemed to have coupled an inept defense with an inadequate offense. As a result, rather than your run-of-the-mill softball scores, our numbers were more in line with what you'd expect if the Chicago Bears played your high school alma mater. In the Super Bowl. For money.

And what of our long-suffering manager? He was frustrated. So frustrated, in fact, that he once threw his glove over the outfield fence in disgust and then had to climb over after it. Fortunately the umpires thought he was chasing another of our opposition's frequent home runs, or it might have jeopardized our chances for winning the league's sportsmanship award. We felt we had a good shot at it for just showing up, week after endless week.

Our manager's dilemma was much the same as that of many of his managerial counterparts in any organization where poor performance is a problem: to train, or not to train? Being of sound mind—at least off the field—he used a training needs analysis to examine his unenviable situation:

∇ **Step 1.** Since performance is made up of part skill and part motivation, which part was causing more of the problem? Since it was obvious to even the most dazed bleacher bums that we were doing our best, insufficient motivation wasn't the problem. Therefore lack of skill had to be the reason.

∇ **Step 2.** Since skill includes both knowledge and experience, which of these seemed to be lacking? Unbelievable as it may have seemed from our box scores, most of our team did know which base to throw the ball to (having someone there to catch it was something else) and where the strike zone was (even if they frequently ignored it). So the performance problem boiled down to experience. In this case, *recent* experience: practice.

∇ **Step 3.** How much was the problem costing us? In our case, not practicing—starting a training program—probably cost us more runs per game than were scored against the St. Louis Cardinals all season.

On the other hand—so what? We were out there for fun, exercise, and camaraderie. Are a few (lucky) runs worth training time taken away from our families or work?

For our team, having completed the above three steps, we decided "no". The training wasn't worth the cost in personal time.

That is not always the case in the business or organizational environment. For example, one of my clients was having a severe turnover problem with middle- and upper-level managers but was reluctant to expand the budget sufficiently to include appropriate training.

In answering the step 3 question, "How much is the problem costing you?" a few minutes with a pocket calculator produced a conservative cost estimate of nearly $500,000 per year! It was quickly evident that appropriate training would be a real bargain.

If you're uncertain about initiating a training program, take the same three analysis steps as our beleagured manager. It will help you answer the bottom-line question: Is training the solution, and is it worth the cost? Unfortunately for our manager, even those three steps didn't produce a fleet-footed, sure-handed, hard-hitting center fielder.

Questions About Training

Once a training needs analysis indicates that training may be the appropriate answer to an organizational problem, there are a number of questions that managers ask. This asking is appropriate. Given the cost of training in time, materials, and instruction, managers often don't ask enough questions before starting a training program or curriculum.

Here are some of the training questions that managers frequently ask, or should ask, before investing in training:

∇ **Is it more cost-effective to train present employees, or to replace them with people who are already trained?** Even if the new employees are completely trained, the cost of employee turnover is greater than is generally realized. Unless the organization is moving in directions that would require extensive retraining, it is usually more cost-effective to train your present employees. This is especially true if you've developed high-performance teams.

∇ **What modes of training are available, and which should I use?** With the accelerated development of training-related technology, there is now a wide variety of training delivery methods available. These are the primary ones, along with some of their advantages and disadvantages:

Self-study. This classic approach is now available in everything from traditional paper-pencil-and-text programs to sophisticated interactive video. Self-study can be used anywhere, depending on the media chosen, and allows learners to proceed at their own pace. Its disadvantages are that there are no other people involved, which makes acquiring skills in some areas more difficult, and that some personality styles are less comfortable studying alone. With the rising cost of travel and classroom training, some form of self-study is probably the wave of the future.

Seminar/classroom. This is probably still the most common form of organizational training. It can be reasonably priced if the participants are not highly paid, but can be very expensive if the participants are also expensive—something too often overlooked in determining training costs. In other words, although the cost of the materials and instruction may be the same, training fifty-dollar-a-day employees for three days costs the organization much less than training two-hundred-dollar-a-day employees for the same length of time.

As instruction, travel, and material costs continue to rise, managers are looking for lower-cost alternatives to bringing everyone together in the same room. Rapid advances in lower cost telecommunication appear to offer one answer, bringing one instructor to many classes simultaneously. Interactive video coupled with small discussion groups is another answer, as it requires no instructor at all.

On-the-job training. This was probably the original form of training, when our ancestral forebears were taught the fine art of sabertooth tiger clubbing or laundry-on-the-rocks scrubbing. With managers' increasing skills in coaching and mentoring, it is still one of the strongest ways to produce applied job skills. Its disadvantages are that it requires managers' time away from other responsibilities, and the typical one-on-one format is an expensive use of time.

∇ **Should we purchase training programs from vendors, or develop them ourselves?** This depends upon four factors:

1. *Which mode will you use?* Development costs for modes such as interactive video can be very high, whereas the cost of developing short classroom courses may be relatively low, although still not cheap.
2. *What size is your organization?* If you are large enough to have the resources and will have sufficient participants in the program over which to amortize the costs, then you may be ahead financially to develop your own training. But crunch your numbers very, very carefully!
3. *What are the time considerations?* Do you need it quickly, or can you afford to take your time? Will you be using the training over a long period of time, or is it to be a one-time event? Would this be the best use of your developer's time?
4. *Does your training need to be highly specialized?* If you know more about the subject than anyone else, it may make sense to develop your own training program. Beyond that, you may be able to sell it to others, if it is not a proprietary subject.

Generally, developing programs *always* takes longer—and costs more—than you predict. Even such large organizations as General Motors, IBM, DuPont, and Bank of America rely on outside vendors to supply important components of their internal training curriculums.

∇ **Should we use off-the-shelf generic programs, or tailor them to meet our specific needs?** If you can afford it, by all means tailor your training programs. Well-tailored programs are generally more meaningful to your employees, help you get at problems that are specific to your organization, and can generate a greater sense of "ownership."

On the other hand, tailoring can also be expensive, depending on the training method used and the extent to which you tailor it. Paper-and-pencil materials are obviously much cheaper to tailor than interactive video.

∇ **For what levels in the organization is training most effective?** Well-designed training can be effective at all levels of an organization, although upper-level managers used to think that they were "beyond that." Their thinking seemed to be, "If I didn't know that already, I wouldn't be here." With the increased complexity of managing modern organizations—especially in the area of "growing people"—this is changing. CEOs are now as likely to be involved in training programs as entry-level employees.

In terms of cost-effectiveness, training can be more efficient with upper-level managers if they make expensive decisions. For example, if it costs a thousand dollars a day to train a manager who is making hundred-thousand-dollar decisions, the realized savings from successful training can be far greater than with five-hundred-dollar-a-day training costs for someone who is making thousand-dollar decisions. These cost considerations help to offset the added cost of the participants' time in upper-level management training.

∇ **How can I get the most for my training dollars?** There are a number of ways to be sure that you get maximum value for your training dollars. Here are several areas that in my experience are frequently overlooked:

Work with the trainers. Let them know the background of the problem that the training is intended to solve, what you want as training outcomes, and what follow-up managerial activities they suggest for you to reinforce the training.

Position the training. Let the participants know, well in advance, the purpose and reason for the training, what the training will require of them, what they can do ahead of time to enhance the training experience, and what benefits they can expect from participating.

I have had participants enter a program, having been notified by their manager to show up at the last minute, not knowing whether they were being rewarded or punished! That is not the way to get maximum value from your training dollars.

Use follow-up. Even the simplest and most basic training program should not be considered a one-time event. The very nature of training can only supply participants with awareness, knowledge, and a limited amount of practice. The real application of the skill is learned when the participant returns to the job. Without adequate follow-up, much of the value of the training is lost.

Several methods of follow-up are helpful:

- Meet with the participant's manager on a regular basis to discuss the application of the training until the manager feels the training has been adequately learned and applied.
- Hold review sessions on a regular basis, usually one to six months after the original training session, depending on the nature of the training.
- Set up small, informal discussion groups, with or without a set agenda, which meet to share experiences with the application of the training in their workplace.
- Have the participants prepare a report or demonstration of the training content to present to the rest of the work unit.
- Have the participants coach co-workers in the application of the new skill.

The last two follow-up methods—teaching or explaining the training to someone else—are two of the strongest methods of reinforcing learning.

Examples set by managers. Employees are quick to learn which side of their paycheck has the butter, and who continues to put it there. If managers don't model what is taught in a training program, the training is generally a waste of time and money. Employees will follow a manager's lead, even if it flies in the face of the most elaborate training, because the manager has the power.

If your managers aren't prepared to practice what is going to be taught in the training process, it is usually best to hold off the training until you can change the managers' behavior and attitudes. If the participants' managers have a "Do as I say, but not as I do" approach, it is unlikely to be a good training investment.

Generally, the best training investment occurs when the training is started at the highest applicable managerial level.

Obtain multiple outcomes. Well-planned training events can have multiple outcomes, if that is considered during the design or preparation stages. For example, a seminar course can not only teach a certain skill, but can also be the vehicle for team-building, reinforcing organizational purpose, organizational development, and a welcome break from normal routine. Because good training can be multilayered, it is important to work with the trainer to be sure that the full potential is utilized.

Use a curriculum approach. The best use of training dollars is usually obtained by looking at the overall picture and designing a series of training events, using appropriate training methods, that is a comprehensive approach. Band-Aid training cures for specific organizational ills are generally not a cost-effective use of your training budget. It is like using the emergency room as your only source of health care—stress-producing and expensive.

∇ **Your place or mine? Where should training occur?** There are several options when selecting the site for training to occur:

Everything in-house. There are distinct logistical advantages to having everything happen "at home," including using an in-house training instructor for seminar sessions. Costs are lower, the in-house instructor is more likely to know both the participants and the specifics of the problem being addressed, and it is easier for managers to monitor the process.

On the other hand, these same plus factors can also be negatives, if the nature of the training is such that sensitive issues may be raised. In that case, too much familiarity may be a problem, with participants not willing to share what's really on their minds.

Import the trainer. This is the best solution if you don't have the necessary in-house resources or want increased objectivity or confidentiality.

Take groups off-site. Although usually more expensive, this gets participants away from their normal distractions and daily patterns, allowing them to focus on the training issues. It can also offer a welcome break from the normal routine and, depending on the site, serve as a team-building reward.

Send individuals off-site. Sending employees to other locations for seminars, workshops, and conferences is generally the most expensive method of all, but may be the only thing to do if there are not enough training participants to make up an on-site group. Aside from that, it also has the advantage of giving the participants a chance to meet counterparts from other organizations and to expand their professional contacts and networks.

In short, where you conduct training is usually determined by the training method you select and the intended outcome. Just be sure to take into account all of the possible training benefits when you make this decision.

∇ **How can I assess the training outcomes?** This is one of the most frequently asked questions in the whole training area. It is often an indicator that the manager may not have been tracking performance very carefully in the first place. By and large, both remedial and preventive training are designed to change on-the-job behavior. If performance behavior hasn't been very well tracked all along, it makes it difficult to determine the impact of the training.

For remedial training—correcting something that isn't working—the assessment question boils down to another question: what were the symptoms or indicators that told you there was a problem in the first place? If those are well-documented, a positive change in those indicators will indicate that the training was helpful.

For example, if the problem indicator for a sales manager was a low sales closings to proposals ratio, then the thing to monitor after the training is the sales closing ratio.

Less obvious and harder to track than sales closing ratios are problems that managers may conclude stem from "poor attitude," such as lateness, excessive absenteeism, or sloppy work. Here again the problem needs to be broken down into observable behaviors: What would employees with a "poor attitude" be *doing*? To the extent that those behaviors change following training, other things remaining constant, the training can be considered successful.

It is almost impossible to measure the effectiveness of training if there is no adequate before and after evaluation of related behavior. Training that claims to improve team-building, attitude, creative problem-solving, motivation, and general employee malaise still requires the tracking of behavioral indicators before and after if it is to be considered successful.

In Conclusion

In a culture such as ours, undergoing an accelerated rate of change, there is no question but that ongoing training and education will always be an organizational fact of life. Recent adult education estimates indicate that there are now more adults in corporate training programs and various other programs than in all of the public schools combined. The only real question for the manager is how to make it cost-effective and pertinent to organizational and personal needs.

To accomplish those vital aims, I strongly suggest that managers spend sufficient time on the front end of the process to diagnose the situation and convert it to observable behaviors. Once that's accomplished, it is much easier to design and implement the training efficiently and to assess the training outcomes.

The fleet-footed center fielder comes later.

∇ ***For additional information, see:***

Chapter 16. P = SOME: The Performance Equation
Chapter 17. Team-Building for All Seasons
Chapter 19. Mapping Career Development
Chapter 22. Performance Appraisal—Who Needs It?

Date______________

∇ Cost of Training Assessment

Note: This assessment gives you the cost-per-participant of various instructional options. This may not be your only criteria for choosing a training program, but it is a basic one.

A. Program: ____

B. Intended outcomes: ______________________________________

____

____

C. Projected number of participants during budget period: ____________

COSTS

INSTRUCTION OPTIONS	Total development costs	Total trainer costs	Equipment costs	Course tuition	Additional materials	Total site costs	Misc. other costs (travel, etc)	**Total Cost of Instruction**	**Cost per Participant***
On-site--our trainer									
On-site--import trainer									
Vendor's program									
We develop program									
Seminar format									
Self-study									
Interactive video									
Individuals off-site									
Group off-site									

*** To calculate, divide Total Cost of Instruction by number of participants ("C").**

Date_______________

∇ Training Program Matrix

TRAINING PROGRAMS

EMPLOYEES											

LEGEND

Program needed and available.

Program not needed.

Program needed, but must acquire.

Program already taken.

∇ Instructions

Used together, the Cost of Training Assessment and the Training Program Matrix give you a simple yet efficient system to get maximum value from your training investment.

Cost of Training Assessment

Completing this assessment will give you the cost per participant for various training options. You can then decide which is the most cost-effective for your specific situation.

A. The title of the program or training situation you want to analyze.

B. The intended outcomes of the program . . . what you would like the student to come away with after the program is over. Focus on behaviors, and be as specific as possible.

C. The number of students you expect to attend the program during the period for which it is budgeted. If it is a one-time event, indicate it as such.

Instruction Options. Once you've decided which options you are going to consider and analyze, determine the costs and enter them in the appropriate columns under Costs.

Add the costs across from left to right to determine the total cost for each instruction option. Divide the total by the number of students you indicated in C and you will have the cost per student for each option.

Training Program Matrix

This matrix lets you see at a glance the training situation for each person in your work unit.

Employees. In this column list the names of employees whose training records you want to track.

Training Programs. List all the training programs your employees are likely to want or need.

Select the appropriate indicators from the Legend to show the training status of each employee with regard to each training program. (Use pencil so that the employees' training status can be easily changed.)

The completed matrix allows you to know at all times which employees need which training, as well as the availability of that training.

∇ 25. Managerial Stress Management

There may be no managerial skill that will do more to improve performance, reduce physical ailments, and generally enhance the quality of a manager's life than stress management. It is a skill that we need from childhood until our final days, but until recently stress management has been overlooked or avoided in almost all educational or training situations.

The price of that oversight has been enormous. Michael Cook, editor of *Training and Development Journal,* writing about excessive stress and its relationship to jobs and illness, states that "last year, American industry lost $25 *billion* due to the premature death of its employees. Another $700 million was lost due to illness and absenteeism." He also points out that heart attacks afflict more than half a million people each year, nine million people suffer from alcoholism or drug abuse, while seventy-five million suffer from chronic back pain and another twenty-five million from hypertension.

If even a small fraction of these tragedies were caused by external terrorists, the military would be on red alert, Congress would be meeting in emergency session, and the airwaves would be clogged with the cries of outraged politicians. Unfortunately, excessive stress is an internal terrorist.

How is stress linked to such appalling bottom-line figures? Karl Albrecht, author of *Stress and the Manager,* points out that medical and stress experts now feel that excessive stress is related to as much as 80 percent of all illnesses. Some hospital officials estimate that as many as two-thirds of all emergency room admissions are stress-related, and the American Cancer Society has stated that research indicates a possible connection between life-style and the onset of cancer.

The late Dr. Hans Selye, who initiated much of current stress research, wrote in *Executive Health* that in 1977 a study commissioned by the U. S. Presidential Science Advisor called stress "a major problem [which] negatively affects the daily lives of scores of millions of Americans. It causes a bewildering array of physiological, psychological, and social malfunctions. On an economic level, the effects of stress probably cost the nation over $100 billion annually. Moreover, available evidence suggests that stress-related maladies are on the rise."

In short, the cost of excessive stress in both private pain and public cost is staggering—and we're just beginning to understand the full range of the workings and implications of stress.

Definitions

What is this internal terrorist? Basically, stress is considered the body's nonspecific response to any demands placed on it. By "nonspecific" is meant the body's unified reaction to both physical and psychological events that throw the body out of equilibrium. This reaction is often called the stress response or the fight-or-flight response. It is the body's attempt to ensure survival in the face of extreme danger or sudden change.

As such, the body responds much the same to a stampede of managerial problems as it would to a stampede of long-horned cattle: it prepares for fight or flight. The internal physical preparations are the same for both:

Eye pupils dilate.
Skin turns white, and hands and feet get cooler as blood leaves peripheral areas.
Muscle tension increases.
Mouth goes dry.
Digestion slows or stops.
Hormone levels and flow change.
Sexual interest/ability lowers or stops.
Adrenalin flows through the body.
Brain chemistry changes.
Blood clotting time shortens.
Breathing rate increases.
Immunization system goes on alert.
Heart rate increases.
Blood is diverted to major organs.
Perspiration increases for additional body cooling.
Sugar is released into blood from liver.

This fight-or-flight response is systemic, in that *all* of these functions occur throughout our entire system when we are under stress. Even a cursory look at the list indicates why chronic stress can have a profound effect on our physical and mental health, as well as our emotions and behavior both on and off the job.

With all of these negative side-effects, is stress actually bad, to be avoided at all costs? No, not really. In fact, not only is it not intrinsically bad, but we couldn't avoid it if we wanted to. Stress is also the body's response to many of the positive things in our lives: challenge, excitement, joy, elation, passion—some of the very things that give our lives value and meaning.

Stress becomes a problem only when it is "dis-stress," either too much or not enough. The stress level needs to be kept within a range sufficient to keep our life interesting and our physical systems functioning, but not so much that it starts to break down those same life-support systems. Selye coined the term *eustress* for this beneficial range of stress.

Stressors are the events that cause the body's fight-or-flight response. They may be either positive or negative as far as the individual is concerned—the body makes no subjective discriminations. Nor does it care if the stressor is physical or psychological. As far as the body is concerned, to paraphrase Gertrude Stein, "A threat is a threat is a threat."

Burnout

Probably no topic in recent organizational history has generated more workshops, articles, and over-coffee discussions than burnout. What is it, and how did it get to center stage?

Burnout is generally defined as the depletion of adaptive energies, usually as a result of chronic stress, to the point that vital functioning is impaired. In other words, we no longer have the energy available to respond successfully to life's normal demands. It can be looked on as the result of going down a one-way energy street, with too much energy going out and not enough coming back in. The fight-or-flight system has been activated for too long. Burnout can affect organizations and individuals alike.

∇ **Organizational burnout.** We can say that an organization is suffering from burnout when it lacks the collective energies to adapt adequately to changing situations or to meet the needs of its employees and customers. It has undergone too many changes too quickly, suffered too many setbacks, put out too many fires.

The burned-out organization may be a victim of future shock—the future got there before the organization was ready for it—or it may be physically and emotionally worn out by overly depleting its energy resources. In either event, the net result is the same: an organization that has lost its verve, its capacity to respond quickly to new situations, its willingness to face and control its future with enthusiasm.

For convenience, let's say there are four basic types of organizations that can lead to individual and collective burnout:

1. *"Quick fryer."* This organization pops you in the boiling oil as soon as you've come on board. It even seems to take a certain twisted pride in its crisis orientation and the high divorce rate of its members.

You can recognize the "quick fryer" organization by its fast-track approach, the "We're all in the hot fat together and isn't it fun?" attitude, and the fact that when you call, everyone is always "away from their desk."

Exit interviews? No one has time to conduct them.

2. *"Microwave."* This organization frys you without your realizing it, because everything is always cool to the touch. No big waves, no apparent problems—and no open communication. Everything is kept safely below the surface.

   You can recognize this organization by its lack of emotion in the face of victories *or* defeats, and by realizing when you walk in the door that although everything *looks* right, it doesn't *feel* right.

   Exit interviews are polite and puzzled, as employees still aren't quite sure what went wrong—except they know it did.

3. *"Slow cooker."* Like a volcano, this organization keeps the lid on things to the point where enough pressure is built up and something blows. There is always an undercurrent of bubbling and rumbling, boiling and grumbling. Employees are passive-aggressive, not confronting higher management with complaints, but not really cooperating or performing well either.

   You can recognize this organization by the black tire marks of rapid and angry five o'clock departures from the company parking lot, the empty rooms at times when meetings are supposed to start, and the dark clouds that hover over areas where disgruntled employees gather.

   Exit interviews are explicit and emotional—finally a chance to vent, on the way out.

4. *"Open pit barbecue."* This organization bathes itself with delicious sauces—but keeps everyone's feet to the flames. The perks are great, but the pace is deadly. Someone once described this type of organization as "a fast-track organization masquerading as a laid-back organization." Employees hesitate to complain about their blistered feet because the sauces feel so good.

   You can identify this organization by the glazed look in the eyes of otherwise smiling employees, the friendly way in which people are fired, and the speed with which ideas and people are basted with golden sauce, consumed, and relegated to the ash heap.

Exit interviews are bitter, as employees get burned when the sauce runs out.

∇ **Individual burnout.** This can be defined as a state in which the individual employee no longer has the adaptive energies necessary to meet physical, emotional, intellectual, and spiritual needs—the well's run dry.

As with organizations, we can identify several types of individual burnout victims:

1. *"Slow suicide."* There are the fast suicides, who make the newspaper, and the slow suicides, who make everyone around them miserable before arriving at the same premature destination. Both are equally effective and lethal—one just takes a little longer.

   Slow suicide individuals smoke too much, drink too much, knowingly eat the wrong diet, don't exercise—and disregard all medical evidence and doctors' advice to the effect that they are shortening their lives.

   Some slow suicides have such a high need to control that they refuse to accept anyone else's advice or the signals of their own body, even if death is the alternative. It is a "Damn the torpedos—full speed ahead!" approach, bravery without a cause.

   Other slow suicides are so highly addicted to their particular version of earthly pleasures that they would rather shorten their lives than give them up or change their life-styles. For others, the self-destructive life-style fits into their own "loser" self-image. To change for the better would require that they look at themselves in an entirely new way. And that may be scarier than continuing to tempt the internal stress terrorist.
2. *"Glowing ember."* Always smiling, cheerful, and in control of themselves, the glowing embers are encased in a fireproof box of their own making. It keeps the fire in, but it also shuts people out. Such individuals often fear that to open the box far enough to let someone close would release a fearful inferno. Better to bank the fires and hope for the best.

   Unless something changes, the glowing ember ultimately becomes a . . .
3. *"Big ash."* Hollow, burned-out, used-up, the big ash burnout victim has

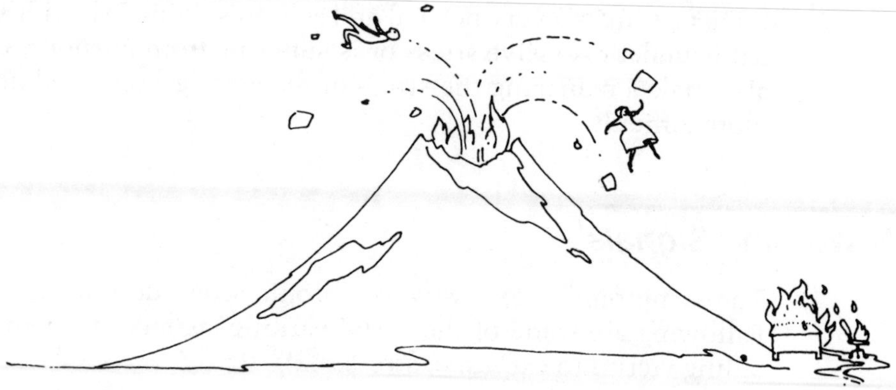

lost creativity, enthusiasm, vitality, and initiative. Without sufficient rehabilitation, at this point they may only be good for low-level bureaucracies. Why did they hang on so long? "Well, there's an excellent pension plan."

4. *"Vesuvius."* Burnout has shortened the temper of these people to the point where they are walking volcanos just waiting to erupt—which they frequently do, often without warning. This eruptive behavior tends to keep family and fellow-workers standing back at a safe distance, as no one is anxious to get buried in hot lava.
5. *"Walking wounded."* These burnout victims soldier on regardless of the pain or injury—even if it was self-inflicted. Ignoring the damage, they don't give it time to heal or pause to consider how to avoid getting caught in the crossfire next time. They're easily identified by their eagerness to tell you war stories and show you their battle scars.

Distancing

Our mind/brain, programmed for survival, will attempt to get us out of any threatening situation. We may not like this rescue attempt. In the case of psychosomatic illness or accident, we may not even survive it, but our mind/brain will try it anyway. It knows no other way to operate. As a result, we may see or experience some very strange ways of rescuing, or distancing, ourselves from excessive stress.

As we might expect, we tend to distance, or put ourselves farthest, from what we perceive to be creating the stress. For example, here are several ways that individuals use to avoid what they perceive to be specific stressors:

Avoid . . .	with:
Family	workaholism, addictions
Work	procrastination, petty details, excessive planning
Work environment	illness, accidents, poor performance (get fired)
People	obnoxious behavior, paperwork, "busy-ness"

Distancing is a very normal and self-preserving behavior when an individual is under excessive stress or is suffering from burnout. Unfortunately, it also makes managing the stress or recovering from the burnout that much more difficult.

Early Warning Signals

The symptoms of excessive or chronic stress do not just suddenly appear. Following are some of the early warning signals that indicate you may be falling victim to excessive stress:

- Negative shift in attitudes without other things having changed.
- Putting down, avoiding, or negating things that were once important.
- Questioning whether things are really worth it, beginning to doubt rewards that once were adequate.
- Feelings of being trapped: job, relationships, career.
- Beginning to alienate those closest to you, those who could help the most.
- Negative changes in physical health.
- Changes in sexual interest or ability.
- Negative changes in your sleep or eating habits.
- Consistent pattern of negative emotions late in the workday or early in the morning, when blood sugar is lowest.
- Starting to believe nothing can be done, that your problems are beyond control.

If you are beginning to notice these early warning signs, there is still time to examine causes and take preventive action.

Causes of Managerial Stress

Here are some of the primary causes of managerial stress, based on a study of three hundred managers in twelve major companies, conducted by Dr. John Howard of the University of Western Ontario.

1. *Poor management* topped the list, including a lack of planning and direction, poor communication by upper management, indecisiveness, and failure to communicate total plans.
2. *Lack of authority* and *blurred organizational structures* was the second leading cause of stress among the three hundred executives.
3. *Feelings of impotence or helplessness* caused stress, for although the managers often recognized and understood problems and developed solutions, organizational constraints left them powerless to carry them out. The inability of a manager—or employee—to influence a situation for which he or she has a solution can be frustrating and very stressful.
4. The *urgency* of situations caused the managers' jobs to be fragmented. In fact, Dr. Howard had discovered that on the average, executives do something different every seven minutes. This makes it difficult to focus on any given managerial task and carry it through to completion—a very stressful situation.
5. *Too much work* without enough time or staff to get it done was another stressor. No amount of good time management will solve the problem if there is just too much to do in the first place.
6. *Ambiguity and uncertainty* were other major stressors, for managerial decision-making is difficult and frustrating when problems are not clearly identified and organizational policies to deal with the problem are ambiguous.

7. *Promotion/recognition concerns* and *company politics* were also found to be major causes of managerial stress among the three hundred managers.

Although this particular study was of managers, other studies indicate that those managers' employees would have had very similar stressors. These are stressors that affect manager and employee alike, with the exception that managers may be in more of a position to do something about them.

Stress Management Strategies

Managing your stress level within optimal limits is much like managing any other part of your job: it requires time, commitment, and attention to detail. I call it a Triple-A approach to stress management:

Awareness. Use the assessments to increase your self-knowledge of the situation. It's hard to manage a situation you're not familiar with.

Antistress strategies. Use the tools that have been found to be most effective in managing stress.

Action. As in any managerial situation, no amount of knowledge or planning really affects the bottom line unless appropriate action is taken. Managing stress is no different.

Following are a number of stress management strategies, all of which have been found effective in keeping managerial stress within productive levels:

∇ **Balance of activities.** All work and no play makes for more than just dull managers, it can also make for very stressed managers. No matter how much managers may enjoy their work, good stress management usually calls for a balance between on-the-job activities and outside activities.

No job is perfect, and few managers have as much control over job-related events as they'd like to have. Outside activities can present the opportunities to do just what they want to do, and how they want it done. Hobbies, volunteer work, organizations, social events—all can provide the sense of reward, social contribution, or accomplishment necessary to balance the stressful elements of almost any job situation.

∇ **Build/maintain a social support system.** Humans are social beings, and to one degree or another, most of us need social contact and support from other people or the stress level goes up. Psychologists say that one of our most basic fears, going back to our first few minutes after birth, is that of being abandoned. It is as though the brain's survival plan is programmed to keep us in social contact with our fellow humans, for it knows that we could not survive alone.

Here are some of the basic needs that a good social support system—our circle of family, friends, and co-workers—helps us meet. Check off those that apply to your current system:

- ☐ Friendship
- ☐ Intimacy
- ☐ Nurturing or physical support
- ☐ Other points of view
- ☐ Listening and feedback on behavior
- ☐ Safety valve—the opportunity to release frustrations or anger safely
- ☐ Advice/teaching
- ☐ Love and affection
- ☐ Emotional support
- ☐ Companionship

How does your system look? As with any other system, keeping your social support system in good condition requires time and energy, something that may be in short supply if you're too far along down the burnout path. The implication, then, is to maintain your system, for if the stress level becomes too high, it may be too late to rebuild it.

One of the difficulties in our culture is that roughly one-half of the population has the cultural expectations and training to maintain a social support system, while the other half doesn't. When a stressful event occurs, women will more typically head for the telephone or the lunchroom to tell someone about it, while men are more likely to head for a bar or punch something. Studies indicate that whereas women are likely to maintain a strong social support system, men frequently have difficulty sharing stressful thoughts and feelings with others, especially other men.

Studies also indicate that women have about one-third the incidence of heart attacks as men, and live approximately 10 to 15 percent longer. A coincidence? Perhaps, but a drive through any retirement center or city in the Sun Belt quickly identifies the survivors in our stress-filled culture. The men are conspicuous by their absence.

∇ **Relaxation techniques.** A number of relaxation techniques have been shown to be very effective in managing the level of harmful stress: yoga, meditation, self-hypnosis, mental imaging, meditative music, and others.

The main thing about these relaxation techniques is not which one you choose—all have proven helpful—but that you *use* one. For example, a study by a major telephone system for its employees indicated that meditation four or five times a week was one of the best stress management strategies of all the available relaxation techniques—but that it needed to be done on a regular basis if it was to be effective. Most employees felt that twenty to thirty minutes a day was a good investment in exchange for fewer harmful stress symptoms and a more productive work life.

∇ **Increase the rewards.** Although it is not always possible to reduce our stress loads, it is often possible to increase the reward side of the balancing scale. I often ask audiences, "If all things were possible, what job would you want to have?" The answers frequently cite some of the most stressful jobs imaginable! Test pilot, large corporation president, race car driver, rock star, astronaut, to name but a few. When asked, "Why in the world would you choose such a stressful job?" each person has in mind a reward, a payoff, that favorably balances the obvious stresses involved.

Remembering that the manager's road to burnout is paved with stressors that outweigh the rewards, how is your reward/stress balance? And what can you do that will improve the reward side of the ledger?

∇ **Setting goals.** One good way to balance out the stressful aspects of any activity is to realize that it is getting you closer to an important goal. This is one of the primary differences between a job and a career: a career has goals and a direction, while a job may only be a result of necessity or convenience. You can put up with more job stress if you know that it is only a necessary step along the way to a career goal, than if you see no future beyond the present job.

It is the same with other goals: if you can see past the present stressful situation to the accomplishment of an important goal, the effects of the stress will be much less significant. The requirement for this to work, of course, is that you have to set the goals.

∇ **Managing your job environment.** There are several things you can do in your job environment to help reduce some of the little stressors that add up to major energy drains by the end of the day:

Provide time blocks. Ever notice, perhaps with some apprehension, how your employees seem to somehow muddle through even when you're out for the day with the flu, or away at a conference? One way to avoid the stress of doing something else every seven minutes is to check out of the office to give yourself a block of time to work on an important project that requires either a period of uninterrupted development or some quiet problem-solving think time.

Some busy managers have found that the local library makes an excellent, quiet, telephoneless second office. In some corporations, "I'm going home to get some work done" is an accepted alternative to spending eight hours of every day in the office.

Optimal scheduling. It sometimes appears that there are two kinds of people in the world: morning people, awake at the crack of dawn and half a day's work done before breakfast, and night people, who don't really get rolling until about noon and then keep at it until well into the late hours. No matter which of these you are—or if you are somewhere in between—you can help avoid stress by scheduling your most difficult tasks at your best times of the day. Don't waste those peak hours on less important activities; use them for things which need your best shot.

Delegating. Although delegating is discussed more thoroughly in Chapter 8, this is just a reminder that appropriately delegating tasks—and leaving them delegated—is a necessary component of a manager's stress-reduction strategy.

Screen phone calls. If your office was in a sidewalk cafe where every passerby could easily interrupt you, it would be no surprise that you couldn't get much concentrated work done. The same thing can happen in your present office if everyone in the known world with a telephone can interrupt you simply by letting their fingers do the walking.

Of course, not every manager has the luxury or opportunity to have phone calls screened, but whenever that is possible, do it. To keep stress at manageable levels, you need an acceptable balance between accessibility and privacy.

This same accessibility/privacy issue arises in the so-called modular offices with partitions replacing fixed walls, where flexibility is accomplished at the expense of privacy and stress-reducing sound control.

∇ **Change self-talk.** What is detrimental about stress is not the stressor itself, but our reaction to it. One manager's minor skirmish may be another's Armageddon. The major difference between the two managers is what they told themselves about the situation.

We are usually unaware of this internal dialogue, our self-talk—we seldom think about what we think about—but it is often the culprit in producing a stress response to an event. It is usually based on our attitudes or beliefs, and may have been with us since childhood.

For example, in a situation involving a late employee, a manager whose belief system says, "Employees should *never* be late!" is likely to escalate the situation into a very stressful confrontation for both manager and employee. On the other hand, a manager whose belief system says, "Extenuating circumstances happen to everyone—I owe it to the employee to check it out first" will probably have a much less stressful session with the late employee. The situation was the same, only the self-talk was different.

To check this out for yourself, start being more aware of what you tell yourself in situations that cause you stress. This is especially true if the same situations don't cause equal stress for others—they're telling themselves something different than you are. If appropriate, ask them. It may provide you with an entirely different, less stressful, point of view.

∇ **The hardiness factors.** We discussed the hardiness factors in Chapter 7, relative to managing change and its related stress. This is just a reminder that these four hardiness factors can contribute significantly to reducing the stressful effects of any given situation:

1. View change as a challenge rather than as a stress-producing threat.
2. Make commitments, rather than avoiding life.
3. Define your goals, values, and priorities, producing a clear sense of mission and purpose.
4. Be aware of the control you have, over both external events and your own life.

▽ **Diet and nutrition.** "You are what you eat" is an adage that has been with us for a long time, but it is only recently that the strong connection between nutrition and stress management has been more fully understood.

Since our daily food intake is something over which we have control, here are a few suggestions for starters:

Eat breakfast. Not only does breakfast get you off to a balanced "fuel intake" start, but preliminary studies indicate that it may also have a positive effect on mental processing through its impact on your blood sugar balance.

If you are not hungry at breakfast, you may be eating too much late in the day—a good bit of which may find its way to your midsection. For those whose metabolism doesn't really turn on until later in the day, even a light breakfast snack of whole-grain toast and some protein, along with appropriate supplemental vitamins and minerals, will help balance your nutritional day.

What many people think is a metabolism issue for not eating breakfast is often just a habit carried over from childhood since many people's eating habits tend to reflect those of their parents.

Control your stimulant intake. This is probably the most abused area in all of American nutritional stress management, for most people take in far more stimulants during the day than they realize. A cup of coffee or two here, a can of cola there, refined sugar in almost everything they eat all day, and a drink or two when they get home from work—it all adds up to a pretty strong drug hit for many people's metabolisms.

Since the reason stimulants stimulate is that they produce a mini-stress response, with all of the physical and emotional characteristics of the fight-or-flight response, the excessive use of stimulants will heighten the individual's stress level. Depending on metabolism, chemical sensitivities, and existing stress level, taking in excessive stimulants can have a pronounced effect on the efficiency of both mental and physical performance.

Here is a list of common stimulants. If you don't think you're addicted to any of them, go without it for *at least* three days. Carefully observe your physical and mental processes. You may find that you are more of an addict than you thought. The rest is up to you.

COMMON STIMULANTS

Sugar	Nicotine
Cola	Caffeine
Chocolate	Alcohol

▽ **Exercise.** One of the primary things that good exercise does for you is help relax muscles that have been kept tense during the fight-or-flight response. A hectic workday can result in a great deal of muscular discomfort. If certain neck and shoulder muscles are tense, for example, a headache is a likely outcome. Exercise—running, biking, sports, aerobics—serves to relax muscles and improve your blood flow.

Another advantage of a good exercise program is the improvement in general body tone. Since the stress response affects the entire body system, anything that improves the body's physical condition will improve the ability to resist the effects of stress.

A more recently discovered benefit of exercise is an apparent change in some of the brain's chemistry. This has the effect of raising spirits and emotional mood. I have asked literally hundreds of people in audiences across the country, "Have you ever felt down, discouraged, blue, or depressed *after* vigorous exercise?" Many had before exercising, but not after. Except for one man—he had lost a championship tennis match! The audience decided that didn't count, so exercise is still batting 1.000.

∇ **Be your own consultant.** One way of stepping back and taking an objective look at the stressful factors in your work or personal environment is to imagine that you've hired yourself to be your own stress management consultant. (You'll find the self-consultant checklist at the end of this chapter.) This gives you the necessary distance from your personal situations to make change decisions. As my Florida relatives tell me, "It's hard to remember that your job is to drain the swamp when you're up to your neck in alligators." Acting as your own consultant gives you permission to climb out of the swamp.

If you find that being your own consultant is too much of a stretch, have someone else be your consultant and use the checklist with you.

On-the-Job Relaxation Techniques

Many European businesses now have a relaxation room where employees can go for a few minutes of relaxation if job situations become too stressful. Kodak-Austria, for example, has a comfortable room to which employees can go for a thirty-minute relaxation break, no questions asked. Kodak realizes that antistress breaks are much cheaper in the long run than having an overly stressed technician accidentally destroy a production run of customers' film.

Here are several relaxation techniques that you can use during your workday. Used regularly, they will not only relieve stress before it gets in the way of performance, but they will also help prevent stress buildup from getting to that point.

∇ **Stress break.** If you have a private office, take a ten-minute stress break: have phone calls held, turn down lights, and find a comfortable location. It is discouraging in how many offices none of these is possible. If that is your situation, just do the best you can.

Some people look out the window, deliberately focusing on nothing in particular. Others stare at a blank area on the office wall, while others close their eyes and take a quick mental trip to a favorite vacation spot.

Relaxing music is helpful. If there are distractions, use a small Walkman-type player and headphones. Music then assists you in creating your own relaxation space. Ideally relaxation music is baroque, with about sixty beats per minute, slightly slower than the normal human heart rate. There is also specially created relaxation music, such as that produced by Jim Oliver or Steve Halprin. Basically, anything that works for you is fine.

∇ **Stretching.** Anywhere that is convenient, go through a stretching routine that appropriately stretches all of your major muscle groups, releasing stored tensions. It can even be done without leaving your office chair by gripping the bottom of the chair and alternately tensing and relaxing muscles up and down your entire body.

∇ **Deep breathing.** At least once each hour, spend a few minutes doing deep breathing. Breathe from both your chest and your abdomen, on a slow count of five for both inhaling and exhaling. This not only relaxes chest and stomach muscles, but it brings additional oxygen to the blood to help counteract the effects of stress.

Some people find they get added value from this method by alternately taking a few deep breaths through one nostril, and then the other. Try it for yourself, and then decide.

∇ **Exercise.** Even if you don't have the opportunity for strenuous exercise during your workday, a brisk walk around the block or up and down several flights of stairs will help relieve muscle tension and improve your circulation.

∇ **Stimulants.** If it is a particularly stressful day, cut back on stimulants—don't add to the problem.

Resisting Positive Change

There has probably been no flood since Noah's that equals the deluge of stress management information, suggestions, and admonitions. Look around at your family, friends, or work environment: has this torrential downpour made any significant change in the stress levels? If not, why not?

To put it in a more personal perspective, if you've read this far, what do you intend to do about the stress areas in your own or your employees' environments? What might block the changes that your managerial experience tells you are necessary?

Here is a list of things which can inhibit stress management changes. Check off the ones which you think may get in the way of you or your employees adopting a less stressful life-style:

☐ Old habits—too hard to break
☐ Peer pressure to continue present stressful ways

- ☐ Magical thinking—"It won't happen to me."
- ☐ Benefits of changing not worth the trouble
- ☐ Methods probably wouldn't work anyway
- ☐ Stress situations beyond help
- ☐ Getting rewards from *staying* stressed:
  - ☐ Sympathy
  - ☐ Less responsibility
  - ☐ Food for conversation
  - ☐ Sick days away from work
  - ☐ All of the above

The checkmarks tell you the areas where your self-talk needs to be changed if you are to make your managerial stress management program a successful reality.

Stress Emergencies

Even the best or most comprehensive stress management strategies can't prevent an occasional stress emergency, when stressful events get out of hand and your stress defences are overwhelmed. Should that occur, the following is a handy stress emergency guide. You should *immediately*:

1. *Acknowledge the problem, your feelings, and that this is a stress emergency.* This may be more difficult for some male managers than for their female counterparts, as our culture has conditioned males not to freely admit problems or difficulties, seeing it as a sign of weakness and vulnerability. Nonetheless, a stress problem can't be dealt with until it is acknowledged.
2. *Improve care of your body: nutrition, exercise, and rest.* In stress emergencies, we unfortunately tend to do the wrong things: reach for the candy bars, alcohol, cigarettes, coffee, ice cream, and junk food, all of which add to the physical stress response. Add to that the likelihood of less exercise and rest during the stressful situation emergency, and we're making sure that stress nails us right between the eyes.
3. *Activate your social support system.* No matter what other ingredients you may have in your stress management program, in a stress emergency most of us need *people.* Call them, see them, or write to them—but do it!
4. *Use relaxation techniques.* Now, of all times, is when you need to use your stress-reduction techniques: exercise, yoga, aerobics, jogging, meditation, and so forth. It is time well spent in the protection of your physical and mental health.
5. *Get help.* If you have a flooded basement, you don't hesitate to call the plumber. Take at least as good care of yourself as you do of your basement—you are far less easily replaced—and get appropriate professional help *at once.* Don't wait for an emergency to become a tragedy.

In Conclusion

A more realistic name for stress management might be life-style management, for the decisions that each manager and employee need to make affect the entire spectrum of life experiences. No one else makes us stressed—it is our personal response to stressors that determines the severity of the stress response, as well as the physical and emotional outcomes. Until we take personal responsibility for our responses, choices, and decisions, we will continue to be stress's frequent victim.

There is an old Spanish proverb that reminds us, " 'Do what you want,' God said, *'and pay for it.'* "

In choosing whether or not to manage our stress, the price is up to us.

∇ ***For additional information, see:***

Chapter 7. The Challenge of Change
Chapter 8. Delegating—The Ultimate Skill
Chapter 18. Poor Performance Comes In for Analysis
Chapter 20. About Time for Time Management?
Chapter 21. Detoxifying the Workaholic

∇ Stress Self-Assessment

Directions: Following are symptoms and causes of personal stress and burnout. To what extent do they apply to you?

Scale: **5-Never 4-Seldom 3-Occasionally 2-Usually 1-Always** (circle one)

Symptoms

1. Do you have colds, flu, or other infectious diseases?	5 4 3 2 1
2. Do you feel overworked, hurried, or pushed?	5 4 3 2 1
3. Do you have headaches and/or backaches?	5 4 3 2 1
4. Do you feel emotionally or physically exhausted?	5 4 3 2 1
5. Do you dread going to work?	5 4 3 2 1
6. Do you feel depressed or down ?	5 4 3 2 1
7. Do you have eating problems--either too much or too little?	5 4 3 2 1
8. Do you feel worried or anxious?	5 4 3 2 1
9. Do you get upset when one of your decisions is questioned?	5 4 3 2 1
10. Do you feel irritable, short-tempered, or angry?	5 4 3 2 1
11. Do you feel you need a drink at the end of the day?	5 4 3 2 1
12. Does it seem nothing can be done about the things that bother you?	5 4 3 2 1

Causes

13. Do you fail to eat a well-balanced meal at least once a day?	5 4 3 2 1
14. Do you feel pressure to make more money?	5 4 3 2 1
15. Do more that two days go by when you've failed to exercise?	5 4 3 2 1
16. Do you have difficulty setting goals for yourself?	5 4 3 2 1
17. Do you feel unappreciated?	5 4 3 2 1
18. Do you feel others can't be depended upon to "do things right"?	5 4 3 2 1

continued

Stress Self-assessment, continued.

19. Do you feel guilty when you want to have time for yourself?	5 4 3 2 1
20. Would those who know you well consider you to be a perfectionist?	5 4 3 2 1
21. Is it important for you to win at golf, tennis, or other sports?	5 4 3 2 1
22. Does a week go by when you haven't had some social activity?	5 4 3 2 1
23. Do you have difficulty asking for help?	5 4 3 2 1
24. Do you feel your occupation has a dead end?	5 4 3 2 1
25. Would other people consider you to be a workaholic?	5 4 3 2 1

Overall rating of your stress situation:

Excellent - 10 9 8 7 6 5 4 3 2 1 - Very poor

Note: If you circled a number of symptoms in the 1-2 area, you may want to look closely at your life style and the effect that stress is having on your health. If you circled a number of causes in the 1-2 area, those are items that may need to be your top priorities for constructive change.

Remember, excessive stress causes a depletion of your adaptive energies. Therefore, the longer you wait to make constructive changes, the more difficult it is likely to be.

∇ Stress Management Consulting Assessment

Directions: Imagine that you have hired yourself to be your own Stress Management Consultant. From that point of view, answer the following questions.

1. What are the first changes you'd recommend to reduce your client's stress level? ________

____

____

2. What rewards would you suggest increasing, to improve the stress-reward balance? ____

____

____

3. What outside-the-job activities, hobbies, or recreations would you recommend? ________

____

____

4. Does it seem that your client is a workaholic? Yes___ No___ If so, what do you recommend? ____

____

5. What changes would you suggest in your client's diet? ____________________

____

6. What changes would you recommend in your client's "self-talk", the internal dialogue that occurs during stressful situations? ____________________

____

7. What changes would you suggest in the way your client manages the job environment?

____

____

Date ______________

∇ Job Stress Assessment

Directions: Following are some specific causes of job-related stress and burnout. To what extent are they applicable to your work situation?

Scale: **5-Never 4-Seldom 3-Occasionally 2-Usually 1-Always** (circle one)

1. Lack of job mobility (feeling trapped). 5 4 3 2 1
2. Little tangible recognition of service or accomplishments. 5 4 3 2 1
3. Low salary, compared with people doing similar work in your or other organizations. 5 4 3 2 1
4. Economically vulnerable--little personal job security. 5 4 3 2 1
5. Inadequate political skills to get ahead in your organization. 5 4 3 2 1
6. Dead-end career path. 5 4 3 2 1
7. Time management problems. 5 4 3 2 1
8. Inadequate communication skills. 5 4 3 2 1
9. Role problems--must wear too many hats. 5 4 3 2 1
10. Low overall organizational morale. 5 4 3 2 1
11. Given responsibility without the authority to carry it out. 5 4 3 2 1
12. Necessity to do jobs for which you were not trained. 5 4 3 2 1

Overall rating of your job stress situation:

Excellent - 10 9 8 7 6 5 4 3 2 1 - Poor

Note: The stressful situations that are circled in the 1-2 area are your greatest opportunity for positive change.

∇ Stress Resistance Test

___ 1. ADD 20 points if you are happily married/related.

___ 2. ADD 20 points if you look forward to going to work at least two days out of three.

___ 3. ADD 10 points if you are not troubled by bills.

___ 4. ADD 10 points if you participate in some social activity at least twice a month.

___ 5. ADD 10 points if you have a hobby that you engage in at least twice a month.

___ 6. ADD 10 points if you engage in some activity that is just for fun at least one hour a week.

___ 7. ADD 10 points if you engage in some activity that completely relaxes you at least three times a week.

___ 8. ADD 5 points for each day of the week that you engage in some sort of exercise for periods of at least 30 minutes duration.

___ 9. ADD 5 points for each day of the week you eat at least one nutritionally balanced meal.

___ 10. *SUBTRACT* 5 points for each day of the week you feel you're hurried or rushed.

___ 11. *SUBTRACT* 5 points for each day of the week that you feel glum or depressed.

___ 12. *SUBTRACT* 5 points for each 10 pounds you are over or under your ideal weight (maximum penalty--20 points).

___ 13. *SUBTRACT* 5 points for each night of the week that you take a sleeping aid.

___ 14. *SUBTRACT* 5 points for each day during the week that you use medications, drugs, or alcohol because they're "necessary" to reduce your anxiety or to help you relax.

SCORING

Maximum = +160 points   **Minimum** = -160 points

90+ = **High resistance**. Defenses in order -- keep up the good work!

60-90 = **Moderate resistance.** Consider changes in areas where you lost points.

Below 60: Vulnerable, support systems weak. You may need to re-examine your habits and life style.

Date ____________

∇ Managerial Interpersonal Stress Inventory

Directions: Circle the number which best indicates your current interpersonal situation with your employees.

Scale: **5-Never** **4-Seldom** **3-Occasionally** **2-Usually** **1-Always**

1. Too much of my time is spent working directly with employees.	5 4 3 2 1
2. I feel I treat employees as if they were objects.	5 4 3 2 1
3. I am not able to deal with employee's emotional situations without getting personally involved.	5 4 3 2 1
4. I feel guilty about the way I have treated some employees.	5 4 3 2 1
5. I am questioning the quality of my managing of people.	5 4 3 2 1
6. I do not enjoy extended contact with my employees.	5 4 3 2 1
7. It is difficult for me to understand how my employees feel about things.	5 4 3 2 1
8. I find it hard to hold my ground when confronted by employees.	5 4 3 2 1
9. It's hard for me to relate to the types of problems my employees have.	5 4 3 2 1
10. I find it difficult to create a relaxed atmosphere with my employees.	5 4 3 2 1
11. I think I've become more callous toward people since I took this job.	5 4 3 2 1
12. I feel that employees blame me for their job problems.	5 4 3 2 1
13. I don't like the kind of person I've become on the job.	5 4 3 2 1
14. I feel I'm not positively influencing other people's lives through my work as a manager.	5 4 3 2 1
15. I worry that this job is hardening me emotionally.	5 4 3 2 1

Note: Circled items in the 1-2 area may indicate the onset of excessive job stress and potential burnout.

Glossary

Air time. The time available for each person to speak in a meeting.

Analogy. The comparison of two essentially different things which have at least one feature or characteristic in common; for example, a chair is like a cheetah in that they both have four legs.

Armageddon. Biblically, the last great battle, still to be fought, between the forces of good and evil.

Assessments. Tools used to obtain information on any given situation or condition. With regard to people skills, they are often in the form of surveys, questionnaires, checklists, or personal inventories. A well-designed assessment should help answer the question, "What's going on here?"

Burnout. The decline of an individual's adaptive energies to the point that he or she is no longer able to effectively adapt to normal physical, emotional, and intellectual needs. It is usually caused by excessive stress or change. It can be accompanied by irreversible physical deterioration in some areas of the body.

Career development. The process of planning the direction of one's career over an extended period of time.

Career path. The explicit course or route an individual follows as a result of career development plans. The designing of the plans is sometimes known as career pathing.

Coaching. The teaching of a given skill, often on a one-to-one basis. Unlike classroom teaching, coaching usually includes a great deal of individual monitoring of actual student performance and feedback during the process.

Consultants. Individuals who bring a particular skill or expertise to bear on a specific problem or situation, usually on a contract basis.

Cross-talk. Individuals talking to each other during a meeting without regard to who has the floor or who has been given air time by the meeting leader. It is considered a disruptive or dysfunctional behavior.

Cultural norms. The beliefs, values, myths, and generally accepted ideas among a group that influence behavior and performance. They are the underlying basis for ". . . and this is the way things are around here."

Curriculum. A specific collection of individual educational programs or courses that have the same general purpose; for example, an engineering curriculum or an interpersonal skills curriculum.

Delegating. The assigning of specific tasks to a subordinate while retaining the overall responsibility or accountability for the outcome.

Due process. The specific method an organization uses to process employee grievances or differences with management, especially in employee discipline issues.

Dysfunctional behavior. Literally, behavior that doesn't work. It is usually used to describe behavior that is disruptive or not in the best overall interests of the person involved. Continually raising objections is dysfunctional meeting behavior, while using drugs is dysfunctional behavior for the individual involved, as well as for the organization.

Enabler. The person with a relationship to an addict who makes it possible for the addiction to continue by covering up the addict's behavior, making excuses, rationalizing, ignoring, avoiding, glamorizing, or otherwise not confronting the addictive behavior.

Facilitator. An individual who guides a process of events through to a conclusion, usually as a result of having special skills in that area; for example, a wage negotiations facilitator or a training facilitator.

Feedback. Information as to how a given process or situation is proceeding; feedback from our physical senses allows us to move more or less safely through our physical environment, while feedback from other people lets us know how we appear to others in our social environment, at home, or on the job.

Fight-or-flight. Our body's prehistoric neurochemical reaction to perceived physical or psychological danger, preparing us for escape or combat. Although archaic in most contemporary interpersonal situations, it still continues to occur.

Filter system. Our internal collection of beliefs, values, and attitudes, unique for each person, through which we pass everything that we perceive, resulting in a given behavior. If our belief is that large dogs are very dangerous, the sight of a large dog may send us scrambling to safety. The person next to us, with a different filter system, may call the same dog over to pet it.

Future shock. A term originated by Alvin Toffler in his book of the same name to denote the adverse effects on individuals and organizations from changes that occur before they are prepared—when the future arrives before they are ready. The physical and emotional effects of future shock are much the same as are caused by excessive stress, change, and burnout.

Grievance procedures. An organization's specific methods or channels for handling situations in which employees have problems with management or other employees; for example, sexual harassment, unwarranted verbal abuse of a subordinate, or violation of a union contract, can all lead to the use of grievance procedures. (Also see **Due process.**)

Grieving process. The almost universal process individuals go through in situations of loss or sudden change. As described by Elisabeth Kubler-Ross, the phases are usually considered to be disbelief, anger, guilt, depression, and ultimately acceptance.

"Head of the messenger." Refers to the classic story of the messenger who brought the fateful news to the king that the royal armies had been defeated in battle. The king was so distressed by the news that he had the messenger beheaded.

Human resource strategies. The advance planning necessary by those responsible for human resources in an organization to ensure that the organization will have adequate managerial and specialty talent available to meet future needs. When done well, it is coordinated closely with individual career development.

Informants. Employees in an organization who have a direct communication relationship with upper management that enables them unofficially or covertly to tell managers what is going on with employees from an inside vantage point. In espionage terms, they would be considered moles. They usually thrive in organizations that have an "us vs. them" employee-management relationship.

Interpersonal skills. The skills that allow an individual to interact successfully with other people. They are usually considered to include, among others, assertiveness, listening, complimenting, giving feedback, confronting, and supporting.

Laissez-faire. Literally, let people do as they please. In management terms, a management style that exercises a minimum of control over subordinates.

Learning modes. The basic ways in which individuals perceive, take in, and process information. They are generally considered to be visual images, visual text, auditory, kinesthetic, and tactile.

Modeling. Presenting a given situation or behavior to others as a positive example; for example, modeling the fall fashions, modeling good listening skills.

Needs analysis. An assessment of specific needs, carried out before making a decision regarding additional resources or training.

Networks. The link of unofficial or informal connections between individuals in different departments or organizations that allows individuals to receive or pass along information more quickly than more formal channels. They are usually established and maintained on the basis of personal contacts, and often cut across more formal hierarchical roles or organizational relationships.

Organizational hierarchy. The normal or formal chain of command through which flow power, authority, decisions, and orders in an organization. It is a direct function of who reports to whom, and can usually be graphically illustrated on an organizational flowchart.

Outplacement. A process in which an employee who is being laid off, replaced, or otherwise released by an organization is helped to find employment in another organization or division.

Performance appraisal. A regularly scheduled session, usually between manager and employee, in which the employee's or the manager's performance is discussed and plans made for growth or improvement.

Problem-solving groups. Small authorized groups of employees who meet on a regular basis to discuss and suggest solutions to problems within the area of their work unit responsibilities; for example, production workers might deal with problems of material flow and handling, scheduling, and quality control. Typically they will make presentations of their proposed solutions to the next higher level or two of management. Experience indicates they function best with the support of upper-level management.

Quit-and-stay. A term describing a situation in which a demotivated or burned-out employee consciously or unconsciously decides to stop performing at maximum potential, yet elects to remain with the organization.

Remediation. A process or treatment that is designed and intended to fix or repair something that isn't working; for example, a remediation program in math or reading for students needing help in those areas.

Role reversal. A situation in which the normal behaviors of an individual or group are transposed, either temporarily or permanently; for example, the custom in some towns or cities in which an ordinary citizen takes over the powers of mayor for a day, or the reversal of expected sex-role behavior.

Sabotage. The conscious or unconscious attempt to ensure that an intended process or function doesn't work or take place; for example, a department that feels slighted in a planning phase may sabotage a new marketing plan by not fully cooperating, withholding needed information, or slowing down a vital part of the implementation process.

Self-study. A program of study that is sufficiently self-contained that it requires minimal or no input or assistance from an outside source, such as a teacher, trainer, or manager.

Self-talk. The ongoing internal dialogue that most of us engage in almost continuously, in either words or images, as a result of our thinking process. We are often unaware of its content—we seldom think about what we think about—but it has a pronounced effect on our behavior. It can be considered part of our filter system. (Also see **Filter system**.)

Seminar. An instructional method, similar to a classroom but usually with fewer people, a shorter duration, more input from the participants, and a tighter instructional focus on a given subject.

Serendipity. Events, situations, or processes that are determined purely by chance, without planning or strategy.

Social support system or network. The circle of family, friends, and co-workers that provides the social contacts and nourishment most of us need to feel we are leading a balanced and complete life.

Stressors. Events or situations that lead an individual to have a stress or fight-or-flight response. Unless it involves an adverse physical situation, it is the individual's self-talk or filter system that determines whether an event or situation is perceived as a stressor; that is, no other person or nonphysical situation can make us feel stressed. (Also see **Fight-or-flight, Filter system,** and **Self-talk**.)

Systemic. A process that involves an entire system, on an all-or-nothing basis, such as the body's physical reactions in the fight-or-flight response.

Value system. Our internal collection of what we believe to be important, vital, or sacred; i.e., those ideas, attitudes, or philosophical positions that we believe to be of value. Our value system is a primary component of our filter system, in part determines our self-talk, and therefore has a pronounced effect on our behavior.

Walk-around management. Also known as M.B.W.A. (Management By Wandering Around), a management technique in which the manager circulates among the employees on a frequent and regular basis. It can serve the multiple functions of improving upward communication from employees to management by making the manager more accessible, allows the manager a less formal relationship with employees, gives the manager better firsthand knowledge of employee activities, and presents an excellent opportunity for the manager to model desired behavior for employees and to keep the organization's mission in front of employees. Not to be confused with M.B.W.O. (Management By Wandering Off).

Win/Win. A point of view in which an individual believes and acts on the premise that in order for one party to a negotiation or situation to win, both parties must win; that there can be no losers for a situation to be satisfactorily resolved.

Work addiction. The compulsive need to work, usually on the basis of fear of inadequate performance or a conscious or unconscious need to use work to avoid other areas of an individual's life.

Index